The New Structure of Labor Relations

The New Structure of Labor Relations

Tripartism and Decentralization

EDITED BY
HARRY C. KATZ,
WONDUCK LEE, AND
JOOHEE LEE

ILR PRESS | AN IMPRINT OF CORNELL UNIVERSITY PRESS
ITHACA AND LONDON

Copyright © 2004 by Cornell University

All rights reserved. Except for brief quotations in a review, this book, or parts thereof, must not be reproduced in any form without permission in writing from the publisher. For information, address Cornell University Press, Sage House, 512 East State Street, Ithaca, New York 14850.

First published 2004 by Cornell University Press

Library of Congress Cataloging-in-Publication Data

The new structure of labor relations : tripartism and decentralization / edited by Harry C. Katz, Wonduck Lee, and Joohee Lee.—1st ed.
  p. cm.
Includes bibliographical references and index.
ISBN 0-8014-4184-6 (cloth : alk. paper)
1. Collective bargaining—Cross-cultural studies.   2. Industrial relations—Cross-cultural studies.   I. Katz, Harry Charles, 1951–   II. Lee, Wonduck. III. Lee, Joohee.
  HD6971.5.N49 2004
  331—dc22
                                                            2003020658

Printed in the United States of America

Cornell University Press strives to use environmentally responsible suppliers and materials to the fullest extent possible in the publishing of its books. Such materials include vegetable-based, low-VOC inks and acid-free papers that are recycled, totally chlorine-free, or partly composed of nonwood fibers. For further information, visit our website at www.cornellpress.cornell.edu.

Cloth printing   10 9 8 7 6 5 4 3 2 1

Contents

Introduction: The Changing Nature of Labor, Management, and Government Interactions   1
Harry C. Katz

1 **The Irish Experiment in Social Partnership**   10
Paul Teague and James Donaghey

2 **The Netherlands:** Resilience in Structure, Revolution in Substance   37
Hans Slomp

3 **Collective Bargaining and Social Pacts in Italy**   59
Ida Regalia and Marino Regini

4 **The Changing Nature of Collective Bargaining in Germany:** Coordinated Decentralization   84
Gerhard Bosch

5 **The Rise and Fall of Interunion Wage Coordination and Tripartite Dialogue in Japan**   119
Akira Suzuki

6 **Will the Model of Uncoordinated Decentralization Persist?** Changes in Korean Industrial Relations After the Financial Crisis   143
Wonduck Lee and Joohee Lee

7 **The Changing Structure of Collective Bargaining in Australia**   166
Marian Baird and Russell D. Lansbury

8 **United States:** The Spread of Coordination and Decentralization without National-Level Tripartism   192
Harry C. Katz

Summary: Reconstructing Decentralized Collective Bargaining and
Other Trends in Labor-Management-Government Interactions   **213**
Wonduck Lee, Joohee Lee, and Harry C. Katz

Notes   **225**

References   **235**

Contributors   **257**

Index   **259**

The New Structure of Labor Relations

Introduction

The Changing Nature of Labor, Management, and Government Interactions

Harry C. Katz

Although it is not clear what explains the enormous economic success of the United States in the 1990s, no one would claim that national-level dialogue, partnership, and forums through which representatives of labor, management, and the government discuss economic policies played any role in U.S. success because such activities are infrequent and inconsequential in the United States. Based on U.S. experience, one might go on to conclude that national-level social dialogue and partnership are irrelevant to economic performance and policy-making everywhere. This book shows that this conclusion is wrong.

In Ireland, the Netherlands, Germany, and Italy, national-level social dialogue and partnership and other national-level interactions between representatives of labor, management, and the government, what is referred to as tripartism, have played a positive role addressing critical economic and social problems. This book shows that there is a spectrum of recent experience with tripartism. In some countries, tripartism is insignificant (the United States), it is on the decline (Japan and Australia), and its use expanded in the early and mid-1990s and then appeared to decline (Italy). In a few countries, tripartism is flourishing (Ireland, the Netherlands, and Germany), and in others it has been used sporadically and with limited success (Korea).

This book shows that the topics addressed and the participants included in tripartite arrangements vary between countries. Tripartite activities are not an invention of the 1990s. In a number of social democratic countries in the 1960s and 1970s, corporatism involving dialogue between representatives of labor, management, and government focused on efforts to control inflation (incomes policy) and often involved political exchanges whereby tax and other government policies were traded for wage (and price) moderation. Yet, while tripartism has some similarities with earlier forms of national-level social dialogue, a number of factors distinguish recent tripartite activities. This book describes how tripartism has come to focus more on working-time flexibility and the promotion of part-time work rather than on inflation. Tripartite dialogue also has expanded beyond traditional corporatist partners to include women's groups, representatives of senior citizens, and other representatives of "civic society."

The nature and role of labor, management, and government interactions are changing in critical ways beyond the replacement of corporatism with more varied forms of tripartite dialogue and policy-making in countries where corporatism flourishes. Chapters in this book, tracing developments in Japan, Korea, Australia, and the United States, find that although tripartism has not been central to economic policy-making in recent years in those countries a variety of other "coordinating" mechanisms provide interactions that help shape employment conditions and labor policy. The fact that there has been so much vibrancy in these coordinating mechanisms goes against the notion, popular in some quarters, that there is an overpowering unilateral decentralizing shift underway in labor-management interactions. These coordinating functions are, in fact, increasing in the face of intensified pressures promoting greater flexibility in work organization and working time.

At the same time, individualization and other, often related forms of decentralization in the structure of labor and management interactions are on the rise nearly everywhere and affect both the processes through which employment conditions are being determined and employment outcomes, including pay, working time, and work organization. So, even within countries, there are complex and somewhat contradictory shifts underway in the structure of labor, management, and government interactions.

CONNECTIONS WITH PREVIOUS RESEARCH

The research outlined in this book has connections to a number of previous research streams in the field of comparative industrial relations and comparative political economy. One link is provided by the question of whether countries with particular structures for collective bargaining perform better than other countries. Calmfors and Driffill (1988), who claimed that countries with either highly centralized or highly decentralized collective bargaining structures were more successful in terms of economic performance (low inflation and strong economic growth), investigated the macroeconomic effects of the structure of collective bargaining. Their research triggered much debate. Soskice (1990), for example, criticizes as overly simplistic the ordering of collective bargaining systems used in the Calmfors and Driffill analysis, pointing out that informal forms of coordinated bargaining, such as *Shunto* bargaining in Japan, are often important and are not captured well in the measure of bargaining centralization used by Calmfors and Driffill. I have argued that recognition of the various components of bargaining structure limits the value of categorizing national bargaining systems along a single centralization-decentralization spectrum (Katz 1993).

Soskice (1990) went on to argue that the extent of coordination within corporate-bank relations and other institutional arrangements produces a critical differentiation between "coordinated" and "uncoordinated" market economies. In a related analysis, Traxler (1995a) claims that a distinction between "organized versus disorganized decentralization" is necessary to account for the widespread nature of the pressures for decentralization and better captures the various paths of national development. Sisson and Marginson's (2002) account of the various forms of bargaining coordination within Europe provides recognition of the increased role that coordinated bargaining plays within and across countries. Other related analyses appear in what has come to be called the "varieties of capitalism" research literature (Hall and Soskice 2001). This literature builds on Soskice's distinction between coordinated and market economies to examine the depth and implications of the various forms of corporate and industrial relations structure that appear within advanced industrial economies.

This book extends the varieties of capitalism debate by providing in-depth analysis of the changing nature of labor, management, and government interactions in a number of key countries. With a common focus, the chapters that follow examine how the structure of collective bargaining has evolved since the early 1980s. The evidence shows that in all countries there was pressure for decentralization and in nearly all countries in the 1990s there were efforts to create some form of national-level tripartism. Exactly how tripartism connected to the more decentralized bargaining that was simultaneously spreading in those countries is one of the key issues examined in the country chapters.

THE PLAN OF THE BOOK

This book includes country chapters written by leading researchers about developments in Australia, Germany, Ireland, Italy, Japan, Korea, the Netherlands, and the United States. The country chapters examine the changing nature of labor, management, and government interactions with a special focus on tripartite dialogue and labor policy-related forums. Early drafts of these chapters were presented at a conference cosponsored by the Korean Labor Institute and the ILR School of Cornell University in Ithaca, New York, on October 5 and 6, 2001. The policy and research questions that motivated the conference are highlighted below.

The Nature of Tripartite Dialogue and Labor Policy Making

With the limited success that incomes policies had in restraining inflation in a number of countries in the 1960s and 1970s, one might have expected that tripartism would have lost its appeal. In this light, the negotiation of prominent tripartite accords in the 1990s in Ireland, Italy, and the Netherlands, and the national employment pact in Germany is quite surprising. What are these tripartite accords and pacts about and what has led to their formation? And, how do these recent pacts compare and contrast with earlier forms of corporatism?

On the one hand, it appears that recent tripartite pacts have much in common with the previous corporatist interactions that occurred in incomes policies. Both give central importance to wage moderation, even though the specific pressure for such moderation, the need for monetary discipline in order to conform to European Union and related monetary union pressures, adds a new twist to recent tripartite activities. On the other hand, with an emphasis on workplace and employment flexibility, promotion of participatory processes, and inclusion of social security reforms, recent tripartite pacts seem to be broader in scope as compared to earlier corporatist agreements. But is this breadth in recent tripartite pacts real and, if so, is the breadth really new?

It also is important to examine how the process of tripartism has changed. For example, are new parties representing the interests of civil society and are new modes of interaction between the various involved parties critical to the operation of recent tripartism? And perhaps most importantly, is there evidence that recent tripartism is working, in the sense that it is meeting the parties' or society's objectives? The analyses that follow shed light on these issues and help identify whether there is one best way to structure or operate tripartism.

There was much theorizing in previous research about the factors that influenced the success of corporatism, including the degree of encompassing interest representation, union democracy, and social democratic political strength (Schmitter 1981, Regini 1997 and 2000, Streeck 1982, Crouch 1985, Baccaro 2000). Schmitter (1979) argues that mechanisms that shielded union leaders from popular pressures assisted corporatism in the 1970s and 1980s. Baccaro (2002), in contrast, claims that it was the spread of internal democracy in unions that was a key to the success of tripartism in Italy in the 1990s. Was union democracy also central to the success of tripartite activities in other countries in recent years? More generally, one of the most important contributions of this book is analysis of how the preconditions affecting the success of recent national tripartite pacts compare and contrast to those that influenced earlier corporatism.

The Decentralization Push of the 1980s and 1990s

Previous research shows that in nearly all countries in the 1980s and 1990s, the locus of collective bargaining shifted downward, often from a national or multicompany level to the firm or plant level. This shift included the breakdown of a national confederation–level agreement in Sweden, the erosion of national tribunal pay setting and the spread of enterprise bargaining in Australia, and the decline of multicompany bargaining in the United Kingdom and the United States. In these and other countries pay was increasingly being set, partially if not fully, at the plant or enterprise level. And where multiemployer bargaining persisted, as in Germany and Italy, its influence declined as sectoral or national agreements in those countries increasingly provided only minimum employment terms rather than contractual standards as in the past.

In nearly all countries, as shown by previous research, the intensity of local bargaining, involving local unions, works councils, or work groups increased dramatically in recent years. Much of this bargaining involved qualitative issues concerning work organization and work restructuring. In some cases local bargaining included increased use of contingent pay methods, as pay in one way or another became linked to plant, firm, individual, or some other measure of economic performance. Informal interactions between labor and management took on greater importance as part of work restructuring, which in some cases amounted to "concession bargaining" (i.e., highly pressurized efforts to stave off a plant closing or layoffs). In the process, work rules, working time, and work organization, often under the rubric of a search for greater workplace flexibility, took on greater importance.

The push for the individualization of pay or work practices provided further impetus to the decentralization of collective bargaining. As pay-for-knowledge, skill premiums, bonuses, and gain-sharing systems spread, any higher-level pay agreements increasingly served as frameworklike pay minima.

In the United Kingdom and Australia, the replacement of collective contracts with individual contracts provided an even more extreme form of bargaining structure decentralization. Even more widespread was the decline in union coverage and strength. In nearly all countries, the percent of the work force covered by collective contracts declined and nonunion employment became the ultimate decentralized way to set employment terms.

There were, of course, some exceptions to these trends. For example, with a longstanding tradition of heavy reliance on enterprise-level bargaining in the private sector, Japan experienced less downward movement in the locus of bargaining, at least as suggested by evidence up until the mid-1990s. Evidence of stability in the locus of wage setting in Japan is seen in the lack of an upward trend in inter-enterprise variation in Shunto wage increases as of the mid-1990s (Katz and Darbishire 2000, 232). At the same time, by the mid-1990s, some signs of increased pay variation did appear within Japanese firms through greater use of ability-based pay and variation in annual bonuses (Katz and Darbishire 2000, 236). Yet, previous research has not clarified whether, in the face of pressures resulting from sluggish economic growth from the mid-1990s on, Japan has begun to experience more extreme changes in the structure of labor, management, and government interactions. Japan is just an illustration of the questions that exist concerning the scope, nature, and implications of recent changes in the structure of interactions in other countries.

The Interaction between Decentralized Collective Bargaining and Tripartism

How has decentralized collective bargaining interacted with tripartite activities and what is likely to evolve in the future? By the mid-1990s in Italy, Ireland, Germany, and the Netherlands, the emergence (or in some cases, reemergence) of tripartite agreements led some to claim that the structure of collective bargaining was being recentralized (Baccaro 2000). Yet it is possible that plant and local collective bargaining will continue to spread while national pacts, focusing on wage moderation and workplace flexibility (and other matters), are forged in these countries. Or tripartism might spur various aspects of decentralized collective bargaining by promoting the development of local labor-management partnerships or through pay or productivity mandates or targets.

Australia provides an interesting case that might shed light on future possibilities in other countries. In Australia, the push for greater enterprise-level bargaining in the 1980s and early 1990s occurred under the rubric of an incomes policy provided through a national union-government agreement, the "accord," which included a number of rounds. To some extent the accord facilitated union acceptance of the simultaneous decentralization underway in the structure of collective bargaining as the Australian labor movement "favored a decentralization of bargaining toward the enterprise level provided this occurred within a strong centralized framework (at national and industry levels)" (Bray 1991). The accord, however, was ended in 1996 by the newly elected conservative government of John Howard. The extent to which the accord provides a precursor or future road map for national tripartite agreements in European countries and elsewhere warrants clarification. More generally, one of the tasks of the research in the country chapters that follow is examination of the interaction between decentralization in the structure of collective bargaining and national-level tripartism.

Another debate that surfaced as collective bargaining decentralization has proceeded concerns the extent to which this shift is transitory. Decentralization is likely to be transitory if it is essentially a mechanism through which employers gain bargaining power advantage. The idea here is that it is the *process* of decentralization that is most important. Employers in this view benefit most from the ability to play plants (and local unions) off against one another, that is, to whipsaw local unions. Yet this might only be a transitory need as, after gaining lower wage outcomes or wider skill differentials through whipsawing, employers then might prefer a return to centralized bargaining because of the advantages it provides (stability, predictability, and economies of scale).

A way to understand the potential temporary advantages to decentralized collective bargaining is to recognize the possibility that employers need decentralized bargaining to gain concessions because central unions are unwilling to grant the concessions employers desire, while local unions are more willing to do so given that they feel more direct pressure from workers threatened by employment losses. The question of whether or not these transitory advantages are critical arises because previous research has not clarified the reasons why employers' favor bargaining decentralization. Examination of recent developments can also clarify whether the structure of collective bargaining truly has been recentralized in recent years and the breadth of any such recentralization.

Shifts in Bargaining Power

In the 1980s and early 1990s, the impetus for the decentralization of collective bargaining clearly came from management. It was management that was either directly pushing for decentralization in its bargaining and public demands, as in Australia, or indirectly promoting decentralization as the device to provide pay and work rule concessions, as occurred commonly in the United States and even in Germany.

As the labor market improved in the late 1990s, however, in many countries labors' relative bargaining power improved and this shift reduced employers' whipsaw leverage. The United States was an extreme example as the labor market strengthened to the point that a debate ensued regarding the extent and permanence of "hyper-mobility" and the associated possibility that highly skilled labor could "call the shots" in the labor market. The bursting of the dot.com bubble in spring 2000 in the United States and the subsequent economic downturn, however, then markedly altered the state of the labor market. As a result, it is a propitious time to examine the effects that economic conditions exert on bargaining structure. For, if the intensity of the pressure for the decentralization of bargaining structure is found to be linked to the state of the economy, then this would lend credence to the notion that a key determinant of bargaining structure is bargaining power.

Furthermore, if relatively stronger labor movements are unable to reverse bargaining decentralization, this may reflect either a shift in labors' preferences (and if so, it would be interesting to know why labor has come to prefer decentralized bargaining) or the fact that it is total and not relative power that drives bargaining structure. Total power concerns the total profits (i.e., economic rents) that are available for distribution. There is some previous economic research suggesting that centralized collective bargaining spreads when total power is high, as in this circumstance labor and management have reason to join together in centralized forums to divide up the large available economic rents and symmetrically, when economic rents shrink, the parties are pushed to decentralize collective bargaining (Hendricks and Kahn 1982). This can explain why the push for decentralization strengthened in the 1980s and early 1990s in the face of globalization and economic deregulation.

Yet it is not clear whether recognition of the role of total power really helps explain recent events and whether the effects of shifts in the parties' total power can be disentangled from the effects of shifts in relative bargaining power. One of the tasks of comparative research is to make use, as best as possible, of variations in labor and management's power over time and across countries to clarify the influence and effects of relative and total power.

Bargaining power is only one among a number of possible causes of shifts in the nature and locus of labor, management, and government interactions. I, and others, claim that work reorganization and corporate or worker interest diversification have been a key pressure for the decentralizations occurring in the structure of collective bargaining and corporations (Katz 1993, Purcell and Ahlstrand 1994). While bargaining power and diversification matter, a strong role also is being played by work reorganization as unions and workers have become "co-managers of the internal labor market" (Streeck 1984). Decentralization has been linked to the elevation in the importance of local bargaining because the process of identifying efficient (or acceptable) team work systems and the successful implementation of new work practices apparently requires the active participation of local actors and local experimentation with new packages of employment practices. Analysis of recent trends thus can help clarify the role played by these and other forces and thereby help identify the causes and consequences of decentralization in the structure of collective bargaining and its extreme variants, individualization and deunionization.

The chapters that follow go a long way in providing answers to the many critical questions identified above. Where currently available evidence remains limited, the chapters at least help clarify the key issues that remain for future research.

1 The Irish Experiment in Social Partnership

Paul Teague and James Donaghey

McDonalds, the fast food chain restaurant, has an outlet just off O'Connell Street, the main thoroughfare in Dublin. In 1987, it advertised part-time vacancies and within a day a huge queue had formed composed of different strata of people all sharing the common desire of getting employment. Fast-forward a decade and the scene is radically different. Traffic in Dublin's city center is in gridlock, and the new prosperity of the country can be seen by the huge amount of construction activity and hustle and bustle of people in the streets. Even if we set aside unhelpful metaphors such as the Celtic Tiger, it is difficult not to reach the conclusion that the economic (and social) transformation experienced by the Republic of Ireland in the nineties was nothing less than spectacular.[1] The country has switched from being a basket case to one that enjoys virtual full employment. A national framework for social partnership has been in place during the economic upturn period. It would be excessive to argue that social partnership was the main driver behind the economic revival. A multitude of factors, positively interacting with each other, fueled the high growth rates. At the same time, social partnership has made an important contribution to economic transformation.

This paper assesses the Irish experience of social partnership. We pay particular attention to what type of coordination was promoted by the various national social agreements. A number of overlapping arguments are advanced. One is that social partnership in Ireland is contained within a multidimensional framework, some parts of which echo traditional "corporatist" practices and procedures while others are more innovative in character. We suggest that the social partnership framework is not exactly a model of coordinated decentralization and is better described as an open method of labor market coordination. A second argument is that while the Irish experience of social partnership holds important lessons for other countries, claims that it represents a new model of labor market governance should be treated with caution. Irish social partnership is a combination of old and new employment relations practices customized to suit domestic economic and political conditions. Third, whether social partnership has fully secured its declared purpose of promoting a form of economic development that combines competitiveness and fairness remains an open question.

The paper is organized as follows. The first section develops our meaning of coordinated decentralization and situates its relevance to Irish social partnership. Then a number of contextual points are developed to set the scene for our discussion of social partnership. Next the wage bargaining element of Irish social partnership is set out and evaluated. After this assessment, the discussion turns to the theme of enterprise partnership and shows how this concept has grown in importance in recent years. The conclusion brings together the various arguments of the paper and makes some observations about the future of the social partnership framework.

COORDINATED DECENTRALIZATION AND THE IRISH EMPLOYMENT RELATIONS SYSTEM

A popular argument is that national employment relations systems in Europe are gravitating in one way or another toward a coordinated decentralization model of employment relations. Coordinated decentralization is usually interpreted in two different ways in the literature. One fairly narrow perspective is that it involves the "loosening" of centralized or sector-level collective bargaining systems. On this view, tightly integrated extrafirm bargains are no longer sustainable in the face of a variety of economic and social transformations that are encouraging greater economic decentralization. The new competitive environment is no place for tight institutional constraints. Organizations must be permitted to make emergency deviations from established industry or national pay rates. Alternatively the centralized bargaining machinery must only produce framework agreements that set indicative guidelines (as opposed to binding rules) for pay increases and improvements in working conditions (Ferner and Hyman 1998; Traxler 1995a). The second view of coordinated decentralization is more expansive in outlook. It is a story of how the *complementarity* and *fit* between decentralized institutions can produce highly coordinated labor markets. On this account, coordinated decentralization gives rise to systems of national institutional comparative advantage, leading to high grade, yet distinctive forms, of economic performance (Soskice 1999).

The evolving system of Irish social partnership approximates neither perspective on coordinated decentralization. On the one hand, it amounts to more than defensive adaptations to employment relations institutions to counter the dissolving effects of globalization, technological innovation, and social change. On the other hand, Ireland does not possess tightly integrated, complementary labor market institutions, which have given rise to a specialized institutional pattern of comparative economic advantage. In the Irish context, achieving close institutional fit between different parts of the employment relations system is neither seen as possible nor particularly desirable. Addressing market (and institutional) failures, the main motivation for seeking coordination in the first place, is still considered important, but it is done by what we call the open method of coordination.

The open method of coordination as developed in Ireland has five properties. First, the governance of wage determination remains the core function of the social partnership arrangement. This is the social glue that holds together the entire system. On carrying out this function, Irish social partnership embodies the same tensions and dilemmas associated with more established "corporatist" methods of wage setting. A second and more distinctive attribute of Irish social partnership has been the emphasis placed on producing a *procedural consensus*, as opposed to building complementarities, between employment relations actors to guide the search for solutions to identified problems. Complementarities between labor market institutions smack too much of seeking a "static equilibrium" within a social partnership arrangement, causing them to be too fixed and rigid in what they do. A procedural consensus, on the other hand, assumes a greater capacity on the part of institutions to change over time so that they are more able to keep pace with fast-changing business and labor market conditions.

The third feature of open coordination is that decision-making inside the social partnership framework does not solely involve tough bargaining to reach an accommodation between competing employment relations interests, but also "deliberative" type interactions that rely more on evidence-based and reasonable discussions to advance policy ideas. In old-fashioned employment relations language, social partnership should be as much about integrative bargaining as distributional bargaining (Walton and McKersie 1965). The motive behind this development is to challenge adversarial attitudes and behavior that have been longstanding features of Irish employment relations and encourage cooperative forms of management and employee interactions. Thus much is made of terms such as *shared understandings* and *joint action* in social partnership circles.

Fourth and notwithstanding the early observation about the centrality of the wage bargain, open coordination has sought to widen the scope of social partnership agreements so that they include public policies designed to promote social inclusion. In concrete institutional terms, this has lead to "new" social groups, such as those representing the unemployed, gaining entry into the negotiating process to conclude social partnership deals. Fifth, open coordination places less emphasis on traditional methods of labor market regulation that use constraining rules to tie employers to particular employment practices. More prominence is given to designing "enabling" or supportive public programs that would advance the competitive performance of organizations while ensuring that employees enjoy decent working conditions.

This open method of coordination that guides Irish social partnership raises a wide range of fascinating questions. For example, can civil associations be integrated into a social partnership arrangement in a manner that confers on them the same "public status" enjoyed by employers groups and trade unions? What types of social inclusion programs have been produced by the social partnership agreements and how do they relate to the pay deals? We do not have the space to address properly these questions despite their obvious importance. Our focus is primarily on the evolution of managerial-employee interactions under social partnership. In addressing this matter we will be concerned with traditional employment relations issues—how have the social partnership agreements affected labor market outcomes, what has been the fate of the unions, and so on. At the same time, we try to shed light on the importance of some of the proclaimed innovative aspects to social partnership in Ireland. In particular we assess whether social partnership is promoting new credible commitments between Irish employers and trade unions and whether the social partnership agreements have balanced equity and efficiency in labor markets. But before we get on to these topics a number of preliminary remarks are required to explain the dynamics of Irish employment relations.

MANAGEMENT-EMPLOYMENT INTERACTIONS IN IRELAND: SOME PRELIMINARY REMARKS

Adversarialism and voluntarism are well-established features of Irish employment systems. To a large extent, this is an administrative legacy of

British rule in Ireland. The organization and behavior of employers and trade unions had a strong "British" voluntarist feel to them. With regard to organized labor, its most pronounced feature was its fragmented structure. Every occupational segment, no matter how small, seemed to have its own trade union organization. Moreover, in many cases, trade unions competed for similar type workers. A second feature of trade union organization was its decentralized orientation. On the one hand, the authority of the Irish Congress of Trade Unions (ICTU), the federal body for organized labor, was carefully circumscribed so that is main role was one of coordination. On the other hand, local shop stewards enjoyed considerable autonomy, thereby ensuring that they were frequently the pace setters on employment relations matters. Employer organizations displayed many of the fragmented organizational characteristics of trade unions. In addition, national employer organizations were relatively weak bodies with little capacity to drive an employment relations agenda from the center. Both employers and trade unions had a predilection for decentralized employment relations relatively free from legal and government interference. Both sides preferred to take their chance in a free collective bargaining tussle rather than allow the government to regulate employment relations through legal procedures and rules.

Before the current social partnership regime, which started in 1987, the Irish system of collective bargaining system lacked order. The institutional level of collective bargaining differed across the economy. In the public sector, bargaining was centralized: wage rates and most terms of employment were set by national negotiations. Some local bargaining did take place, but this was usually limited to matters such as working conditions, the availability of overtime, or changing job rules. In some spheres of the market economy, most notably in the construction industry, sector-level bargaining prevailed. Again, a certain amount of supplementary enterprise bargaining took place. Overall, decentralized, enterprise-level bargaining was the norm in the private sector. Various efforts were made to bring order to this fragmented bargaining system by promoting centralized incomes policies, especially in the 1970s, but without much success (Hardiman 1988).

Unlike some "continental" European countries, Ireland has no legal extension rule that ensures that all "relevant" workers are covered by a collective agreement. No reliable data exist on collective bargaining coverage, but the consensus view is that sector-level agreements led to more spreading of bargained terms as compared to other contract forms. Where enterprise bargaining was the norm, the picture appears patchy: a going-rate of sorts emerged in some industries, but was absent from other industries. A minimum wage was only introduced in 2000. Before then, low-paid workers received a certain level of protection from two wage-fixing mechanisms, the Joint Labour Councils (JLCs) and the Joint Industrial Councils (JICs). These two bodies established a floor for pay and working conditions in certain low-wage sectors. Since the early 1980s a notable trend has been the steady growth of a nonunion sector. An important driver behind this development has been the arrival of new multinational companies in the country, particularly those based in the United States. All in all, before the mid-1980s Irish employment relations were voluntarist in character and the structure of collective bargaining was fragmented.

Another important contextual point to note is the extreme openness of the Irish economy. In Ireland's formative years, Irish governments sought national self-sufficiency through a strong program of protectionism (Mjøset 1992; Lee 1989). This policy was a wholesale failure. In the fifties, the political and administrative elite engineered a complete policy reversal and introduced a regime of unfettered economic openness. Generous tax incentives were created to attract foreign direct investment and many multinationals, particularly those based in the United States, took up the offer. The result is that foreign companies now dominate the tradable sector in the country. Economic openness was advanced by Irish entry into the European Union (EU) in 1973. Deeper economic integration with the rest of Europe exposed many parts of Irish indigenous industry for the first time to international competition. The process of economic openness has continuously increased ever since. As a result, Ireland is probably the most-exposed EU economy.

This has led to two powerful dynamics, one of constrained discretion and the other of guiding economic policy-making. Placing such an emphasis on attracting foreign companies to advance industrial development has encouraged governments to act in a self-restraining manner. For example, an unwritten assumption is that the labor market cannot be regulated too much as it might discourage multinationals from moving to the country. At the same time, public policy has been designed to maximize the positive spillover effects that can be derived from foreign direct investment. A case in point is the range of programs developed to build "backward linkages" between foreign and domestically owned companies. This policy mix of constrained discretion and guiding has left an imprint on Irish employment relations. On the one hand, the adversarial orientation of the "British" model of industrial relations sits uneasily with efforts to project Ireland as a warm home for multinationals. On the other hand, the disorganized character of the employment relations system may hold back the capacity of organizations to "appropriate" new ways of doing things.

THE SOCIAL PARTNERSHIP EXPERIMENT

While the preceding contextual remarks provide the necessary background to discussing the evolution of social partnership, it is important to stress the contingent nature of the birth of this arrangement. Social partnership owes a great deal to the election of a Fianna Fail minority government in 1987. The political hue of this political party is right-of-center. Nevertheless, it was strongly committed to tackling the dire economic and social situation prevailing in the country through a program of social consensus (Manseragh 1986: Fianna Fail 1987). A national pay deal was seen as the centerpiece of this economic strategy. A national consensus quickly formed with a bipartisan approach being followed by the two largest parties, Fianna Fail and Fine Gael (also a center right party and the largest opposition party) in the area of economic policy. Both trade unions and employers were supportive of this move toward a centralized wage agreement. For the trade union movement, national pay determination was a way of avoiding a Thatcherlike offensive, which was causing big damage to organized labor in the United Kingdom. For employers, centralized bargaining held out the promise of stable employment relations. Moreover, they did not want to be seen standing apart from a "national effort" to pull the country back from the economic abyss (MacSharry and White 2000). In addition to dealing with the country's domestic economic difficulties, the social partners and political parties were of the view that a consensus-based employment relations system would better place the country to become a member of a European monetary union (Teague 1995; MacSharry and White 2000). Thus a variety of pressing internal and external economic pressures pushed employment relations actors toward national wage setting.

Altogether there have been five separate national agreements. The process got under way in October 1987 with the Programme for National Recovery (PNR). The PNR was followed by further agreements in 1990 (Programme for Economic and Social Progress, PESP), 1993 (Programme for Competitiveness and Work, PCW), 1996 (Partnership 2000), and 2000 (Programme for Prosperity and Fairness, PPF) (Government of Ireland 1987, 1990, 1993, 1996, 2000).

The first three agreements more or less replicated centralized wage agreements as practiced elsewhere. The key representatives of employers and trade unions—the Irish Congress of Trade Unions, the Federated

Union of Employers, the Construction Industry Federation, the Confederation of Irish Industry—and four agricultural organizations (three for the PNR in 1987) negotiated the terms of these agreements. By 1994, all of the five parliamentary parties in the Dáil (Irish parliament) had been involved in governments that oversaw social partnership agreements. This covered a broad ideological spectrum involving the left-wing Democratic Left; the center left Labour party; the center right parties, Fianna Fail and Fine Gael; and the right-wing Progressive Democrats.

After the negotiation of the PCW in 1993, the institutional complexion of social partnership changed. In particular, a fourth community pillar was introduced into the social partnership framework. The bodies included the National Women's Council of Ireland, the Irish National Organization for the Unemployed (INOU), and the Council of Religions in Ireland (CORI). CORI and the INOU are highly vocal on the issue of social exclusion. Nominally these groups participated with full social partner status in the negotiations that produced in 1996 the fourth social agreement, Partnership 2000. But the trade unions, employers, and government negotiated the core element of the agreement, the pay deal, alone.

The civil associations had greatest influence on the "social wage" component of the national agreement. Like other "corporatist" wage deals in Europe, the Irish government makes a number of commitments on public expenditure and taxation to facilitate the pay deals concluded by the employers and unions. In the literature, these commitments are referred to as corporatist quid pro quo. A feature of these commitments is that the design, implementation, and evaluation of the public expenditure commitments usually remain "in-house" concerns of the relevant government departments.

Bringing civil associations into the social partnership framework opened up this relatively closed form of public policy-making. A new deliberative form of policy-making was introduced, allowing civic associations a more active role in the decision-making cycle (NESF 1997). The hope was that these associations would improve the quality of public programs through their possession of greater knowledge of the various dimensions of a particular social problem (O'Donnell and Thomas 1998). Unfortunately, no convincing research has been completed that assesses whether this initial expectation has actually been realized.

WAGE BARGAINING AND IRISH SOCIAL PARTNERSHIP

Since 1987, wage bargaining has been the mainstay of the various social partnership agreements. Table 1.1 describes the basic terms of the wage

TABLE 1.1. BASIC PAY TERMS OF NATIONAL PAY AGREEMENTS

Year	Basic pay increases	Other pay and tax features
I: PROGRAMME FOR NATIONAL RECOVERY, 1988–90 INCLUSIVE		
1988	2.5%	Special pay awards for public servants delayed.
1989	2.5%	Tax cuts of £225 million agreed over three years.
1990	2.5%	Low-paid workers given "special consideration".
II: PROGRAMME FOR ECONOMIC AND SOCIAL PROGRESS, 1991–93		
1991	4.0%	Special rates for the low paid: year 1; 4.25 in year 2; and 5.25 in year 3 for the low paid.
1992	3.0%	Local bargaining of 3% permitted in "exceptional cases".
1993	3.75%	£400 Million in tax cuts promised.
III: PROGRAMME FOR COMPETITIVENESS AND WORK, 1994–96/7		
1994	2.0%*	Public service pay deal: 3.5 years: 5 month pause; 2% in year 1; 2% for year two; 1.5% for next four months; 1.5% for next three months; 1% for final 6 months.
1995	2.5%*	Tax cuts focusing on low and middle earners.
1996	2.5% for first six months* 1% for next six months*	Special consideration for the low paid after year 2.
IV: PARTNERSHIP 2000, 1997–2000		
1997	2.5%	Public service pay deal: Phase 1: 2.5% of first £220 basic for nine months, then 2.5% of the balance of full basic pay for 3 months. After first year, as private sector.
1998	2.25%	Provision for local negotiation of further 2% rise in years 2 (private sector) and 3 (public sector).
1999	1.5% for 9 months, 1.0% for 6 months	£1 billion on full year cost basis to be made available for tax relief.
V: PROGRAMME FOR PROSPERITY AND FAIRNESS 2000–2002		
2000	5.5%	Further tax cuts.
2001	5.5%	Public service pay issue to be resolved by benchmarking body: 4% to be allowed for substantial change in public sector organization.
2002	4% for the next nine months	National minimum wage established to have reached £5 per hour by the end of the PPF.

* Private sector excluding construction.

settlement contained in each agreement. It shows that all five agreements have contained relatively low increases to nominal wages in Ireland. A feature of all the wage deals has been the link between the pay awards and projected economic growth rates. In addition to these basic terms, three of the agreements—the PESP, Partnership 2000 and the PPF—included local bargaining clauses. Under these local bargaining clauses wages were capped: a ceiling was placed on what pay increases an employer could give at the enterprise level over and above the pay award set out in the national agreement.

Figure 1.1 suggests that some wage drift, particularly with regard to the manufacturing sector, occurred during the life span of the various agreements, but it never got out of control. Since 1990, the correlation between the pay increases recommended in the agreements and actual manufacturing wage increases are relatively close. The greatest degree of drift occurred in 1996 (the final year of the PCW) and 1999 (the final year of Partnership 2000). These figures, however, should be read with caution, as official Irish wage statistics are not always accurate. Moreover, a certain level of deviation from negotiated rates was only to be expected in the context of super economic growth and a tight labor market. But the consensus is that social partnership did deliver wage moderation.

The various pay agreements have delivered real product wage moderation. Figures from European Economy (2001) show that for most of the 1990s productivity increases outstripped wage increases, causing unit labor costs to fall. This is supporting evidence for those who claim that the social partnership agreements helped produce a super-competitive economy in Ireland. Falling unit labor costs amounts to a real depreciation of the Irish wage system vis-à-vis other economies, particularly those of the EU, thus allowing the country to steal a march on their rivals. At the same time, real wages have increased for Irish workers. Although workers in some industries have fared better than others during the lifetime of the partnerships, nearly all types of workers have experienced substantial improvements in their living standards. All in all, under social partnership wages have been increasing above inflation, allowing real take-home-pay to improve, but at the same time have not been keeping pace with productivity improvements, thereby contributing positively to economic competitiveness.

A debate has flared in recent years about the distributional effects of the pay agreements. There are two overlapping parts to this argument. One is that while the share of profits in gross domestic product (GDP) has increased significantly, the wage share has fallen. Figure 1.2 shows that that since the start of 1987 the general trend has been for the share of

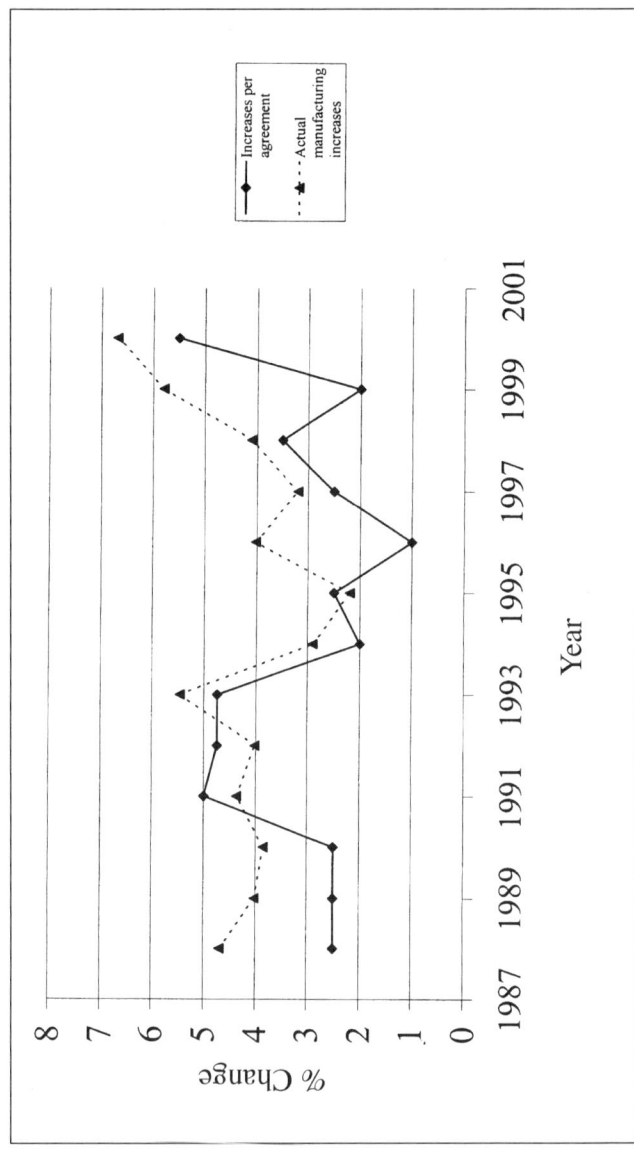

FIGURE 1.1 ACTUAL MANUFACTURING WAGE INCREASES COMPARED TO WAGE INCREASES PROVIDED IN AGREEMENTS

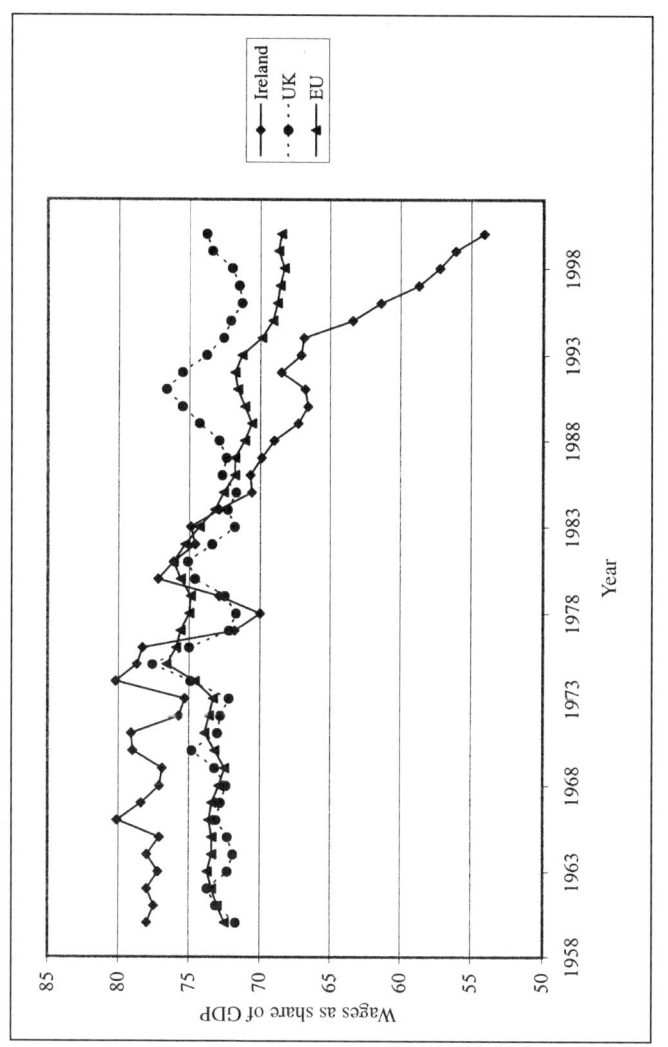

FIGURE 1.2 WAGES AS PERCENTAGE SHARE OF GDP

wages in national income to decline across Europe. But the fall appears to have been sharper in Ireland than elsewhere, particularly since the mid-1990s. Even the United Kingdom, one of the homes of neoliberalism, has not experienced such a marked shift from wages to profits. These figures should be treated with caution. Ireland has a low rate of corporation tax for multinationals—the lowest in the EU. Some foreign companies with operations in the country tend to register profits in Ireland but shortly afterward repatriate them to the "home" country. Transfer pricing policies of this kind inflate GDP figures and thus distort the proportion of wages (and profits) in this set of national account calculations. Nevertheless, even allowing for these shadowy accounting practices, the trend tarnishes the claim that the social partnership regime is producing an equitable distribution of the fruits of economic growth. Workers have experienced real improvements in living standards during the lifetime of the present agreements, but employers appear to have fared better. This should be a cause for concern.

The second part of the argument is that wage inequality has increased under social partnership. It is widely accepted that income inequality increased during the 1990s, but this is also true for wage inequality (Barret et al. 1999; Cantillon et al. 2001). A popular argument normally made about "corporatist" wage bargaining systems is that they insert both a floor and ceiling into pay structures, thereby compressing wage differentials. The Irish national pay deals appear not to have produced such solidaristic wage outcomes. This trend has been used to support the argument that social partnership as practiced in Ireland is essentially neoliberal in character (Allen 2000). This argument is an overstatement. The Irish labor market has not followed an "Americanized" path characterized by impressive job generation performance alongside stagnant real wage growth for many low-income workers. As mentioned above, most workers have experienced an appreciable increase in wages in Ireland: there has been a rising tide of economic prosperity.

Nevertheless, rising wage inequality is a troublesome development, but whether it is regarded as one in policy circles is a moot point. This observation is an important point for it touches on a critical debate on the economic and social content of "Third Way" European social democracy. Supporters of this approach are coy on the matter of wage inequality, but there is a suspicion that they regard it as acceptable for some workers to receive higher wages than others, provided that everybody is progressing up the wage curve. Increased wage differentials between employees are interpreted as a sign of the new diversity in occupational structures brought about by the growth of service industries and an indication that meritocracy and effort are being rewarded in the economy. Not everybody is happy with this approach: social democrats of a more traditional orientation suggest that to accept increases in wage inequality is to abandon commitments to social justice. This debate is likely to continue for some time in Ireland and indeed in other EU countries. Our assessment of this debate in the Irish context is that the increase in wage inequality is a matter of concern as it threatens the survival of the entire social partnership framework.

SOCIAL PARTNERSHIP AND LABOR MARKET PERFORMANCE

At the start of the present round of social partnership, the Irish economy faced two major problems: high public debt and high unemployment. In 1987, public debt stood at 118.2 percent of nominal GDP and unemployment was at 16.8 percent. Ireland's economic mess began in the 1970s with traditional Keynesian expansionary policies being pursued. Of the two problems identified, the poor fiscal state of the country was seen as the priority for remedial action. Over a fifteen-year period, due first to an austere stabilization program and then a prolonged period of revenue enhancing economic growth, Ireland has reduced significantly its public-sector debt. In fact, Ireland was able to enter the European Monetary Union (EMU) in 1998 with a fiscal performance superior to any of the other participating countries with the exception of Luxembourg.

When social partnership was initiated in 1987, unemployment stood at 16.8 percent. In addition, emigration was running at a frighteningly high level as people left the country to secure a better life elsewhere. This situation has been dramatically turned around. In 2002, unemployment stood at 4.2 percent, half the EU average. Moreover, to relieve labor market shortages, Ireland has started "importing" labor to the extent that immigration now exceeds emigration. Behind this big fall in joblessness has been a hugely impressive employment-generation machine. To the extent there has been a miracle of any description in the country it has been on the employment front. As figure 1.3 shows, since 1987 Ireland has been one of the EU's star performers in terms of job creation. Market- or business-related services have been the main source of the new jobs.

Ebbinghaus and Hassel (2000) argue that a motivation behind many of the recent social pacts in Europe has been to bring about welfare state reform. Countries like Germany and Italy are seen as financially overcommitted in terms of pension provision and other social benefits. As a result, social partnership agreements are being used to reduce the fiscal demands made by these social protection systems. But this has not been

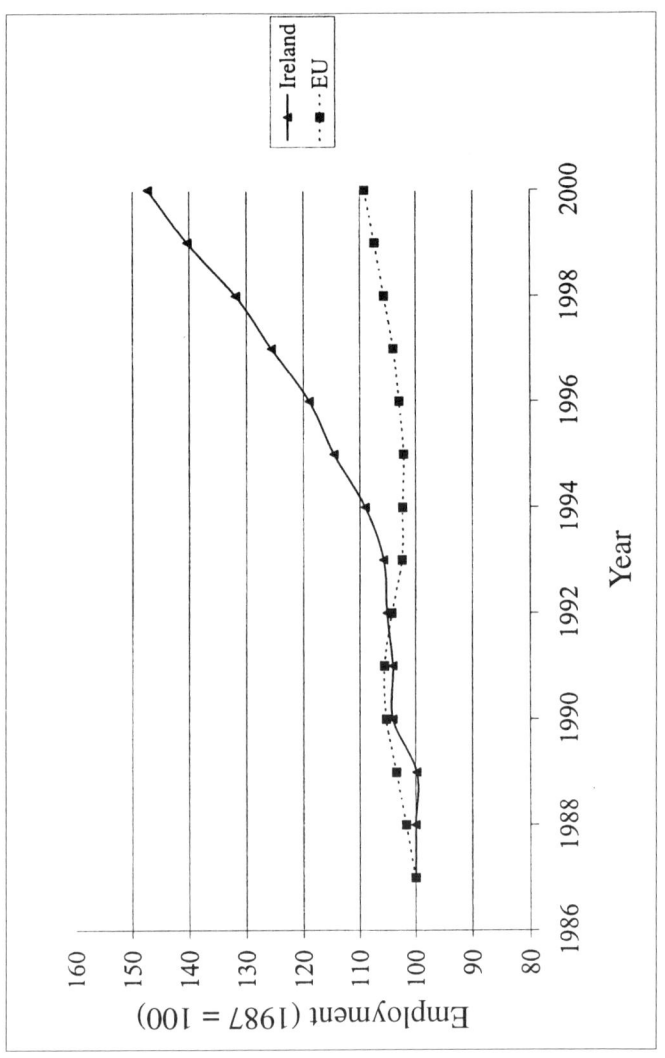

FIGURE 1.3 EMPLOYMENT GROWTH 1987–2000

an issue in the Irish context, as the country never really developed a Swedish or German type welfare system. Rather, a feature of successive national agreements has been a trade-off between wage moderation and tax reductions. The focus on tax cuts has been designed to improve the take-home pay of workers. In 1987, the lower tax rate was 35 percent whereas those in the upper tax bracket paid 48 percent. In 2001 these figures had dropped to 20 percent and 42 percent respectively. The plan is that by the end of 2002 those earning the national minimum wage are likely to have been taken out of the tax net completely. One argument gaining ground is that too much emphasis has been placed on tax reductions and in the future social and health provisions need expansion by increasing public expenditure.

EMPLOYMENT RELATIONS UNDER SOCIAL PARTNERSHIP
The Fate of the Trade Unions

As outlined above, the Irish trade union movement has traditionally been highly fragmented. However, since 1980, mainly as a result of mergers, the trade union movement in the Republic of Ireland has undergone large-scale reorganization. Between 1981 and 1999, the number of trade unions fell from eighty-six to forty-six. A merger in 1989 created Ireland's biggest union, called SIPTU. In 1999 this union had a total membership of 226,659, which amounted to just over 45 percent of the membership of trade unions that hold negotiating licenses. The top three unions, SIPTU, IMPACT, and MANDATE, have 59 percent of total trade union membership while the ten largest unions make up 86.4 percent of total union membership. The absolute numbers of those in employment and belonging to a trade union have increased over the past few decades. Yet when we turn to trade union density levels, the figures are less comforting for organized labor. Since the mid-1980s, Irish trade union density levels have been declining, from a high of nearly 48 percent in 1983 to just over 35 percent in 1999. If the period of social partnership is specifically examined, trade union density has fallen from 43.8 percent to 35.0 percent.

Although social partnership cannot be said to have been disadvantageous to organized labor, it clearly has not been as supportive as some would have wished. Two different views exist about the cause of the decline in trade union density. One view is that the decline is due to employer union avoidance and substitution strategies (Gunnigle 2000; Gunnigle, O'Sullivan, and Kinsella 2001). The other view is that trade union membership has simply not been able to keep pace with the quite spectacular increases in employment. While both factors have been at play, our view is that the second explanation is the more convincing as an explanation for the decline in union density.

Trade union recognition has been a hot issue during the social partnership period. One argument is that trade union recognition procedures are too weak and favor employers. Ireland's heavy reliance on inward investment is seen as source of this problem (Gunnigle 2000). Many trade union activists point to a deep paradox in successive governments' employment relations strategies. On the one hand, governments have promoted social partnership, thereby giving trade unions unprecedented access to national economic and social decision-making. On the other hand, they have adopted policies that have made it difficult for trade unions to recruit at the company level. All in all, the social partnership years have not been entirely blissful for trade union organization.

The Role of Employers

Important changes have occurred in the organizational structure and role of employer bodies under national social partnership. Traditionally, employer interests have been represented by a wide number of bodies. But as a result of a number of mergers and reorganization, one strong body, known as the Irish Business and Employers Confederation (IBEC), has emerged as the effective voice for employers. IBEC is an effective organization. First of all, it has carried out efficiently the "encompassing" functions normally associated with employer groups in a corporatist wage regime: it has policed the various national pay deals very effectively. Second, it is a highly disciplined organization. Rarely, do you find internal disagreements spilling out into the public arena. In fact, it is very difficult to gain an insight into the internal debates and workings of IBEC. Third, the organization is highly proactive and forward-looking in developing a public policy agenda that coincides with the interests of its members. Thus, for instance, the members of IBEC have been willing participants in public programs to advance enterprise partnerships on the grounds that such action will reduce the demand for legislation on employee involvement. Overall, IBEC has played an important role in sustaining the current social partnership regime.

Employment Disputes

Social partnership has produced a stable employment relations environment. The number of days lost due to industrial action since 1960 (figure 1.4) show that the period since 1988 has been by far the most stable since 1960. When the current phase of social partnership is compared with the

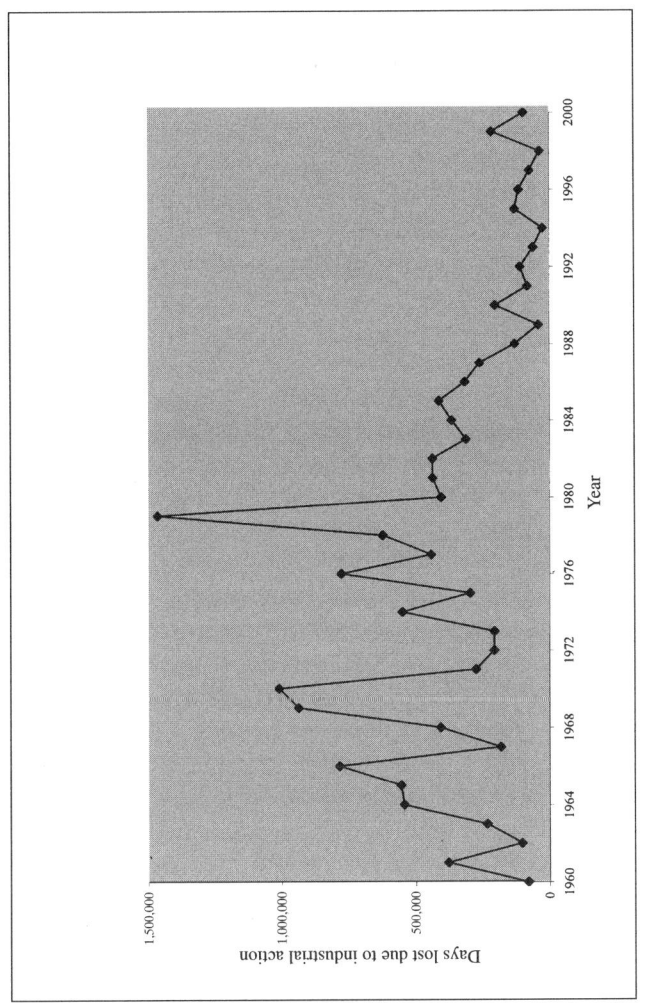

FIGURE 1.4 DAYS LOST DUE TO INDUSTRIAL ACTION

previous round of centralized agreements in the 1970s and early 1980s, the data show that the current regime has experienced fewer employment disputes. Actually the most peaceful years during the earlier regime (1971, 1972, 1973, and 1975) just about compare with the worst years of the current phase of social partnership (1990 and 1999). Admittedly, such comparisons are crude; nevertheless they give some indicator about why there is such strong support for the continuation of social partnership in Government.

This story of high stability in labor relations under the recent social partnership agreements is corroborated by the figures on the numbers of days per year lost because of industrial action over the past four decades. Two features stand out from the data provided in table 1.2. First, the decade with the highest number of annual days lost because of industrial action was the 1970s—during the life of the previous attempt to create wage coordination. Second, the 1990s is the best decade, with a lower number of annual days lost because of industrial action than any of the three previous decade: for example, the average loss of days was just over 100,000 in the 1990s, compared to over half a million days during the 1970s.

A mixed picture emerges from this overview of employment relations outcomes during the recent period of Irish social partnership. The scorecard reads full marks on employment performance, but could do better on the equity front. One of the consequences of these ambiguous employment relations trends is that ample ammunition has been provided for those eager to develop either excessively optimistic or pessimistic accounts of Irish social partnership. Those who promote the optimistic view point to remarkable employment growth rates and the durability of the national partnership deals (Sweeney 1999). Others seeking to paint a darker portrait invariably focus on the falling share of wages in national income and rising income inequality (Allen 2000). Against the evidence set out in this paper both positions seem too partial. It is simply inappropriate to write-off Irish employment relations as neoliberalism disguised by a social partnership façade or to promote it as a model that other countries should

TABLE 1.2. INDUSTRIAL DISPUTES IN IRELAND

	1960–69	1970–79	1980–89	1990–99
Average days lost per year	420,498	585,103	31,140	109,722

Source: Figures from the Department of Labor and Central Statistics office.

rush headlong to emulate. Although not particularly flamboyant, the most accurate conclusion lies somewhere between these two extremes.

PROMOTING SOCIAL PARTNERSHIP AT ENTERPRISE LEVEL

The first two national agreements were mainly concerned with macro-economic matters such as securing fiscal consolidation and advancing Irish entry into European monetary union. By the mid-1990s, however, trade unions had become increasingly anxious that a narrow focus on macro-economic targets was leading to the neglect of social partnership at the enterprise level (NESC 1996; Roche 1997; Teague 1995). To address this worry, the third agreement, Partnership 2000, established a framework for fostering enterprise partnerships. A rather loose and open-ended definition was used to foster such arrangements. The agreement stated that enterprise partnership should be viewed as

> an active relationship based on recognition of a common interest to secure the competitiveness, viability and prosperity of the enterprise. It involves a continuing commitment to improvements in quality and efficiency; and the acceptance by employers of employees as stakeholders with rights and interests to be considered in the context of major decisions affecting their employment.
>
> Partnership involves common ownership of the resolution of challenges, involving the direct participation of employees/ representatives and an investment in their training, development and working environment. (Government of Ireland 1996, 62)

The Programme for Prosperity and Fairness built on this definition by identifying nine areas as being "particularly relevant" to the partnership approach.[2] This "open" approach to enterprise partnerships rests on two key assumptions. One is that such arrangements cannot be imposed, legally or otherwise, on organizations, but have to be "owned" by the various constituencies of the enterprise. The other is that public policy has an important role in providing managers and employees with knowledge on how to embed partnership activity inside organizations. The public support framework, which is largely organized by the National Centre for Partnership and Performance, has four overlapping components.[3] One component is the sponsorship and coordination of learning networks so that companies setting up partnerships can connect with one another and share experiences. These networks are closely monitored so that more useful diagnostic instruments and training modules can be developed. The second component is the promotion of research and dissemination. A variety of focused research projects have been sponsored to deepen understanding of the partnership process in action—the extent to which employee and management attitudes change with the introduction of collaborative employment practices for example.

A third function is building verification and assurance focal points outside the organization. Very often employees and managers inside organizations seek assurance from external agents, usually national trade unions and employer associations, that meaningful value-added activities will emerge from developing an enterprise partnership. To facilitate this demand, IBEC and ICTU, the national employer and trade union bodies, respectively, have developed a number of important projects and advisory services. These initiatives are important as they guarantee organized labor a central role in the supportive framework for enterprise partnerships. In addition, the National Centre for Partnership and Performance, also acts as an external verifier. In essence, this role involves the center giving its imprimatur to various training agencies and experimental actions that organizations and trade unions regard as a quality standard. The fourth function can be called experimental public policy. For the most part, this involves the NCPP coordinating new joint action by different arms of government and semipublic bodies to advance partnership at enterprise level.

It cannot be claimed that enterprise partnerships have spread widely across the Irish economy. At the same time, interviews with trade unions, employers, and public officials who are actively involved on this matter as well as some selective case studies suggest that the enterprise partnerships that have been established broadly follow the following institutional design (see figure 1.5). It is important to emphasize that this design operates as a reference point that employment relations actors touch base with when setting up partnerships.

An enterprise partnership normally is established by an agreement involving managers and employees (typically represented by a trade union). This agreement outlines the institutional character of an envisaged arrangement. It is normally signed only after managers and unionists have carried out a lengthy diagnostic review. A diagnostic review is a set of procedures that organizations conduct to give managers and the union a better understanding of the type of partnership agreement an organization can "hold" in prevailing commercial circumstances. Furthermore, a review provides an opportunity for employees and managers to forge a consensus about the shape and character of a prospective partnership deal. A partnership agreement is less an elaborated model of how the organization should be and more the institutional expression of the consensus reached by managers and employees during the diagnosis review. At the

The Irish Experiment in Social Partnership

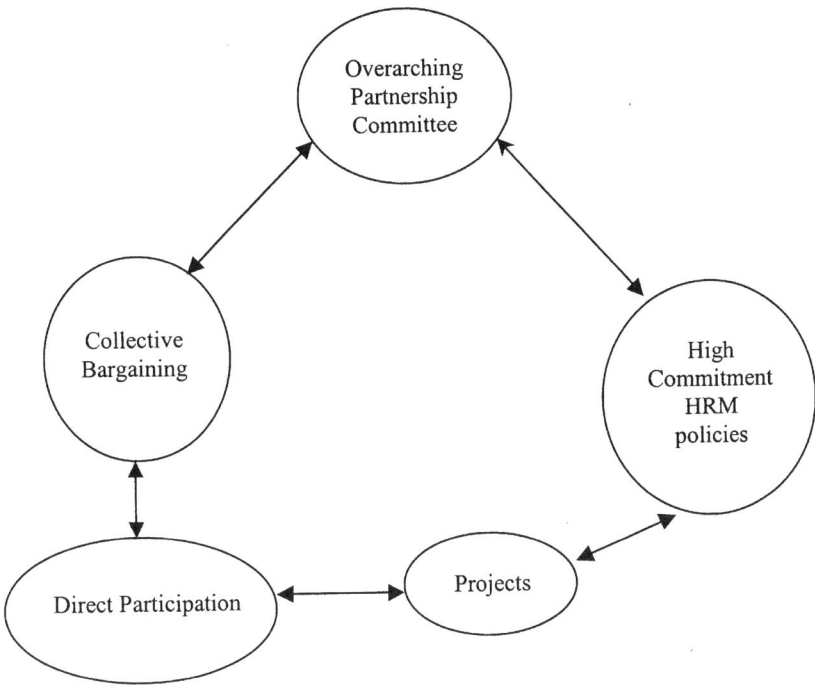

FIGURE 1.5 DESIGN FEATURES OF ENTERPRISE PARTNERSHIPS

same time an agreement usually sets up a companywide partnership forum or committee. Invariably, the partnership forum established is an overarching, open-ended, arrangement charged with the responsibility of initiating, coordinating, and reviewing partnership activity.

To advance these objectives, partnership committees frequently establish subgroups or projects. Case study evidence suggests that well-functioning subgroups are key to a successful enterprise partnership (O'Donnell and Teague 2000; O'Dwyer et al. 2002). Project groups work on matters such as reforming the company pension scheme, devising a new financial participation arrangement, and establishing the ground rules for the introduction of new employment practices such as teamwork. By working on specific tasks, or attempting to invent solutions to agreed problems, these bodies drive purposeful joint action between managers and employees. Subgroups, which encourage managers and employees to search for superior ways of doing things, make enterprise partnership simultaneously process- and task-driven: the boundary between process and outcome becomes blurred. Enterprise partnership is thus a distinctive trust-creating institution in that the search for greater fairness and cooperation is placed in the context of working life. It is at least tacit recognition that matters relating to fairness at work can only be agreed, analyzed, and changed in the context of addressing concrete problems. The operating assumption is that a shared understanding between management and workers can fulfill its promise only if it can be translated into practices that guide actual behavior.

The emerging "model" of enterprise partnership stands apart from, but nevertheless is associated with, both the "works council" and "human resource management (HRM)" approaches to employee involvement and participation. These two established approaches use distinctive and contrasting practices and procedures to organize the employment relationship. First, work councils are representative and indirect forms of worker participation, and thus epitomize collective employment relations. In contrast, HRM approaches espouse decentralized forms of involvement that tend to focus on the individual. Thus, the HRM approach puts greater stress on direct forms of involvement. Second, whereas work councils cover strategic matters as well as operational and implementation matters, HRM tends to concentrate on the last two matters. Third, an important function of work councils, at least those in Germany, is to oversee the implementation of substantive and procedural rights proscribed in German labor law, whereas the HRM model is about solving problems that arise in the day-to-day running of the business or productive system. Fourth, work councils are mandatory institutions in the sense that managers are obliged by law to follow a proscribed list of rules and procedures when consulting with employees. HRM, on the other hand, is an instrument of management that leaves the depth and scope of any employee involvement scheme more or less in the hands of the managerial team. Fifth, the "value system" underpinning works councils is integrative bargaining whereas HRM is heavily orientated towards "empowerment" and performance (Muller-Jentsch 1995).

The "Irish" version of enterprise partnership contains elements of both the works council and HRM approaches, but cannot be considered a full-blown version of either. It is a "borderland" institution that interfaces with both approaches. It is fully compatible with new employment practices such as direct participation, teamwork, total quality management, and job rotation. At the same time, there is a collective and strategic dimension to its activities. Thus, for example, projects or subgroups of the enterprise partnership have the potential to deal with matters that are once removed from the immediate operation of the business and have far-reaching implications for the organization as a whole—a new pension scheme or a new system of work-sharing, for example. To properly design and introduce such work innovations requires managers to share information of a strategic kind with employees.

All in all, the value system of the Irish version of enterprise partnerships is a hybrid of the work councils and HRM approaches, as it seeks improved organizational performance and competitiveness through procedures and relationships closely associated with integrative bargaining. If this model of enterprise partnerships is implemented in full then the distinction is blurred: between direct and indirect participation; between operational and strategic matters; between expertise and authority; between process and outcomes; between bargaining and cooperation.

The case-study evidence suggests that few partnerships have all these attributes (O'Donnell and Teague 2000; O'Dwyer et al. 2002). This is hardly surprising as many studies find a gap between the stylized model of a workplace innovation and the configuration of the arrangement actually introduced—how many fully autonomous teams have been introduced by organizations? A number of other important findings emerge from the (patchy) evidence. First of all, enterprise partnerships still face a big "buy-in" problem. On the one hand, managers are reluctant to engage with social partnership at the organizational level, as they fear it might undermine their authority. On the other hand, trade unionists on the shop floor fear that workplace partnership might weaken collective bargaining.

Second, partnerships are mostly found in organizations where there has been a history of employment relations difficulties: partnerships are used to improve manager-employee interactions in cases where they have become embittered. This is very worthwhile, but it does mean that the employment practices associated with a partnership arrangement tend not to be particularly innovative. Third, most of the enterprise partnerships focus on operational matters and only intermittently deal with strategic matters. Fourth, enterprise partnerships that have established meaningful projects sometimes do not connect them properly with the wider employee involvement system. As a result, the projects tend to become a working party consisting of an elite group of employees and managers, albeit doing a worthwhile task.

Thus, advancing social partnerships at the organizational level has not been problem free. The negative externality associated with promoting cooperative management-employee interactions seems to at play. Freeman and Lazear (1995) suggest that employees and employers may not engage in mutually advantageous cooperative interactions even if it is in the self-interest of both parties to do so. This is because a range of negative externalities, mostly in the form of information asymmetries, prevents the creation of adequate incentives to install institutionalized forms of employee involvement. On the one hand, management will vest them with too little power. On the other hand, workers will demand more power than is considered optimal by managers. As a result, a type of market failure arises that is difficult to reduce.

Highlighting the problems that have emerged with advancing enterprise partnership is not a criticism of the national agreements or efforts at promoting this organizational model. But it does suggest that there is no automatic correspondence between the emergence of shared understandings about social partnership at the national level and the diffusion of the same principles at the organizational level. The lesson is that only through sustained public support will a new consensus emerge between managers and employees about cooperation at the workplace.

CONCLUSIONS

The evolving system of Irish social partnership bears some resemblance to traditional continental European neocorporatism and indeed earlier tripartite agreements in Ireland. The narrow process of centralized wage bargaining is not particularly innovative. For its success, it has relied on traditional features of corporatist wage bargaining, most notably the ability of encompassing trade union and employer organizations to police effectively the negotiated pay deals. At the same time the social partnership framework stands apart from corporatism of the past both in terms of content and process. We called this approach the open method of coordination. The open method of coordination is distinctive. It is not like most HRM models that seek to internalize the governance of the employment relationship inside an organization. HRM assumes that there is little need for an active public policy regime to help shape and guide enterprise-level employment practices. The open method of coordination emphasizes that a public framework for employment relations is essential, not the least to address labor market (and institutional) failures. But it departs from the traditional social democratic model of labor coordination, which relies heavily on constraining laws and procedures. Open coordination emphasizes support structures over constraining rule, pragmatic problem-solving over distributional bargaining, social consensus over adversarial mobilization.

Despite its innovative character, the open method of coordination has made it difficult to interpret employment relations developments in Ireland. First, it has proven all but impossible to identify the exact contribution social partnership has made to the high economic growth rates experienced by the country since the mid-1990s. Second, although real wages along with general living standards have risen significantly and the growth in jobs has been spectacular, the failure of the system to combat income and wage inequality is a disturbing trend. Third, even though the number of trade union members is at an all-time high, the continuing fall in union density is a serious cause for concern for organized labor. Fourth, although much is made of building shared understandings and cooperative relations between management and unions, there is ample evidence to suggest that a "them-versus-us" attitude still prevails in the employment relations system at the enterprise level. Thus Irish employment relations are characterized by old and new procedures, and by benign and malignant features sitting side by side.

One key lesson from the Irish experience is that it is hard to reconcile social partnership and openness to international investment. For instance, there have been occasions when the government has been obliged to put the country's image as an attractive site for inward investment before social partnership considerations. The Irish government, for example, opposed the adoption of the recent EU Information and Consultation Directive, even though it sees itself as an active supporter of enterprise partnerships. The government's desire to signal to U.S.-based multinationals that it will not pursue policies that excessively intrude on multinational operations in Ireland explains this apparent paradox. Economic openness places constraints on the regulatory dimension of social partnership. Another uncomfortable lesson from the Irish experience, with implications for the unfolding debate about "third-way" employment relations within Europe, is that while the "open method" of labor market coordination may create superior policy-making procedures, these may not block adverse employment relations outcomes.

Squall clouds are beginning to gather over Irish social partnership. One open question concerns whether the current pattern of wage setting is compatible with European monetary union. The argument is that efforts to more or less fix pay increases over two or three year periods may be out of step with the need for greater labor market flexibility in Europe. A second problem is developing a package of social measures that doesn't replicate the organizational shortcomings identified in other welfare systems nor overburdens the public budget, yet is comprehensive enough to satisfy the demands of trade unions and other social groups. Third, is the need to establish a wage-setting procedure that has credibility with unions and employers and produces orderly comparisons between private- and public-sector occupations. In 2002 and 2003, these difficulties manifested themselves in the negotiations for the latest agreement, Sustaining

Progress. Though an agreement was reached in 2002 and ratified early in 2003, neither trade unions nor employers were willing to commit themselves to a pay deal in excess of eighteen months—half the norm of the previous deals. Thus, social partnership in Ireland is facing multiple pressures, and it is not at all certain that current arrangements will survive. But then again partnership may survive by reinventing itself.

2 The Netherlands

Resilience in Structure, Revolution in Substance

Hans Slomp

Since the "discovery" of corporatism by researchers in the mid-1970s, the Netherlands (Holland) has been classified as a typical exponent of it, only slightly less corporatist than the Scandinavian countries and Austria. At first, the high degree of corporatism was appreciated as a device to weather the storms of the 1973–74 oil crisis. Later, when attention shifted to the degree of centralization of wage bargaining and its effect on economic performance, analysts viewed the country as a leader in wage coordination at the industry or sector level, again behind the more centralized Scandinavian nations. Some critics blamed the modest degree of centralization for the bad performance of the Netherlands following the 1979–80 oil crisis, when unemployment reached 14 percent (Calmfors and Driffill 1988).

The country's ranking in degree of corporatism and centralization of wage bargaining has hardly changed since then. The Dutch economy is still regarded as one of the more "coordinated" economies of the Western world (Soskice 1999). In the meantime, the economic performance of the Netherlands improved; it had one of the highest unemployment levels in the European Union (EU) in the early 1990s, but by 2002 the Netherlands had the lowest unemployment level in the EU, below 3 percent. This leap in the Netherland's relative economic performance illustrates the drawback of static international comparisons, which focus on average economic performance during fixed periods rather than on developments over time. The improvement of Dutch economic performance has also been interpreted as evidence of the importance of (deliberate) policies in contrast to the role played by economic and bargaining structure (Visser and Hemerijck 1997).

This chapter analyzes the driving forces behind the various policy changes that have taken place in the Netherlands. To summarize, while the traditional structure of collective bargaining has persisted, the contents of the negotiations and of state policies have changed dramatically—not due to pressures from globalization, but rather as a result of the EU. The structure of collective bargaining matters, but the contents of bargaining matter even more, and the EU matters most of all.

THE POLDER MODEL AND ITS ACTORS

Since the mid-1990s, the widely acclaimed "Polder model" has been a key influence on Dutch collective bargaining. The model began with the 1982 Central Agreement (Wassenaar Agreement), by which trade unions promised to forego large wage increases in exchange for a reduction in working time. It was not until the mid-1990s, however, that significant reductions in unemployment began to occur. Over the last twenty years, severe cuts in social security were carried through, which contributed to the ending of the national government's budget deficit in 2000. In addition to wage moderation and the fact that budget cuts were generally not contested, the enormous expansion of working time flexibility, mainly in the form of part-time jobs for women, drew praise to the country as a leading economy in Europe (Visser and Hemerijck 1997). The more than 20 percent growth of gross national product (GNP) that took place in the Netherlands in the 1990s was surpassed in the EU only by Ireland and Denmark; the decrease of government debt as a percentage of GDP that occurred in the Netherlands was exceeded in the EU only by Ireland; and no other EU country reduced unemployment as much as the Netherlands did.

Most changes in the Netherlands, including those brought about by the Polder model, are accomplished through *overleg*. This term denotes a harmonious interchange that may range from consultation to bargaining with the sincere intention on both sides to compromise without any conflict. In the Netherlands, no collective-bargaining related activities are undertaken, of whatever kind, without previous *overleg* with those involved. Only where collective bargaining involves industry bargaining is the word *onderhandelen* (bargaining) also used as a descriptive term.

At the national level, the national government is an active participant. From 1994 to 2002, the Netherlands was governed by a left-right "purple" coalition, in which "red" Social Democrats and "blue" Conservative Liberals were the main participants. This composition constituted a complete breach with Dutch tradition, since the Christian Democrats, who had dominated government for almost the whole previous century, were left out. As the Christian Democrats were most attached to close contacts with all kinds of voluntary organizations that make up "civil society," this shift favored the government's "independence" in contacts with employers and trade unions (the "social partners").

On the social partners' side, the employers' association VNO/NCW organizes more than 80 percent of all enterprises. The unionization rate has stabilized at 27 percent since the mid-1990s, after a steady decline from about 40 percent during the 1980s. The trade union movement is divided along religious/ideological and status lines. The dominant Social Democratic confederation FNV (1,227,000 members) is flanked by a Christian confederation (356,000) and an organization that mainly caters for middle and higher echelon workers (235,000).

For tripartite as well as bipartite business/labor *overleg*, the government and the "social partners" interact through two institutions: the SER (Social and Economic Council) and the STAR (Foundation of Labor). Unlike Ireland, in the Netherlands other types of organizations have never claimed or been offered a seat in these discussion forums. The SER is a formal advisory body to the national government, and it includes a number of independent outsiders, most of them university professors and increasingly also former politicians. Among the latter are the president of the National Bank and of the Central Planning Bureau, which regularly issues reports and outlooks on economic conditions in the country. The SER is a typical example of the Dutch tradition to tackle difficult issues and depoliticize them either by leaving them to the organizations affected, or by basing policy on "objective" scientific data—or even, preferably, by a combination of these devices. The STAR is a joint business-trade union body, without any outsiders. Employers and trade unions use this small institution to prepare for each new round of collective bargaining and to conclude agreements on specific topics. Twice a year the STAR and the government meet in the so-called spring *overleg* and autumn *overleg*.

The main overall goals of Dutch corporatism, served by the tripartite and bipartite *overleg* interactions promoted through SER and STAR, are economic competitiveness and social inclusion. Wage equality and full employment have never been priorities in their own right (Slomp 2001). Increasingly, however, Dutch-based multinational enterprises (MNE's) investing in the United States have been pressing for less *overleg* and more room for the free market. These MNE's point to the advantages of less restrained Anglo-Saxon capitalism, including the large bonuses paid to top executives. In the past, the primary promoters of such views were U.S.-based MNE's operating in the Netherlands.

Contacts between the leaders of employers' organization, trade unions, and the government are not confined to the monthly full SER meetings, in which ministers occasionally show up, or to the STAR. In between there is a lot of formal and even more informal contact. Great value is attached to good personal contacts within this small elite. Trade union leaders also regularly move to leading posts within public administration. As high public officials a few of them have even served as employers' representatives in public-sector collective bargaining. Wim Kok, prime minister from 1994 until 2002, for example, was a former FNV president, and one of the signatories of the 1982 Wassenaar Agreement.

THE STRUCTURE OF BARGAINING

Some of the famous Dutch seventeenth-century landscapes are dominated by a sky covered by dark clouds. The clouds fill three quarters of the total canvass, leaving only a small margin at the bottom for the landscape, in which people are sailing on a river, or are leading a few cows along the riverbank. Although the sky usually seems as though it is about to rain, a few rays of sunshine often illuminate the landscape. All participants in collective bargaining have such a painting in mind and first wait for the weather forecast, which in the Netherlands invariably includes lots of clouds, chances of showers, and at the most one hour of daily sunshine.

The Central Planning Bureau produces the leading economic forecasts twice a year. These economic outlooks are based on econometric models and depict the competitiveness of the Dutch economy. The annual bargaining round starts with tripartite and bipartite peak level *overleg*, based on an economic forecast, which in and of itself is rarely disputed, but which may give rise to diverging conclusions.

The national employer confederations do not engage in collective bargaining, but both separately and in common *overleg* issue noncompulsory recommendations to their member organizations and to the managements of companies that negotiate their own labor conditions. Even when a majority of employers is convinced of bright prospects, the VNO-NCW usually only focuses on the clouds in the forecast. Regularly, the VNO-NCW speaks about the imminent dangers facing the Dutch economy, like inflation, unemployment, and the loss of world market position. The national government invariably joins the employers in their focus on the dark clouds in the forecast and warns that wage moderation is required.

The trade union confederations typically discuss the clouds in a forecast, point to the activities going on, and to the rays of sunshine, and publish their general wage claims, as a voluntary guideline for their member organizations. Like the Planning Bureau's Economic Outlook, the FNV's wage claim is based on economic criteria, a combination of productivity growth and price increases.

This sequence means that the trade unions have the widest focus; they point to dark clouds as well as to the rays of sunshine. The employers mainly engage in cloud-spotting, the national government is also a cloud-watcher rather than a sunbather.

The next step in the process is the autumn *overleg* that occurs in STAR, in which all parties discuss the weather forecast and their initial response to it. Sometimes the social partners conclude an agreement, or a "covenant," or issue a "statement of intent," which tends to stress the need for wage moderation, to be compensated by working time reductions, extensions in training facilities or other improvements in secondary labor conditions. Then annual or biannual rounds of collective bargaining at the industry and enterprise levels take off. Although enterprise bargaining typically makes the headlines more than industry bargaining, industry agreements predominate. In both industry and company bargaining, unions that are affiliated to the trade union confederations represent the employees.

As a rule, industry and company agreements are concluded without strikes. Compromise is facilitated by the broad range of subjects covered by collective bargaining, including subjects like social security benefits, employee participation, employability provisions, child care facilities, internships for apprentices, jobs for ethnic minorities, and even the effects of production on the environment. Negotiations may be broken off for some time and the unions may announce workplace actions, but strikes are rare. The country's low strike profile is on a par with the German one. Moreover, once agreements are concluded no further strikes are allowed until the next round of collective bargaining.

A strict line of division is drawn, enforced by law, between collective bargaining, which is an exclusive trade union right, and employee participation within the enterprise, for which elected works councils exist. Most works council members are trade union members. Works councils do not have the formal right to discuss subjects covered in industry or company agreements or to call strikes, since that would intrude on trade union rights. Informally, however, many works councils are involved in the process of negotiating a company agreement, and their involvement can lead to elaborations of the industry or company agreements to some extent.

REVOLUTION IN SUBSTANCE: THE MAIN SUBJECTS OF CENTRAL OVERLEG

Although central *overleg* has dealt with a wide range of issues, over the last fifteen years three major concerns have dominated the agenda of tripartite and bipartite contacts: wage moderation, the mounting costs of social security, and the low labor force participation rate.

Wage Moderation

Wage moderation, considered to be the main source of national competitiveness, has been at the heart of Dutch corporatism since 1945. Wage developments in Germany, and to a smaller extent in Belgium, serve as yardsticks. Wage restraint was abandoned in the Netherlands during the 1970s, and was resumed, under pressure from rapidly mounting unemployment and from government threats to intervene in collective bargaining (Visser and Hemerijck 1997), with the 1982 Agreement of Wassenaar. During the 1990s two STAR-agreements set the pace for collective bargaining: "A New Course" in 1993 and "Agenda 2002" in 1997. In both agreements, the trade unions once again promised a "responsible wage costs development," while employers conceded more room for all kinds of leave and more funds and time for employee training. A new agreement in 2001, "More is Needed," expressed concern with the upward pressures on wages being produced by the tight labor market. This agreement recommended a continuation of the policies set out in prior agreements.

The general wage claim issued by the FNV, and followed by the CNV, served as a voluntary guideline, but in practice it has functioned as a ceiling for the unions in various industrial sectors, which showed these unions' compliance with wage moderation. A second sign of compliance was the almost complete disappearance in the course of the 1980s of automatic cost of living increases. A third sign was the widespread introduction of new and lower wage rates that were closer to the minimum wage for unskilled and untrained workers. This was a response to the government threats not to declare agreements legally binding if the lowest wage rates were far above the statutory minimum wage.

The public-sector unions displayed a more stubborn attitude toward the recommendations for wage moderation during the 1990s. After wage cuts for a number of years, in view of the growing pressure on the labor market for teachers and nursing personnel, and in light of the pressures public-sector employees faced at work, these unions demanded exceptions for their members, which was one of the reasons strikes followed these negotiations.

The overall impact of the Agreement of Wassenaar has been a downward movement and compression in the annual wage increases received in various industries (see figure 2.1) (Van der Wiel 1999). Compression in industry wage increases has not prevented an economywide increase in wage inequality since the early 1980s. Inequality has been promoted by the low wages received by poorly skilled workers, the fact that the legal minimum wage was not increased fully in line with price increases, and the absence of moderation in managerial and other high salaries not covered by collective agreements. Despite all the efforts to maintain wage moderation, the tight labor market recently has put upward pressure on wages, contributed to a rising inflation rate, and been a factor in a gloomy economic forecast in 2002. This all served to reinforce the priority placed on wage moderation in *overleg* discussions.

Social Security

The second key focus in central talks, the cost of social security, became acute when the country needed to reduce the central government's budget deficit and the public debt as preconditions for participating the European Monetary Union (EMU). The two largest groups affected by social security savings were the unemployed and the almost 1 million people (out of a total labor force of under 7 million) who received a disability benefit. Unemployment ceased to be a major problem in the second half of the 1990s, but disability remained on the agenda. The SER issued a number of divided (and abortive) reports on social security reform, but the government on its own imposed a reduction in disability benefits, while leaving intact the traditional goal of social inclusion. A second government move was to shift responsibility for compulsory sickness and disability insurance from the social partners to the individual enterprise, with the possibility to reinsure the risks involved. Disability continued to be a hot issue, with new reports almost every year, but the lower benefits succeeded in terms of cost reduction, although not in terms of promotion of labor market participation. Yet, the total number of disability recipients continued to climb and was expected to exceed 1 million in 2002, which led to the commissioning of a new series of study reports.

Participation and Part-time Work

The third key policy concern was the low rate of labor force participation found in the Netherlands. Criticism for this low rate focused on the large number of disability claimants and on the number of women who were not active in the labor market. Women's role in the labor market has been

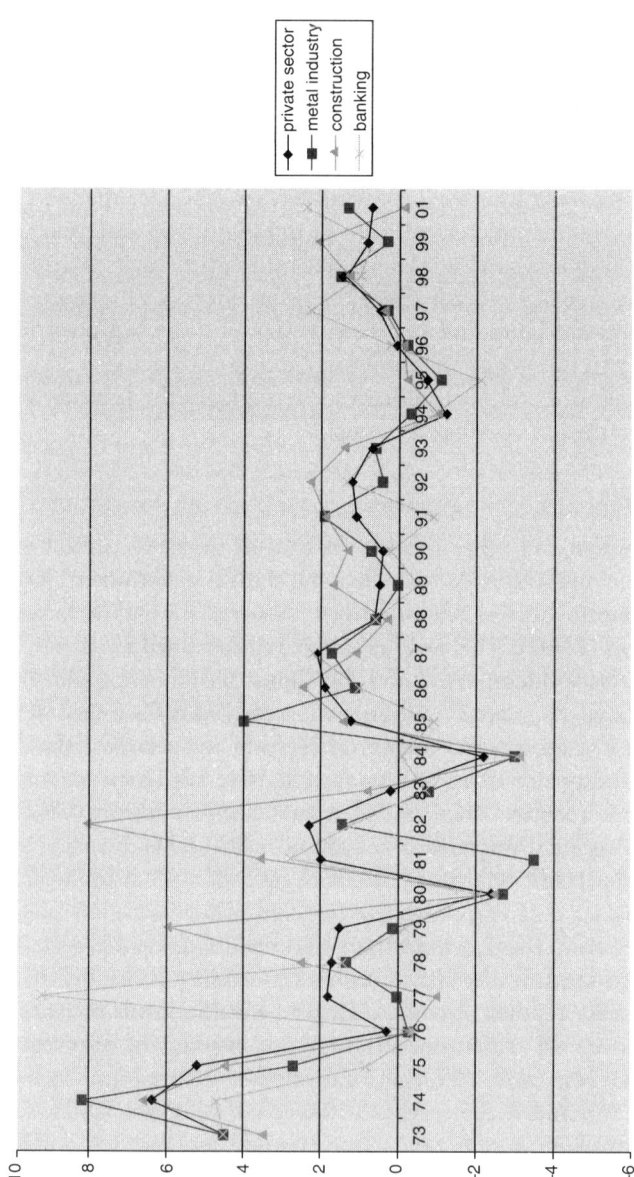

FIGURE 2.1 WAGE INCREASE IN THE PRIVATE SECTOR AND THREE CORE INDUSTRIES, 1973–2001 (AS PROVIDED IN COLLECTIVE AGREEMENTS, ADJUSTED FOR INFLATION)

Source: CDS: Sociaal-economische maandstatistiek 1985–2002

at the heart of debates about the Polder model. In the 1970s and 1980s women started to enter the labor market, which affected traditional Dutch labor culture, with its division of labor between male "breadwinners" and married women working as housewives. Social policy reinforced this division; keeping married women at home was an explicit government aim. Only slowly has the country come to terms with the new position of women as employees. The first step was gender equality in wages and other labor conditions, which was raised by the EU directives on gender equality. The Dutch government trailed other EU countries in applying the directives, and it did so only when the European Commission threatened to bring the country before the European Court of Justice (Van Vleuten 2001).

Even more crucial than equal pay was equal access to the labor market. In 1980, the female participation rate was still a meager 35 percent, compared to over 50 percent in the surrounding countries. The country slowly caught up with the rest of Western Europe, but it was not until 1990 that the issue was fully addressed by the government and the social partners, this time under pressure from the opening of the internal EU-market in 1992 and the Netherlands' admission into the EMU. In 1990, a report by a scientific consultative council, followed by a very alarming SER report argued that the low labor participation rate of women was the main weakness in the Dutch economy. These reports advocated a fast rise in female labor force participation as a crucial condition for the improvement of national competitiveness. The country then officially changed its policy and started promoting equal access to the labor market.

The rapid growth of female employment that followed was not due to government policy or peak level recommendations, but rather, resulted from the spread of part-time work, the core of a new and "flexible" economy. The expansion of part-time work had begun in the 1980s, and since the end of that decade the country has led the EU in the incidence of part-time work, 69 percent of female employees and 18 percent of men in 1999. Part-time work was not state-sponsored, rather it spread as a managerial response to the desire for such working time arrangements by women eager to enter or reenter the labor market. The predominance of supply factors in the spread of part-time work is shown by the fact that the country also has the highest rate of *voluntary* part-time employment in the EU (Eurostat 2001). In particular, public services like education and social work, as well as commercial services (except for banking), pioneered in the use of part-time jobs.

Private employers sometimes sought part-time work in combination with (or in exchange for) longer operating times. Employers' attitudes were shaped by pressures from globalization and adaptations to lean production, but they also represented a "flexible" response to trade union demands for working time reductions. The spread of flex-time changed the issue of working time, which had been on the collective bargaining agenda since 1982. At first, the unions had demanded a thirty-eight-hour workweek, as a means to reduce unemployment by a better redistribution of work, and to compensate for wage moderation. In the mid-1990s, under conditions of rapidly declining unemployment, the unions demanded a thirty-six-hour workweek, this time mainly as a means to reduce work stress. The massive entry of women into the labor market, however, served to support the employers' demands for working time flexibility, rather than uniform changes in the length of the workweek. The trade unions soon also embraced working time flexibility as a priority, as long as it implied working time reductions for full-time workers.

Part-time work greatly contributed to the influx of women on the labor market, but it did not unleash that movement. At the root of the labor market changes was the fast and radical social and political shifts that changed the Netherlands in the course of the 1970s from a rather closed and religion-oriented society, divided among Catholics and Protestants, into one of the most open and tolerant societies in Europe. An influential feminist movement and EU-pressure for labor market equality contributed to the expansion of female labor force participation. The change that occurred in labor culture is reflected in public attitudes toward the employment of women with small children. In 1965 over 80 percent of men and women had objections to such work, thirty years later less than 20 percent felt the same way (Niphuis-Nell and de Beer 1997).

The enormous expansion of female labor market participation that took place by means of part-time work made the country a leader in workplace flexibility (de Beer 2000; Plantenga 2000). Flexibility is highly gender-specific, however, and part of a new gender division of labor between part-time working women, crowded into lower status (and lower paid) employment, and full-time working men, who still monopolize better-paid jobs. The separation between the two is not a total one, though. First, the share of men working part-time in the Netherlands is the highest in the EU. Increasing numbers of young men, for whom a two-earner family is an attractive new feature of household work patterns, are following the example of females and are opting for part-time jobs.

The new labor culture of a two-earner family also contributed to the broad acceptance of wage moderation. Second, differences in labor protection between part-time and full-time work have been reduced. In 1996, a STAR-agreement improved the rights of part-timers, while slightly reducing those of full-timers. Third, from an initial separation between two standards, full-time and part-time work, the country is increasingly characterized by blurred standards in working time. The individualization of working time became a popular topic in collective bargaining, and the 2001 STAR agreement explicitly drew attention to individual working time arrangements, with the option to "buy" or "sell" working time. Fourth, because of the large influx of women into the labor market, work and family issues, including "care leave" and the shortage of child care facilities, have become prominent policy issues.

THE RESILIENCE OF STRUCTURE: DEREGULATION

State involvement in wage bargaining in recent years has been more limited than it has been in the previous fifty years. Since the Agreement of Wassenaar (which was concluded under threat of government intervention), the national government has pressed for wage restraint but not interfered directly in wage bargaining. In spring 2001, for example, the government firmly stated that "we must fully jam on the brakes." Even after the September 11 terrorist attacks in the United States led to much economic uncertainty, the Dutch government has not announced any kind of direct or indirect intervention in collective bargaining. Repeatedly, the government reconfirmed its confidence in the ability of the social partners to handle wage setting in a responsible manner, and consequently, the government was willing to leave wage negotiations to them. The government has even relinquished the statutory right to interfere directly in wage bargaining—a complete breach with the past. Notwithstanding, the government in recent years has used two indirect instruments and incidental tax measures to reward wage moderation.

One indirect instrument the government used to stimulate wage moderation is the *koppeling* (linkage) between private and social transfers: an automatic increase in social security benefits provided by the national government in step with increases in the average market wage. The unions, which claim to represent the many nonmembers and benefit-recipients as well, are very attached to this expression of national solidarity. On the other hand, this device allowed the national government to press for moderation in private-sector bargaining by arguing that if the social partners would not moderate private-sector wage increases, the government would be "forced" not to apply the *koppeling* in social security. Although public-sector wages are now formally negotiated at decentralized levels, the *koppeling* to some extent still applies to them as well. The main parameter used to set public-sector wage increases is the rate of change in private-sector wages.

The second policy instrument used by the government to encourage wage moderation is the threat to no longer declare collective agreements binding on enterprises that are not affiliated to employers' associations. Partly due to this threat, many collective agreements introduced lower wage rates for unskilled and poorly educated young workers in the early 1990s.

In the area of working time, the national government has played a more active role, as a promoter of the spread of part-time work. The government has sought to encourage working time flexibility by means of deregulation in some cases, and even more extensively, through reregulation. The prime example of deregulation was the 1996 Working Hours Act. The act abolished some of the restrictions from the 1919 law on the eight hours working day. The new law allowed a ten-hour workday and a forty-five-hour workweek (as an average over a three months period), but each had to come about only as the outcome of collective bargaining, and a nine-hour day and a forty-hour week in cases where no collective agreement was prevailed. Saturday became a normal working day, for Sunday work labor restrictions were partially lifted. Working time deregulation was hailed by the government as a step in the direction of less-restrained Anglo-Saxon capitalism, while retaining the best elements of organized labor relations and labor conditions.

At the same time the government enacted a series of measures to promote flexibility, even in the face of employers' opposition. In 1997, the legal right of parental and other forms of leave was extended, and in 2000 a new Working Time Adaptation Act provided employees with the right to reduce or extend the length of their workweek. The employer could deny such requests only if there were very serious company interests that made such measures inappropriate or unaffordable. Employers resisted this new "one-sided" measure as superfluous, claiming that the social partners, and company management and employees, could handle these matters well on their own. Another law on career-interruption for the purpose of educational leave or sabbatical leaves promoted working time reductions and flexibility, and also encouraged employee training and employability. The extension of "care leave" also became the subject of state action (Delsen 2002).

Noninterference in wage setting and the promotion of working time flexibility also were linked to the reregulation of social security. With regard to social security provision in the Netherlands, a strict division is made between state responsibility and the more limited role the social partners play as consultants to any policy changes in this area. Facing a large budget deficit, the government tried to use the freedom of action afforded by this division of responsibility by reforming social security in the 1980s and early 1990s.

The rise to power of the purple coalition in 1994 (without Christian Democrats) led to an even greater brake with traditional tripartism and its blurred responsibilities (Slomp 2001). The government imposed strict state control on social security funds, after public investigation had shown too lavish spending by the social partners.

Summarizing, deregulation and reregulation went hand in hand. Non-interference in wage setting was matched by active promotion of working time flexibility and limits on social security spending.

THE RESILIENCE OF STRUCTURE: DECENTRALIZATION

The revolutions occurring in female labor market participation and working time did not affect the structure of collective bargaining. The main trend has been toward rapid expansion of individual differentiation in working time options and pay in collective labor agreements, but without a concomitant decentralization of the structure of collective bargaining.

Generally speaking, the reach of industry agreements has remained stable in the Netherlands. Although the number of enterprise agreements has steadily grown from just over 600 in the early 1980s to more than 750 at the turn of the century, industry agreements have continued to cover five times more employees than enterprise agreements (5.27 million employees covered by industry agreements versus 855,000 covered by enterprise agreements in 2000). These data do not even show the full degree of coordination that exists in both industry and enterprise collective bargaining, as out of the total 963 collective agreements, the largest single union, FNV-*Bondgenoten* (FNV-Allies) is the main trade union signatory of more than 600 of the agreements. This union is the product of a recent merger of four FNV-trade unions, in industry, food processing, services, and transport. This merger was the main change made in union structure during the 1990s.

On the employers' side, the multi-industry AWVN, affiliated to the national employers' association, participates in more than five hundred collective agreements (though not the most important ones). Opting out of industry agreements by leaving the employers' association, as happens in Germany, is highly exceptional, due to the common legal extension of industry agreements to all companies in an industry. One can describe this coordinated system as pattern bargaining where the FNV-*Bondgenoten*, the metal working employers' association, and two leading firms, Philips (the largest private employer except for the postal services) and Akzo Nobel, a chemical MNE, act as pattern leaders.

Labor market changes have affected how, and the extent to which, workers are covered by collective agreements. The shift from industry to services is reflected in the expansion of agreements in commercial services. The catering industry, with 227,500 employees, now has the largest agreement in the private sector, a position traditionally occupied by the metal working industry and the electromechanical industry, whose coverage has decreased to 187,000 employees. New and growing service providers, such as commercial temporary employment agencies (225,000 employees) and the information technology industry have added to the growth of collective agreements in the services sector. Less obvious is the growth and professionalization of funeral services that encouraged undertakers and crematoriums to conclude their first collective agreements in 1998. The sports sector followed in 1999, with a separate agreement for paid soccer players.

A second labor market development that has affected the coverage of collective bargaining is the growing number of highly trained employees. In a few industries, like metal working and construction, and in a number of companies, including Philips, separate agreements apply to staff employees. At Philips, Agreement A applies to twenty-five thousand production workers, and Agreement B to twelve thousand staff and technical personnel. These employment numbers have changed almost every year in favor of staff agreement coverage.

In addition to labor market changes, outsourcing has also affected bargaining coverage. Outsourcing has increased the reach of industry bargaining, since most workers involved are covered by industry agreements. Conspicuous examples are the agreement for catering and cleaning services, and the agreement for temporary workers (who now make up 10 percent of the labor force at Philips and Unilever).

Companies have come to apply different agreements for work outside the core business, even when subcontractors do not perform the work. This kind of differentiation is also increasingly found in industry agreements. Many workers in the construction industry that are actually doing work that is closer to that done in the metal working industry are no longer covered by the construction agreement, but rather, are covered by the metal working agreement. Such a shift may be due to pragmatic choices of job descriptions and wage scales that better fit various jobs; sometimes it is motivated by lower wages or lower social security contributions in particular agreements. In the metal working industry, for example, enterprises tried to move from the metal working agreement ("big metal") to the industry agreement covering small workshops ("small metal") because of its lower pre-pension contribution. The sector organizations then established a joint committee to outline the conditions for such a move (Tros 2000).

In contrast to these bargaining shifts, a total decentralization from industry to company bargaining is rare. The only major example where an industry agreement has been replaced by enterprise agreements is the banking industry. In 2000, the three biggest Dutch banks, which employed 80 percent of those working in the banking industry, for the first time concluded company-level collective agreements. The primary background factors that led to this development are the fast expansion and internationalization of Dutch banking and the mergers occurring between banking and insurance companies. The spread of part-time employment did not serve as an important catalyst for company-level bargaining, since the banks were already discussing flexible working time by the mid-1990s within industry bargaining.

The shift of bargaining to the company level in the banking industry started with the privatization of the Postbank in 1986 and its merger in the 1990s with a major insurance company. That induced the new company (ING-Bank) to combine the banking and the insurance agreements that regulated employment conditions for the firm's employees, into a company-level agreement. The other two large banks, also products of recent mergers, had very different markets and working cultures. Once the ING-Bank left the banking industry bargaining table, the two other banks also concluded company agreements. The FNV union had tried to stimulate decentralization in the form of a "layer-agreement," which would have involved various "layers" of collective bargaining, but the shift to company agreements made this impossible (Tros 2000; Tijdens 2000).

Decentralization from company level to subsidiary or plant levels also is exceptional in the Netherlands. Only a few company agreements have broken up completely and been replaced by lower forms of collective bargaining. The only major example was the separate agreement for the telecommunications part of the privatized postal services formed in 1999, a long-awaited and logical step in view of the widely different labor markets and labor conditions within the two parts of the postal/telecommunications provider. Despite the split, the agreement for the sixty-six thousand postal workers remained the largest company-level agreement.

A more widely discussed example of the breakdown of company-level bargaining is Unilever, where the unions tried to stop the "exodus" of noncore employees from the main collective agreement by bringing all nonproduction personnel under that agreement. In a long and intensive sequence of *overleg*, Unilever and the unions then decided to opt for a single company agreement with wide coverage, to be applied in a decentralized way. In this "cascade model," introduced in 1998, five levels of *overleg* were distinguished: company, division, plant, department, shift, and the individual employee. The new system implied a more active role for the works council in wage negotiations (Snijkens and Miltenburg, 2000).

Decentralization in collective bargaining often has come about in a less conspicuous manner. In some cases, while the overall structure and coverage of an industry agreement was maintained, the scope of the industry agreement was modified to provide more latitude for decentralized elaboration. Even this type of "coordinated" decentralization is very limited. Mr. Rojer, a high-ranking official of the Ministry of Social Affairs and Employment, has even spoken of the "myth" of decentralization (Rojer 2000).

Very little decentralization has occurred within pay determination in the last decade (Tros 2000). The basis for wage scales typically remains formal systems of job rating, described in industry agreements. Since 1994, the metal working agreement offers employers the option to pay less (or cut pay more) than the agreement, but only after consent by the bargaining parties. The employers' association has been almost as hesitant as the unions to allow any such exception, even in case of the threat of plant closure or mass layoffs. An often cited, yet rarely imitated, case of decentralization in collective bargaining where industry bargaining was retained is the graph industry. This industry is involved in a fast process of technological change and the spread of new media. In 1997, six branch agreements merged into one general agreement for "media production," but the new general agreement was intended to serve merely as a framework ("coat") contract, leaving job rating and other subjects to the enterprises, within limits provided in the industry agreement (van den Toren 1998).

Like wages, working time generally remains a subject of industry control. Working time was reduced in the course of the 1980s, but industry rules set limits on annual working time. While the overall impact of the relaxation of maximum daily working time is limited, legal extension of shop opening hours in 1996 had some decentralizing effect in the supermarket sector, which left opening hours more or less to the individual supermarkets.

The small impact of labor flexibility on the structure of collective bargaining means that the role of works councils in wage bargaining is still limited, except in some information technology firms. Most works councils tend to guard their autonomy from the unions. They do so because of the existence of three competing trade union confederations, the presence of unorganized members, and the role of independent consultancy and training firms in works councilor professionalization (Slomp 2000). This autonomy was one of the reasons the unions objected to works council involvement in collective bargaining, but that opposition is weakening somewhat. Unions now frequently offer assistance to works councils and allow a works council to become involved in bargaining where the company has a good record in social and personnel policy. FNV-*Bondgenoten* has developed a "social policy test" for that purpose. In matters other than wages, the works councils typically get involved in the elaboration of the details of the collective agreements, for instance, in working time arrangements, social provisions like child care, and employability plans. The wider range of subjects covered by collective agreements has tended to increase works council activities.

Interestingly, works council involvement in wage bargaining in information technology (IT) firms has not weakened, but rather, has reinforced the position of the unions. Most IT companies started without any kind of trade union presence or collective agreements, but after some time company management contacted the works councils to engage them as bargaining partners. Later, both management and the works councils recognized the advantage of union involvement, a development from "nonunion firms" to some form of indirect or even direct union participation.

The most important change occurring in formal collective bargaining has been the shift from government directives to formal wage negotiations in the public and nonprofit sectors, a kind of "decentralization" in collective bargaining. The sector agreements in education are now by far the largest agreements, with a total number of 350,000 employees. Although the public sector and the "care sector" are formally free to bargain any change in labor conditions, the employer (a government agency or ministry) uses a "reference model" to determine the available budget for each of these sectors, with private-sector wage agreements serving as the point of reference. This often leads to an obscure (and in fact still rather centralized) procedure in which the government first sets the available budget, and then starts collective bargaining.

In 1999, the public sector was affected by a series of strikes in education and local services, with the unions trying to attain wage increases that were in line with increases being provided in the private sector. The discussions surrounding determination of the employment conditions of police and teachers were the most contentious. The police collective agreement set the tone for the public sector, but it led to an outcome that exceeded the available budget, due to an accounting failure on the employers' side (whose delegation included a previous FNV leader). The role of pattern setter then shifted to the teachers' agreement, and from the Ministry of the Interior to the Ministry of Education.

A few other industries, such as health care and local public transport, are part of the "state-subsidized" or "contribution-financed" sector, with theoretically even more freedom to bargain. But in fact, bargaining in these industries involves obscure procedures that in practice matter much. Until 1999, in these industries the employers first negotiated with the government to fix the available budget for increases in labor costs. That system did not work satisfactorily and sometimes even aroused joint employer/employee protests to increase the budget. Since 1999, an independent committee has set the budget. Since the split up of the agreement for hospitals and homes for the elderly, also in 1999, the hospitals' agreement (155,000 employees) has acted as a key pattern setting agreement in the care sector, leading the way for separate agreements covering mental welfare, home care, homes for the elderly, and smaller branches.

Partly due to the spread of collective bargaining in the public sector, the share of employees under agreements has risen in the course of the 1990s. About 750,000 employees, some 12 percent, are covered by collective agreements in an indirect way, because of the legal extension of industry agreements. The main reason for the initial lack of collective bargaining coverage within these firms is the fact that these employers do not belong to their respective employers' associations (those associations conclude the industry agreements), and these employers also choose not to negotiate their own labor agreements. Legal extension is granted in these cases as a routine matter at the request by either of the signatories of the industry agreement. Only about 10 percent of all employees are not covered by any collective agreement at all—excluding higher staff and management with salaries more than fifty thousand dollars, whose labor conditions are often determined in individual negotiations.

INDIVIDUALIZATION

The "part-time revolution" and the spread of variations in working time have hardly affected the bargaining structure, but they have exercised a profound effect on the contents of collective agreements. The spread of part-time work has favored a rapid individualization of working time, both for women and men. Individual working time options were first applied in the IT industry but soon spread to other industries. By the mid-1990s, the thirty-six-hour week had been implemented (or its introduction planned) in one third of all agreements (as measured by an official survey), applying to almost 40 percent of all workers under an agreement. Most of the agreements offered a variety of options, such as four working days of nine hours each, one day off every two weeks, shorter working days, or additional days off during the year (Arbeidsinspectie, Najaarsrapportage 1996). By 1998, flexibility in saving days for longer periods of leave had become a possible option for 40 percent of employees in the IT industry. The primary motivations for use of this option were pre-pension and educational leave, with care leave playing a minor role.

The buying and selling of days off also quickly became a significant new element within working time flexibility. In 1998, 16 percent of employees could buy time, in some agreements even up to fifteen days of time. The option of selling days off applied to almost 20 percent of employees, in spite of trade union objections to time selling, on grounds that it undermines working time reduction (Arbeidsinspectie, Voorjaarsrapportage 1999). Labor shortages encouraged the selling of time off, however, in the late 1990s (Paping and Tijdens 2000). Consistent with Dutch traditions, one of the minor options used consists of selling time off in order to spend the extra (and untaxed) salary on a bicycle—as a government-sponsored means to reduce car traffic.

A few leading enterprises have paved the way in the individualization of working time. While they generally accept various forms of working time flexibility, preferably in combination with performance-related pay, unions advocate collective working time reduction and training to improve employability. Conflicting priorities regarding working time flexibility have mostly been conciliated without overt conflict, but tensions have arisen over the issue in a few firms, including Philips and Akzo Nobel. At Akzo Nobel, the thirty-six-hour workweek had been agreed to in principle in 1995, but the company was not content with the outcome of various working time experiments and wanted to stop them by 1997. Even the prime minister appealed to the company not to counter the ongoing trend of working time reduction, if only because it would endanger wage moderation. After long negotiations, the company implemented the thirty-six-hour workweek through the use of extra days off.

The most significant form of individualization, performance-based pay, is still in its infant stage and is far less popular than traditional profit-related bonuses. In the second half of the 1990s, working time flexibility encouraged employers to broach the subject of pay flexibility as well, in the form of profit-based bonuses, or performance-based wages. Unions only consented to bonuses on top of regular salaries. The 1997 STAR agreement recommended differentiation of wages in the form of nonrecurrent pay increases, either related or not related to enterprise profitability, in addition to uniform pay increases. The title of the 2001 collective agreement, "More is Needed," explicitly referred to the need, in view of uncertain economic conditions, for (collective) flexible pay that was related to enterprise performance, in the form of incidental bonuses as well as stock options for all employees.

In 2000, 10 percent of all collective agreements, affecting 10 percent of private-sector employees provided for such pay. Flexible pay was encouraged by the individualization of working time and by the trend toward increasing wage inequality. Most of the agreements involved, however, postponed actual implementation until further *overleg* or joint investigation of the matter (Arbeidsinspectie, Voorjaarsrapportage 2001).

The company-level agreements for the five largest banks in 2001 share a gradual transition toward performance-related pay. In one bank the process includes the introduction of competence management and is controlled by a joint company/trade union committee. Salary increases are divided into three parts: a collective base for all employees, a periodical rise based on employee competence, and incidental bonuses based on employee performance.

Except for a few IT firms, including Philips-offspring Origin, recent wage agreements at Phillips involve the strongest thrust in the direction of individualization of working time and wages. The two Philips agreements contain uniform job rating systems, with ample room for differential application for individual employees. Plant managers may cancel annual wage increases to individual employees, dependent on individual performance, but such a measure may not extend beyond two consecutive years. Philips introduced other forms of flexible extra pay in the 1980s, then abandoned these procedures in 1990 in favor of a fixed additional month of salary and a system of incidental individual bonuses that may amount to 2–4 percent of regular salary. Individual differentiation, in combination with employability proposals, proved contentious as early as 1996, when only a minor union was willing to sign the company-level collective agreement. In 2000, a few strikes in some of the Philips plants resulted in a combination of a general wage increase and performance based pay—a typical Dutch compromise (van der Meer 2000; FNV 2000). Even in the face of these shifts to flexible pay, Philips does not pay any profit-related bonuses (except to top executives).

CONCLUSION

This analysis of Dutch collective bargaining highlights three points, the importance of structure, policy learning, and the impact of the EU. There have been no significant changes in the decision-making procedures and structures that regulate collective bargaining, yet great changes in decisions regarding the content of collective bargaining have occurred in the Netherlands. The shift from an unemployment-plagued economy to conditions of fast growth and full-employment did not lead to a concomitant change in the structure of collective bargaining. Traxler's earlier rating of the Netherlands as a country that did not experience major alterations in collective bargaining structure still fits (Traxler 1995a). Decision making on labor conditions continues to take place at industry and company levels, and is coordinated by the national level. There have not been great shifts from industry- to company- or plant-level collective bargaining. Given the individualization of working time, and increasingly also pay, the trend might well become one of "strongly coordinated individualization" without collective bargaining decentralization.

The revolutionary breach with the past that has occurred in female employment and in part-time jobs makes clear, however, that focusing on (collective bargaining) structure has its limits. Similar structures may well hide great variations in content. The "bargaining regime" does not tell all about the "labor conditions regime." The national government and the social partners followed the growth in female employment and part-time jobs and only belatedly took steps to coordinate these developments. The parties essentially tried to adapt to rather than lead these developments. Moreover, central level *overleg* followed what had already been discussed or laid down in industry agreements. This confirming, rather than initiating, position is in line with the general thrust of central agreements as well as legal rules in the Netherlands: formal rules follow new practice, they hardly ever initiate new practice. The experiences of working women attest to the tradition of government adaptation to social change rather than government initiative in bringing about change. For a long time women had to wait for positive incentives for part-time work, and they still await improvements in child care provisions.

The highly praised performance of the Dutch economy is mainly due to the combination of wage moderation and increases in female labor force participation. In the early 1980s, the country returned to a traditional instrument, corporatism, and wage moderation, which had not occurred for fifteen years, returned. It did so under pressure from mounting unemployment. In the early 1990s, the country shifted away from a national goal of social inclusion and moved instead toward a goal of labor market participation. The influx of women into the labor market was made possible by satisfying their desires for part-time work. When making the policy changes that affected women, the government and the social partners acted under strong EU pressure.

Visser and Hemerijck (1997) describe the Polder model as a model of successful "policy learning." The return to wage moderation and the transition to female labor market "inclusion" may even be called examples of strategic choice. Both changes, however, were brought about by very strong pressure from high unemployment and the EU. A pupil that only starts learning under the threat of a cane can hardly be an example for other pupils. Learning under that condition looks more like the successful reduction of tension and redress than as real learning aimed at improving national qualities.

Policy learning in employment policies largely was a response to EU directives on labor market equality and to the EU conditions for joining the EMU. It did not take the form of "imitating best practices" (Streeck 1995) but rather, of adapting to EU rules, with the EU as an old-fashioned headmaster, glancing at the cane. This forced learning suggests a more "positive" view of the EU's cross-national harmonizing impact as compared to voluntary adaptations to other national economies that serve as models to be imitated. The headmaster has a cane and that combination works (contrary to what some observers claim).

The Netherlands finally has taken seriously and literally Katzenstein's notion of the "flexible response" of small nations to world markets (Katzenstein 1985). The Dutch revolution in female flex-time could be a transitional stage toward full-time employment of women. The voluntary nature of their part-time employment and the spread of part-time work to men might also mean that the only Calvinist country in the European Union is heading toward a new and post-Calvinist work ethic.

3 Collective Bargaining and Social Pacts in Italy

Ida Regalia and Marino Regini

The revival of the tripartite dialogue that occurred in Italy in the 1990s and, in particular, the tripartite agreement of 1993, were widely seen as marking the beginning of a new phase in Italian industrial relations. This phase was distinguished by declines in the importance of the following traditional features of Italian industrial relations: (1) relatively little regulation of procedures and of relations among highly organized actors; (2) instability and unpredictability in industrial relations practices and frequent recourse to conflict in order to define power relations and bolster support for interest organizations; (3) frequent and haphazard oscillation between centralized and decentralized collective bargaining structures; and (4) difficulty activating processes focused on rationalization and reform (reorganization indeed did eventually come about, and often through joint agreements, but it occurred on an informal and piecemeal basis and had little visibility).

As a result of the tripartite agreements in the early and mid-1990s a number of improvements in Italian industrial relations appeared to have been achieved, including: (1) greater formalization and explicit definition of shared criteria, rules, and procedures that could resolve conflicts over representation and distributive issues such as incomes policy; (2) increased predictability in industrial relations practices and close coordination in the actors' objectives, with a substantial reduction in industrial conflict; (3) formation of a more stable and orderly two-tier bargaining structure—with both centralized and decentralized levels; (4) significant public policy reforms of public-sector employment, the pension system, and the labor market accomplished with the involvement of the social partners (labor and management).

And yet, at the end of the 1990s, the new Italian system of industrial relations proved to be less consolidated than had first appeared. On the one hand, the factors responsible for the success of centralized tripartite dialogue either attenuated or disappeared, and endeavors to create arenas for local-level tripartite dialogue faltered. On the other hand, the shortcomings of weakly institutionalized labor relations reemerged. The electoral victory of a center-right government in 2001 then prompted fundamental reappraisal of the industrial relations reforms that had been adopted in the early and mid-1990s.

The next section provides a brief survey of the traditional characteristics of Italian industrial relations and then discusses the development of tripartism in the 1980s and 1990s. A description of the structure and outcomes of the bilateral collective agreements reached in the same period follows. Discussion of the problems that continue to plague Italian industrial relations and the lessons that can be learned from Italy's experiences are presented in the concluding section of this chapter.

THE TRADITIONAL FEATURES OF THE COLLECTIVE BARGAINING SYSTEM

The structure of collective bargaining in Italy has oscillated between centralization and decentralization with unusual frequency. This is explained by the "voluntarist" traditions within Italian industrial relations, which led to infrequent direct state intervention in industrial relations. As a result, collective bargaining was heavily affected by shifting power relations between labor and management, and this produced frequent changes in practices and heavy reliance on informal arrangements.[1]

The industrial relations system included a highly centralized level of negotiations with agreements between union confederations and the employers' associations that addressed very general issues. In addition, collective bargaining occurred at two main negotiating levels: the industry (or sectoral) level—devoted to the periodic determination of pay and conditions for an entire industry or sector[2]—and the company or plant level—devoted to negotiations about specific workplace problems. It was not until the tripartite agreement of 1993 (see below) that the competencies, procedures, and issues pertaining to the two levels were clarified. Prior to this agreement, the balance between the various levels of collective bargaining frequently changed according to circumstances.

A key factor that promoted the oscillation between centralized and decentralized collective bargaining was the interest representation system. In the post–World War II period, the three main trade unions—Confederazione Generale Italiana del Lavoro (CGIL), Confederazione Italiana Sindacati Lavoratori (CISL), and Unione Italiana del Lavoro (UIL)—competed for representation and influence on the basis of ideological differences.[3] All three unions were organizationally structured along two dimensions. One dimension of union structure was "horizontal" (i.e., geographical), which corresponded with an encompassing representation logic. The other dimension of union structure was "vertical" (i.e., industrial), which corresponded to the articulation of different sectoral interests, more affected by economic fluctuations.[4] Given the weak regulation of Italian industrial relations, this complex structure enabled trade union initiative to switch rapidly between the center and the periphery, and between more general union strategies and more sectoral ones. This served to promote frequent change, and also made it possible for different strategies to be pursued simultaneously. A similar, although less ordered, pattern characterized the structure of employers' associations, with Confindustria (Confederazione Generale dell'Industria Italiana) functioning as the principal representative for private-sector firms.

The shifting balance between centralized and decentralized collective bargaining depended on power relations. There was a tendency for negotiations to be decentralized in periods of economic growth, when labor had greater power to enforce its demands and when it was in the interest of firms to agree to concessions in order to avoid conflict. Conversely, the structure of collective bargaining tended to recentralize during periods of sluggish economic growth when the unions focused on standardizing the terms of employment (Cella and Treu 1998).

In the late 1970s, however, the unions started pushing for a recentralization of the structure of collective bargaining. They did so from a position of strength aided by large memberships and substantial political influence at the height of the economic crisis that had hit all the Western economies. Membership within the CGIL, CISL, and UIL, then allied in a Unitary Federation, were at an all-time high in 1978, with the unionization rate climbing to 50 percent of the labor force (Visser 1992). Another strengthening factor at this time was the spread of works councils ("factory councils") in the private sector, a spread that started during the collective mobilization in the "hot autumn" of 1969 with support from the unions (Regalia 1995). Unions were able to exert great influence on employers and the government in the mid- and late 1970s. Particularly important was the 1975 agreement between the unions and Confindustria on the *scala mobile* (the wage-indexation system) and other welfare provisions, by which the mechanism of automatically inflation-linked pay increases was revised and extended to the whole economy.[5]

Unions pushed for central-level agreements through various initiatives, including the negotiation of social reforms with the government and the first attempts to develop a tripartite social pact. A social pact was proposed that would have involved a trade-off between wage restraint and job creation, better regulation of the labor-market and of company restructuring processes, and development of the Mezzogiorno (southern Italy) region (Regini 1995). The unions were promoting a redefinition of industrial relations in which the central level of negotiation would acquire the capacity to coordinate demands, and thus follow the "European model" of industrial relations (Streeck 1993).

However, the union efforts to promote centralized and tripartite bargaining in the late 1970s either were not reciprocated by employers and the government or produced few results. In exchange for exercising wage restraint at the bargaining table, powerful unions were not adequately compensated. Furthermore, the legislation introduced under union promptings to regulate restructuring processes and promote employment fell short of union demands. The result was frustration and disappointment, especially among the unionists who had pressed hard for innovation (CGIL) and rank-and-file militants in the most unionized large companies, who saw their power undermined. The traditionally adversarial nature of Italian unions revived, although as clarified in the next two sections, surprising developments followed.

THE DEVELOPMENT OF TRIPARTISM AND THE REGULATION OF COLLECTIVE BARGAINING IN THE 1980S AND 1990S

Following two oil-shocks in the 1970s and the ensuing strong pressures for large wage increases promoted by highly mobilized unions, inflation in Italy rapidly rose to a two-digit rate. Even more than economic recession, inflation became the main concern for policymakers as well as for industrial relations actors. As in other European countries, governments looked for a consensual solution to the inflation problem, and incomes policy emerged as an attractive policy option. Thus, in the early 1980s, national-level tripartism developed as both the most important level of industrial relations as well as the key method of economic policy-making, focused on the search for an "anti-inflation pact." The first outcome of this laborious negotiated search was a tripartite agreement signed in January 1983. In exchange for a jointly agreed revision of the *scala mobile* and a more flexible use of the labor force, the government offered state-financed benefits to labor and management; subsidies for social security contributions to employers; tax reductions; and an increase in family allowances.[6] The role of the government in this pact was to use public funds to compensate firms and workers for any costs they incurred by complying with the agreement.

Although that agreement was hailed by many observers as marking a crucial stage in relations between labor, management, and the government, it did not in fact give rise to stable social dialogue. An attempt was made in the following year to repeat the experience, but this was only partly successful as neither the government nor the unions could replicate the role they had performed in 1983. After being widely criticized for using public expenditure to gain consensus, and faced with a huge public deficit, the government found it more difficult to offer compensation to unions and employers for the "sacrifices" required of them. The unions, for their part, had run into difficulties in their relations with the rank and file, and they were especially vulnerable to internal splits created, among other things, by the divergent policies pursued by the political parties with which they were associated. The center-left government sought to acquire social legitimation by means of a new tripartite agreement, which the majority block of the CGIL, closely linked to the Communist party (PCI), was unwilling to accept. As a result, although the two "minority" unions accepted the proposal offered by the government, CGIL, the "majority" union, did not. The outcome was a flawed agreement, which the government sought to remedy by issuing a "decree law," imposing the terms of the agreement in full.

Irrespective of their varying degrees of success, the two social pacts of the early 1980s can, with hindsight, also be viewed as a determined effort to institutionalize Italian industrial relations by means of a mix of associative and state regulation. Although, as said, the main policy concern was inflation, with employment and welfare benefits being of secondary concern, this method of political bargaining had the more general aim of replacing the traditional adversarialism and informality of relationships among labor and management in Italy with stable, centralized, and institutionalized cooperation. The objective was to create a model that would be imitated at more decentralized bargaining levels. On this score the parties' efforts failed miserably.

However, while relationships between unions, employers' associations, and the government were permeated by a sense of paralysis and adversarialism at the central level, in the periphery of the industrial relations system a practice of "hidden microconcertation" spread. This spread was especially significant in large firms and in regions where small firms dominated (Regini 1995, 111–25). This form of dialogue provided "voluntarist" and negotiated solutions to the problem of how to add more flexibility to the rules governing the employment relationship. In many cases, dialogue evolved into a genuine, though informal, comanagement of industrial adjustments. In several firms, in fact, industrial restructuring was carried forward, not in open conflict with unions, but rather, in a sort of continuous discussion of problems as they arose at the workplace.

What arose in the 1980s, therefore, was tacit acceptance of the existence of two distinct spheres of industrial relations action. The central and official level continued to be dominated by difficult and often adversarial relationships. Meanwhile, at the local firm or industrial district level, the search for joint regulation, even if only informal and voluntaristic, prevailed. Thus the largely unstructured bipolar character of Italian industrial relations still persisted. Since there was little institutionalization of rules and practices, instability and uncertainty increased as the importance and extent of the matters to be regulated jointly increased.

It was only in the 1990s that the search for social pacts, which had ceased after the failed tripartite agreement of 1984, was resumed with vigor and a mechanism was found to create institutionalized practices and procedures. The most significant events were the two tripartite agreements in 1992 and 1993, which settled negotiations over incomes policy and the structure of collective bargaining. These agreements were followed by political negotiations over pension reform, which gave rise first to a severe social conflict and then (in 1995) to an agreement between the government and unions. This was followed by a "pact for employment" in 1996 and the "Christmas pact" of 1998, which ended a decade-long series of social pacts (see table 3.1).

Incomes Policies and Collective Bargaining Reform

What made it possible for the parties to reach a series of social pacts in the 1990s was that the parties found a way to reform the *scala mobile* (the wage indexation mechanism). The *scala mobile* effectively had shielded wages from the risk of inflation (until the mid-1980s, wages were automatically adjusted to cover about 80 percent of the inflation rate) and thus it created labor cost problems for firms. For the unions, on the one hand, the *scala mobile* had great symbolic significance, since it was the outcome of previous waves of collective mobilization and the main indicator of their ability to resist change in power relations. Yet, on the other hand, the *scala mobile* created severe problems for unions as it left them with very narrow margins to negotiate wage growth and pay differentials.

Hence, when negotiations over the cost of labor and the collective bargaining structure were resumed in 1989, the issue of the *scala mobile* seemingly blocked any possible progress. The two tripartite agreements signed in 1990 and 1991 acknowledged this deadlock by restricting themselves to declarations of principle while postponing reform of the indexation system. However, the political situation changed radically in 1992, the year in which the *Mani Pulite* (Clean Hands) investigation was launched.[7] The April 1992 elections brought the collapse of the old political system, and the new "technocratic government" headed by Amato faced a fiscal and monetary crisis. It was this climate of national emergency that enabled the government to mobilize the consensus necessary for the most drastic attempt to balance the state budget since the late 1940s.

The tripartite agreement reached in July 1992, which abolished the *scala mobile*, was spurred by this climate. Not only was the *scala mobile* abolished, but company-level bargaining on wages also was frozen for the period 1992–93. The core of the agreement was therefore the curbing of wages growth without the compensatory measures that had accompanied the political trade-offs made in the early 1980s. The goal of reducing inflation was achieved as the rate of inflation fell from 5.4 percent in 1992 to 3.2 percent in 1993, to 2.5 percent in 1994, and to 2 percent in 1995.

Despite the resignation (later withdrawn) by the leader of the CGIL, who had signed the 1992 agreement, and notwithstanding considerable pressure from CGIL members and numerous wildcat strikes mounted in the most unionized factories, the 1992 agreement was generally hailed as a turning point in industrial relations. Yet this agreement was incomplete because it did no more than temporarily halt company-level collective bargaining and failed to introduce new rules and procedures into the collective bargaining system.

These problems were tackled in a new agreement reached the following year involving the new "technocratic government" led by Ciampi. The agreement signed by this government, unions, and employers in July 1993 was not the simple emergency measure many had expected, but instead delineated a new structure of incomes policies and collective bargaining. In addition to confirming the abolition of the *scala mobile*, the agreement set out an incomes policy based on commitments by the parties to constrain wage setting to limits imposed by the expected rate of inflation. For this purpose, two annual meetings were set up, in order, respectively, "to define common objectives concerning the expected inflation rate, the growth of GDP and employment" and "to verify the coherence of behavior by the parties engaged in the autonomous exercise of their respective responsibilities."

The agreement also confirmed the bipolar character of the Italian collective bargaining system, which consisted of a national industry level and a company (or local) level, as described above. Furthermore, the roles of the two levels of collective bargaining were clarified, and the relations between them given clearer definition in order to overcome previous jurisdictional overlap and ambiguity. The national industry contract (of two-year duration with regard to wages and four-year duration with regard to other matters) adjusted pay scales to the expected rate of inflation with accommodation to the average productivity increases occurring in each respective industry. The company contract (for large firms) or the territorial contract (for small firms) were expected to provide additional wage increases where there were higher than average local productivity increases, as well as to deal with the consequences of technological and organizational innovation. At the same time, local adjustments were not to alter any concessions included in the national level agreement (see the next section for an assessment of the results). In order to render this second level of collective bargaining viable, a reform of workplace representation was envisaged; a reform, in fact, that was later sanctioned by an agreement between the unions and the employers' associations.[8]

Negotiations over Pension Reform

After the Second World War, the Italian pension system grew steadily in an incremental manner, with the progressive extension of coverage to workers in different occupations. The pension system for each industrial sector developed a particular relationship between contributions and benefits and often included separately managed funds. Reform of this chaotic system had long been on the policy agenda in response to concerns about the need for cost containment, rationalization, and equity.

In the 1990s, the problem of curbing expenditures on social security grew especially dramatic. Although in Italy total spending on social programs as a share of gross domestic product (GDP) was (and still is) below the European average, the proportion of that spending allocated to pensions far exceeded the average.[9] Pressure also came from the huge public debt and the steady declines occurring in the population and labor force. As a result of these pressures, reform of the pension system had become the cornerstone of Italy's economic recovery strategy.

The Amato government (see table 3.1) was the first to seriously address the pension system's problems with a 1992 decree that raised the age of retirement, increased the minimum number of years a person had to make contributions into the system in order to qualify for a pension, made it more difficult to combine a pension with other work-related income, and introduced other changes. An even more complete "structural" reform of

TABLE 3.1. SOCIAL PACTS AND GOVERNMENTS IN OFFICE SINCE 1990

1992	Amato "technocratic government." Tripartite agreement on the abolition of the wage indexation system.
1993	Ciampi "technocratic government." Tripartite agreement on incomes policy and collective bargaining structure.
1994	Berlusconi first center-right government. Failed negotiation on pension reform.
1995	Dini "technocratic government." Negotiated pension reform.
1996	Prodi center-left government. Tripartite "pact for employment."
1998	D'Alema center-left government. Tripartite "social pact for development."
2002	Berlusconi second center-right government. "Pact for Italy" not signed by CGIL (the majority union).

the system, which would have replaced earnings-related pensions with a contributions-related scheme and abolished "seniority pensions" (that enabled employees to retire at any age as long as they had made contributions into the system for thirty-five years), was considered, but not adopted. Factors limiting the extent of reforms included the "acquired rights" of many categories of workers and the role and power of the unions, who held a majority of seats on the board of directors of INPS (the institute that manages the pensions of private-sector employees). Consequently, it was extremely difficult to deal with these problems until a consensus was achieved among the various interest organizations.

The first Berlusconi government, installed in May 1994, seemed initially to recognize the need for social consensus when it asked a committee of experts and representatives from labor and management to formulate proposals for pension reform. However, given the unwillingness of this committee to suggest specific policy reforms and go beyond agreement on general principles, the government decided to act unilaterally by including provisions in the budget law that would effectively eliminate seniority pensions. The center-right government tried to change the unwritten rules of the game that had hitherto regulated social security policy-making in Italy. The government decided, that is, to use the issue of pension reform, the focus of strong pressures from the financial sector and a broad political consensus, to test what it perceived to be altered power relations. The Berlusconi government also sought to test whether it was possible to cut public spending without the agreement of the unions.

However, it was precisely the fact that this initiative was perceived as a test for a new mode of policy-making that gave special impetus and incisiveness to union mobilization. Although the reform proposals that the unions drew up were not greatly dissimilar from those proposed by the government, a general strike was immediately proclaimed and followed by wide social mobilization and a series of public protests. Even Confindustria, which had explicitly supported the government's proposals, watched these developments with disquiet. The result was a defeat for the government, which in an agreement reached with the unions, removed the provisions on pensions from the budget law and postponed them until the following year.

At the beginning of 1995, the center-right Berlusconi government was replaced by yet another "technocratic government," led by Dini. The Dini government included reform of the pension system in the policy program it intended to put in place before new elections were called. The new effort to reform the pension system recognized that consensus with the unions was necessary.

The government and the unions then engaged in bargaining over reforms based on a project report drawn up by union experts. An agreement between the government and the unions was reached in May 1995. Although the employers' associations were involved at various stages in the long and difficult talks, Confindustria was generally critical of the eventually adopted reforms, deeming them insufficiently radical while regarding the forecast spending cuts as inadequate, and employers refused to sign the agreement. The government later converted the text of the agreement into a bill that it submitted to Parliament, while the unions conducted a referendum at the workplace level over pension reforms. After a tough campaign, the union pension referendum passed with significant majority support. The bill was finally approved by Parliament in July 1995, and the new "negotiated" law was hailed as one of the spurs, along with the tripartite agreements of 1992 and 1993, of Italy's subsequent economic recovery.

Because it rationalized the entire pension system, standardized coverage and benefits, abolished or at least reduced privileges, and prepared the way for change (albeit gradual) to a contributions-based system, the reform of the pension system was one of the most radical reforms in the history of the Italian welfare state. At the same time it is important to note that the immediate effects of the reform on spending were quite limited. The key condition that led to the unions' support for pension reform was retention of the previous pension system for elderly workers, with the introduction of a new and more rigorous system for less senior workers.

This obviously meant that savings would only accrue gradually. In a policy-making system like Italy's, which is based on incremental change, the reform of social security represented a quite unusual policy innovation (Lange and Regini 1989, 249–72).

Social Pacts from the Mid-1990s: A Broadening of Scope and Decreasing Effectiveness

Employment policy was another important topic of tripartite dialogue. In September 1996, a "pact for employment" was signed to promote job creation, especially in the less-developed areas of the country. This new tripartite agreement involved reforms of education and training systems, promotion of temporary work and working-time reductions, and perhaps most importantly, "territorial pacts" to promote new investment in economically underdeveloped regions. The employment creation provisions of the "pact for employment" were implemented through a 1997 law, which for the first time formally allowed temporary agency work, addressed fixed-term employment, and provided incentives for part-time work and the redefinition of working time schedules. New rules were also introduced to relaunch the apprenticeship system and to develop work and training contracts and supplemental training.

"Territorial pacts" were also sanctioned by the 1996 pact. These territorial pacts were to be based on formal agreements involving a local government, unions, employers' organizations, and other important local actors such as banks and universities. The territorial pacts involved innovative forms of decentralized social dialogue, aimed at the consensual planning of local initiatives for economic and occupational development. A form of territorial pacts introduced subsequently by legislation were the so-called "area agreements," especially targeted on less-developed regions, primarily though not exclusively in southern Italy. While intended to mobilize local resources, these area agreements typically stated the intent to promote wage and labor market flexibility; however, sharp divisions among unions emerged on these issues.[10]

The outcomes produced by territorial-level collective bargaining were less impressive than expected. While several case studies (Bolocan Goldstein, Pasqui, and Perulli 2000; Ballarino et al. 2001; Barbera 2001; Regalia 2003) describe examples of success, the overall attempt to decentralize tripartism and to broaden its scope has been hampered by divisions between unions and a lack of sufficient resources from local institutions devoted to these efforts. More important, employers have in most cases been lukewarm participants to these efforts and generally have not cooperated actively in them. The main reason for employers' behavior is that they perceived territorial tripartism as yet another burdensome level of collective bargaining, at a time when they were becoming increasingly unhappy about the two levels of collective bargaining set up by the tripartite agreement of 1993.

Employers became convinced that the distinction between issues to be discussed at various bargaining levels made in the 1993 agreement did not prevent the emergence of substantial confusion and overlapping negotiations. Curiously enough, in a period in which average real wages in Italy were growing less than in the other EU countries (largely an outcome of the incomes policy established by the 1993 agreement), shifting to a "one level of bargaining only" system became a key employer demand, along with a desire for greater flexibility in dismissals. Employers saw no need for two levels of bargaining since a sharp drop in the rate of inflation had deprived industry-level bargaining of its main content, and distributional demands stemming from increases in productivity were supposed to be dealt with at the local level of bargaining. While employers' associations demanded a shift to a "one level of bargaining" system, however, employers could not agree on which level should be retained. Most employers favored decentralized (local) bargaining (at the firm level for large- and medium-sized firms, or at the territorial level for small firms within industrial districts), but some other employers preferred industry-level bargaining.

The employers' one level demand set the agenda for the new tripartite agreement eventually signed in December 1998, but largely because of the divisions among employers, the final text of that agreement did not even mention the structure of collective bargaining. Nor did it deal with the two other hot issues in Italian industrial relations in the late 1990s, namely, the rules that protected workers from dismissal and pension reform. This agreement did, on the other hand, contain a very ambitious program on a wide range of issues including measures to foster growth and employment, education, and other supply-side policies. Yet the measures adopted confronted the usual implementation problems and in the end were not very effective.

This illustrates the main lesson stemming from the recent attempts at tripartite social pacts. As the scope of these pacts broadens, in terms of both the issues covered and the levels of operation (national, regional, and even local), their effectiveness decreases. In fact, objectives such as employment creation, training, and labor market and welfare reforms, are far more difficult to pursue through social dialogue than are traditional incomes policies. In some cases a tentative solution to these difficulties may be to enlarge the number of actors involved in the political negotiation process and the levels of negotiations (i.e., calling on local institutions to provide their own resources in a wider political exchange as in the territorial pacts). But this solution often brings its own set of problems, since a negotiation involving several actors is more difficult to complete and any outcomes are likely to be more difficult to monitor. The commitment of each actor to common goals may weaken as the number of actors increases, and each actor may be less willing to take on responsibility for difficult decisions as the number of negotiating parties increases.

The outcome of these trends has been a growing loss of enthusiasm by policymakers and especially employers for social pacts. It has not been difficult for the current center-right Berlusconi government to capitalize on this widespread feeling and to state that, while what is now termed tripartite "social dialogue" remains the preferred method in Italian industrial relations, "modernization" must continue even in the absence of social dialogue. This has led to a new division among the three union confederations. Eighteen years after the tripartite agreement of 1984, signed by CISL and UIL, but not by the majority trade union (CGIL), in 2002 a new "separate" agreement, the "pact for Italy," was reached by CISL and UIL. The issue that split the union confederations was differences in their views toward the (rather mild) relaxation of the rules regulating dismissals. Even deeper differences are to be found in the views of the three union confederations regarding the possibility that tripartism can maintain a viable role given the presence of an openly proemployer government. Perhaps more importantly, both Confindustria and the center-right government may have seen the 2002 agreement more as a means to divide the labor movement than as a testament to the virtue of tripartite dialogue over economic policies. If this is so, then the central role that tripartism has played in Italian industrial relations may rapidly decline and even end.

THE STRUCTURE OF BILATERAL COLLECTIVE BARGAINING BEFORE AND AFTER THE TRIPARTITE AGREEMENT OF JULY 1993

In the 1980s it was not fully clear which issues were to be addressed in industry-level collective agreements and which issues were appropriately resolved in local bargaining. Nevertheless, there was a substantial amount of standardization in the content of industry-level collective bargaining agreements across industries. Typically the duration of agreements was three years and there was a lot of similarity in the negotiating procedures and agreement contents. Over time, industry-level collective bargaining had standardized the employment conditions of workers in various industries (or within sectors in industries where sector differences were important) and assured minimum protections. In other words, industrywide contracts came to perform the role fulfilled in other countries by minimum wage legislation (Cella-Treu 1998, 217).

The negotiation of industrywide agreements also provided the opportunity for demands to be aggregated, harmonized, and then ordered, while unions simultaneously validated their role and support in each industry/sector by means of the debates and information exchanges that surrounded agreements. Unions did not use formalized and explicit systems to coordinate their demands, although a certain amount of coordination was achieved by means of informal contacts, as well as through the influence of the decisions taken and agreements reached by the union confederations when bargaining was centralized in the late 1970s and early 1980s, as discussed in the previous section.

Industry-level bargaining in the 1980s generated significant trends toward making pay and working hours more flexible, a process that continued in the 1990s. The pay structure in Italy has always been highly complex (the basic wage is supplemented by a wide variety of allowances and bonuses) and characterized by a large amount of deferred components (including end-of-service allowances and pension benefits) and automatic pay increases (seniority increments and the *scala mobile*). The process that led to the abolition of the wage-indexation system is discussed above. Other pay reforms included a 1982 law that scaled down the end-of-service allowance, while automatic seniority increments were progressively reduced by means of industrywide bargaining. The overall result was an increase in the variable, and negotiable, part of pay and a widening during the 1980s of pay differentials (among sectors, among companies of different sizes, and among jobs). As for working hours, the most significant feature of industrywide bargaining in the 1980s was the tendency, as in other European countries, for contractual hours to diminish, which was achieved through references to annualized rather than the previously used, weekly hours. This had the effect of facilitating in Italy, earlier than elsewhere, considerable flexibility in working hours, which catered to the needs of firm restructuring. Not by chance, working time issues were at the top of the agenda for company-level collective bargaining, which grew increasingly common in the second half of the 1980s.

According to several surveys, one may estimate that company-level collective bargaining in unionized private-sector firms takes place in approximately 25–35 percent of firms with 15–50 employees, in 40–50 percent of firms with 50–150 employees, and in 60–75 percent of larger firms (Cella and Treu 1998, 240–41). Informal understandings (i.e., without written agreement) that in some cases supplement the terms of formal agreements, or in some other cases substitute for formal agreements, are also reached in a number of firms.[11]

The Impact of the 1993 Reform

Overall, the reorganization of the collective bargaining system promoted by the 1993 agreement appears to have been largely successful. Analysis of wage dynamics and various macroeconomic indicators indicates the following outcomes (see table 3.2): the 1993 agreement contributed to wage restraint by helping to balance economic accounts and the public debt; the agreement led to wage increases that held purchasing power steady; pay differentials between the export (i.e., manufacturing) sector and protected sectors such as public services and public utilities (electricity, gas, and water) tended to decline; business profitability increased in the 1990s (and was particularly high in 1998 and 1999), in large part because of modest increases in the cost of labor (less than the rate of productivity improvement); and wage restraint contributed to the stabilization of employment in the first half of the 1990s and to employment growth in the late 1990s (Trentini 2001).[12] According to ISTAT, the National Statistics Institute, the unemployment rate finally returned to below 10 percent in March 2001.

As a result of their extremely broad coverage, industry-level agreements emerged as the best guarantor of basic employment conditions and also proved capable of augmenting and improving the capacities for centralized coordination of industrial relations and economic policy-making. Particularly important in this regard was the fact that industry-level agreements standardized employment conditions and reduced agreement fragmentation. There were strong tendencies in opposing directions coming from the liberalization of markets and the privatization of previous public monopolies, which were taking place in the 1990s. Market pressures called into question the traditional negotiation of separate agreements for private and public firms. A clear purpose came to be served by broader agreements that redefined and standardized employment conditions. One of the most noteworthy cases was the collective agreement for the telecommunications industry that brought order to a particularly unruly sector. Similarly, an attempt to establish more orderly relations by centralized collective bargaining was carried on in the transport and public utility sectors. Agreement simplification and coordination was also

TABLE 3.2. TRENDS IN REAL CONTRACTUAL WAGES AND MACROECONOMIC INDICATORS
(AVERAGE ANNUAL PERCENTAGE CHANGES)

	1976–82	1983–92	1993–2000	1996–2000	1999	2000
Real contractual wages*	2.3	0.7	−0.3	0.6	n.a.	n.a.
Manufacturing output	2.5	0.5	0.0	0.5	n.a.	n.a
Gross domestic product at 1995 prices	3.3	2.3	1.7	1.9	1.6	2.9
Public debt (stock)	22.6	16.7	5.3	2.1	1.7	1.4
Productivity	2.2	1.8	1.7	1.1	0.8	1.4
Productivity-wage differential**	0.0	1.0	1.5	0.5	0.0	0.6
Wage and salary earners	0.6	0.5	0.2	1.0	1.3	1.5
Total employment	1.0	0.6	0.0	0.8	0.8	1.5

* Blue-and white-collar household deflator for the whole economy.
** Pay levels deflated with the same deflator as production (GDP defl.)
Source: IRES calculations on ISTAT and Bankitalia data (Birindelli and D'Aloia 2001).

enhanced in industries that were unaffected by privatization, as with the unification of what were previously three separate collective agreements in the banking sector.

Industrywide agreements also were used effectively to regulate employment conditions in new sectors. One of these was the collective agreement for temporary work agencies signed in 1998; another was the national agreement for the market research sector signed in 2001 with the newly formed union representing atypical workers (the latter became the first national labor contract for self-employed workers in Italy) (Ballarino 2002).[13]

Turning to decentralized, or "second-level," bargaining, the distinction between in-company bargaining and territorial bargaining is critical. In Italy, company-level bargaining has always been limited by the fragmented nature of market and corporate structures and the associated predominance of small firms. ISTAT data from 1995–96 on bargaining practices in firms with more than ten employees indicate that 10 percent of firms had, and 40 percent of employees were covered by, company-level agreements (i.e., larger firms were relatively more likely to have a company-level agreement) (ISTAT 1998). The percentage of firms that had engaged in company-level bargaining ranged from 3.3 percent in firms that had ten to nineteen employees to 61 percent in firms that had more than five hundred employees. In general, moreover, company-level bargaining was less frequent in the southern region as compared to the center-North and Northeast regions, and was less frequent among service firms as compared to manufacturing firms. Company-level collective bargaining was widely diffused within the small industrial firms of the Northeast.

Larger estimates of the diffusion of company-level bargaining are provided in the findings of a survey conducted in 1997 by Federmeccanica (the employers' association in the metalworking sector). This survey finds that 45 percent of sampled firms had company-level agreements, and that 90 percent of the firms that had more than two hundred employees engaged in company-level bargaining. The Federmeccanica survey also furnishes data on the most sensitive issue raised by the 1993 reform, namely, the possibility of bargaining only supplemental wage increases based on productivity in company-level agreements. The survey finds that where pay increases were provided in company-level agreements, in only 18.4 percent of these cases were pay increases not justified by, or linked to, company economic performance (and this mostly occurred in small firms) (Federmeccanica 1997).[14]

Yet, overall the net effect on pay of company-level collective bargaining seems to be modest. A study by the Bank of Italy (on a sample of manufacturing firms that had more than fifty employees) found that the pay increases provided in national- or industry-level collective bargaining made up 85 percent of the total pay increases received by workers. In the firms included in this survey the remainder of the pay increases were determined through company-level bargaining, and only 3 percent of these company-level pay increases were linked to company economic performance (Casadio 1999). The Bank of Italy survey does find that company-level bargaining was used effectively to address workplace issues. This was particularly common in the more developed regions of the country, where unions were well established. Most often company-level collective bargaining was used to address employment issues, labor market problems, and "atypical" jobs. The focus in company-level bargaining on these issues was encouraged by the 1996 Employment Pact and legislation adopted in 1997, both of which increased labor market flexibility (Lizzeri 2002).

According to most observers, company-level bargaining seems to have grown to a larger extent than was envisaged at the time of the 1993 agreement, when it was thought that the limits imposed on decentralized bargaining with regard to pay would have discouraged it.

The fact however that company-level bargaining was extremely rare in small firms was a key reason why unions were unwilling to accept the employers' request to make it the main, if not the only, level of collective bargaining.

On the other hand, small firms may participate in two other types of local collective bargaining—territorial bargaining (widespread in the crafts sector and in numerous industrial districts), and provincial bargaining (widespread in agriculture and the construction industry), as well as the already-mentioned experiments in territorial social dialogue concerning local economic development and employment creation.

Whether in territorial or provincial bargaining, the main aim of these "second-level" negotiations is to improve employment conditions established by national agreements, or to implement contractual rules by defining arrangements appropriate to the local context (regarding matters such as work hours or the organization of work). The main purpose of territorial social dialogue is to consider concessions from the standards set out in national agreements regarding pay, job classifications, working hours, employment contracts, or workforce deployment. These concessions are typically granted in exchange for assurances that jobs will be created by specific projects and investments. These practices are similar to the "opening clauses" found in German industrywide agreements (CNEL 2000, 266). Debate commonly surfaces among the unions about whether economic conditions warrant acceptance of concessions, as happened when CGIL opposed the Milan Employment Pact of 2000 (Bolocan Goldstein 2002).[15]

Precise estimates of the diffusion of territorial bargaining are not available; however, it appears that collective bargaining occurs infrequently at this level. An interesting exception is Veneto, a region with a high incidence of small firms, where company-level bargaining often is combined with territorial bargaining (see table 3.3). Overall, in this area territorial bargaining seems to cover as many firms and employees as company-level bargaining (Giaccone 2001).

Changes in Public-Sector Collective Bargaining

Finding an appropriate way to regulate the pay and conditions of public employees was one of the central policy problems left unresolved in the early 1980s, when the traditional balance between statutory regulation and trade-union involvement had broken down. In the early 1980s, the use of collective bargaining to set employment terms had spread in an uncoordinated manner. The fact that public employers did not face market constraints created space for wage drift, widespread conflict, and a militant opposition to the "moderate" policies pursued by the union confederations. As a result, radical rank-and-file unionism (the *Cobas*) spread (Bordogna 1994). The first effort to rationalize collective bargaining in the public sector (by means of a framework law) occurred in 1983. This law formally allowed collective bargaining in the public sector, but passage of the law did not lead to stable labor relations. Continuing instability in labor relations spurred a push for the privatization of the employment relationship of civil servants, which was finally initiated in 1992. As a result of this reform, the tripartite agreement of July 1993 became the first agreement to be applied to both the private and public sectors (Barbieri 1995, 295–307; Garofalo 1994, 163–95).

The privatization process stimulated extensive consultation and negotiation involving the unions and the government. As a result, collective bargaining was empowered to extensively regulate the employment relationship of civil servants. The influence of collective bargaining has been constrained, however, within a legal framework that imposes controls on public spending and defines the bargaining subjects. The greatest innovation was the creation of the Agenzia per le relazioni sindacali (ARAN), a technical agency with legal status that replaced the traditional committees nominated by the public ministries. The agency took over the task of representing the government in its role as employer in collective negotiations. The goals of the reorganization that followed the 1992 reform were to

TABLE 3.3. THE COVERAGE OF SECOND-LEVEL BARGAINING IN VENETO*

	Industry & Agriculture		Services		Total	
	1994–97	1998–2001	1994–97	1998–2001	1994–97	1998–2001
Company-level agreements	27.8	23.8	17.1	16.0	22.3	19.7
Territorial agreements	41.4	19.4	7.7	19.6	24.3	19.5
Other local agreements	3.2	3.8	7.7	8.3	5.5	6.2
Total	72.4	47.0	32.5	43.9	52.1	45.4

* Also included in the 1998–2001 data are cases where negotiations were in progress at the time of the survey.
Source: Giaccone (2001, 113).

provide centrally coordinated collective bargaining and separate political and administrative responsibilities in order to reduce patronage and public spending.

The privatization process was completed in 1997–98 with further legislative measures that clarified the organization of workplace representative bodies, RSUs; measured the representative capacity of unions; and extended the applicability of public-sector collective bargaining agreements. This legislation also extended to the public-sector provisions, allowing for supplementary local bargaining to the public sector, thus strengthening the two-tier bargaining model (D'Antona 2000). As a result, employment conditions in the public sector no longer differ significantly from those in the private sector, and in fact, labor relations in the public sector in general have become more methodical and more structured than labor relations in the private sector. This has helped control public expenditures and substantially reduced industrial conflict in the sector.

CONCLUSION

As some authors (Damiano and Giaccone 2001) point out, four variants of two-tier collective bargaining currently operate in Italy. The four variants differ according to how the lower (local) level of collective bargaining performs and interacts with industry-level collective bargaining. One type of collective bargaining, which can be labeled as "decentralized" bargaining, is characterized by either extensive company-level bargaining led by the respective RSU and territorial unions (mainly in manufacturing enterprises), or by territorial-level bargaining usually involving territorial trade unions (mainly within industrial districts and craft sectors). This variant corresponds most closely to the goals held by those that framed the 1993 agreement.

A second type of collective bargaining is also decentralized in character, but includes an even more significant role for the RSUs and comanagement of the workplace. This variant is especially prevalent among autonomous local agencies in the public sector (e.g., hospitals).

A third type of collective bargaining, which can be labeled "centralized" (or highly coordinated), includes a lower level of bargaining that is substantially controlled by the respective national union. This variant is typical of large organizations (firms or government agencies) that include numerous small- and medium-sized local units scattered across the country. It appears in the private sector (among banks, telecommunications firms, large retailers, and automobile manufactures) and in the public sector (in various ministries).

In a fourth type of collective bargaining, the lower level of bargaining is de facto either absent or almost entirely constrained by the respective industry-level agreement. This variant is typical of the bargaining that occurs in very small firms (such as professional offices, cleaning firms, construction firms, and farms).

Overall, the structure of collective bargaining has adapted creatively to the competitive and structural changes and the specific composition of the work force within organizations. New external and internal factors, however, have emerged recently that may upset the equilibrium that had been achieved. One key external factor looming as a potential significant influence is the European Union (EU) directives on aspects of work and employment. Another external factor is the recently enacted constitutional law on federalism, which gives regional administrations concurrent legislative powers on employment protection measures.

The EU directives on issues such as work hours, overtime, part-time work, parental leave, and fixed-term employment contracts has spurred legislation that enables experimentation and the determination of standards at the company level, thereby eliminating one of the roles previously played by national agreements. Since the national agreements are renegotiated only every four years, they have not always been able to keep pace with normative innovations. This has produced a downward shift in bargaining power and initiative, and a "disorientation among union officers (officials and RSU's) in company-level regulation, accustomed as they are to take their bearings from the national agreement" (Damiano and Giaccone 2001, 62).

The constitutional law on federalism (no. 1/01), which defines the matters reserved to the state and those on which concurrent legislation may be introduced on the initiative of regional governments, has been called a "veritable revolution." It has introduced a "complete reversal of perspective" in which the regions may become the lead actors (Biagi 2001). Although the state has competence on fundamental principles (in addition to specific issues such as compulsory social security), at least in principle differences among regions are possible on numerous important issues, which may further reduce the role and significance of industry-level collective bargaining.

From within the bargaining system itself, an internal factor that may have destabilizing effects is the way in which change has so far occurred. With the notable exception of the changes that occurred in the public sector, reform of the bargaining system has been accomplished on the basis of negotiated agreements between the actors, but without statutory definition of bargaining rules. In this way, the substantially voluntarist character of Italian labor relations has been supported. As history has shown, however, although voluntarism facilitates change and adaptability, it also leaves the door open to instability and unpredictability.

It is too early to draw firm conclusions. But it is already clear that the future is likely to involve more than just further consolidation of the bargaining system along the lines promoted by the tripartite pact of 1993.

What can we learn from the Italian experience discussed so far? Analysts argue that the emergence of social pacts in some European countries reflect centralizing tendencies in wage bargaining and in other aspects of industrial relations that run counter to the previous trend toward decentralization, a trend still very visible in other countries (European Commission 2000). However, close inspection shows that the recent social pacts in most cases are not products of centralizing processes. The tripartite agreement of July 1993 in Italy shows this clearly. As discussed above, this pact did not seek to create top-level bargaining of the classic Scandinavian type. Rather, the 1993 pact establishes rules and procedures for the conduct of collective bargaining, but does not fundamentally constrain industry- and company-level negotiations; nor does it prevent firms from designing idiosyncratic pay structures.

Although the institutional mechanisms differ, the logic that inspired the 1993 Italian pact is the same as the logic that inspired the Austrian system. In both the Italian and Austrian systems, while the central level of bargaining influences overall wage dynamics, at the same time the task of determining relative wage levels is left to decentralized negotiations. Traxler (1996) conceptualizes this trend as "organized decentralization," contrasting it with the "disorganized decentralization" characteristic of the collective bargaining systems in Britain, the United States, and New Zealand.

Moreover, although collective bargaining has become more decentralized in Italy and other European countries, an influential role is being played by various informal mechanisms that coordinate wage dynamics. The role played by coordinating mechanisms in these countries suggests that it is appropriate to categorize these countries as "coordinated market economies" which, according to Soskice (1990), respond to common challenges in ways markedly different from "liberal market economies." From this point of view, the incomes policy devised by the tripartite agreement of 1993 in Italy is nothing but an instrument to reinforce the central coordination of wage dynamics.

While collective bargaining became more decentralized in the 1980s in many countries, in the 1990s bargaining decentralization moved in two very different directions. In some European countries, industry- and company-level negotiations occurred more commonly in the framework of a coordinated collective bargaining system. This was the case in Italy, while other authors detect similar developments in the Netherlands, Ireland, Greece, Portugal, and Spain (Fajertag and Pochet 1997). On the other hand, in a number of other countries the trend toward decentralized wage bargaining was in no way steered by the center, nor counterbalanced by the strengthening of coordinating mechanisms.

Why did social pacts become the dominant form of collective bargaining in Italy and in a few other European countries? Why were they successful in the 1990s, while they generally failed in the previous decade, and why have these pacts been less effective in the last few years and once again come under sharp questioning? A tentative answer to these questions, which fits Italy especially well, focuses on the process of monetary unification in Europe. In the early and mid-1990s, to gain admission to European Monetary Union, European countries were required to satisfy a set of economic performance standards concerning the rate of inflation and the size of the government fiscal deficit. These came to be known as convergence criteria or "the Maastricht parameters." Countries that were marginal to the European integrated economy (Ireland, Greece, Portugal) and those that were further from meeting the Maastricht parameters (Italy, Spain) resorted to mobilization of their citizens, interest groups, and institutions to generate support for their admission to the European Monetary Union. Social pacts, in various forms, were the main instrument that governments used to deal with this national emergency (Fajertag and Pochet 2000). The more the policymakers needed, and were able to mobilize, national consensus by advancing the idea of a national emergency only resolvable through cooperative efforts, the more recourse to social pacts was possible and the more likely their success.

Why then have social pacts been questioned, and why have they become increasingly ineffective in the last few years in Italy? The main reason is that the goal of meeting the Maastricht parameters has been achieved, and as a consequence the ability of Italian policymakers to mobilize labor and management in pursuit of a shared objective requiring mutual restraint has decreased. Also, since inflation appears to be under control among the European Monetary Union member countries, the need for an incomes policy of the kind that motivated tripartite agreements has become less pressing.

The new imperative for advanced political economies, like Italy, is to increase their global competitive standing. It is difficult to predict the extent to which policymakers will be able to translate this imperative into a new national emergency that requires cooperative efforts by labor, management, and governments. The first decade of the new century may well see a new differentiation between those economies that follow a path based on some form of social accord and other countries in which economic adjustment is achieved primarily through the market. Membership in these camps may not follow along traditional lines and over time countries may shift from one camp to the other.

4 The Changing Nature of Collective Bargaining in Germany

Coordinated Decentralization

Gerhard Bosch

Collective bargaining takes place in Germany mainly at the industry level. Collective agreements, however, lay down only minimum conditions, which can be exceeded at the company or plant level. As a result, it is customary for large or highly profitable firms to pay more and offer better working conditions than small or less profitable firms. In the 1960s in particular, the so-called "second pay bargaining round," conducted at the company level, was often more important than industry-level collective bargaining between trade unions and employers. Labor was in very short supply at the time and firms were forced to try to attract and retain workers by offering high wages. These higher wages were negotiated by works councils, and not by unions. The consequence was substantial wage-drift. At that time, the unions were concerned that company-level bargaining would undermine industry-wide bargaining. Unions considered introducing so-called "opening" or "authorizing" clauses into collective agreements in order to regain the bargaining power they had lost to works councils at the company level. The idea was that such clauses would permit the negotiation at the company level of upward exceptions from the provisions of collective agreements. However, after heated debate the unions rejected authorizing clauses, fearing that they would lead to the collapse of industry-level collective bargaining. The employers' associations also opposed such clauses because they would have conveyed to company agreements the status of collective agreements.[1]

At the end of the 1980s the decentralization of collective bargaining was once again on the agenda, although this time in completely different circumstances. The issue at stake was no longer the safeguarding of wage drift negotiated at the company level, but rather, reductions in employment conditions below the minimum standards provided in industry-level agreements, and delegation of certain bargaining topics to the firm level.

In the industrial relations literature, the globalization of markets is generally identified as the main reason for this development. It is argued, quite rightly, that in global markets wages cannot be taken out of competition as they can in protected national markets. Thelen (2000, 139) points out that the industrial relations literature offers "a continuing overabundance of ('globalization') theories that tell us why these systems should be breaking down, when in fact we need a more robust explanation for why, despite these strains, many of these systems are holding together at all." However, Thelen's investigation is too restricted in scope since she, just like virtually all of the other researchers on industrial relations in Germany, considers only the engineering and metal industries and not the system as a whole. In fact, German unification has had at least as a big an impact as globalization on the evolution of the German industrial relations system. Moreover, industrial relations in other industries are evolving in completely different ways as compared to the engineering and metal industries, and in many industries trade unions are facing the difficult task of reconstructing, or even building up from scratch, structures capable of supporting collective bargaining.

In a country in which industry-level collective bargaining predominates, the social reconstruction of industry bargaining structures, namely, the process of defining the industrial affiliations of companies, employees, developing institutions, and representative actors able to engage in collective negotiations, is crucial to the system's survival. The evolution of collective bargaining in Germany is being shaped by concurrent trends toward uncontrolled decentralization, coordinated decentralization, and recentralization. However, uncontrolled decentralization is not the dominant trend. There is not widespread erosion of the German industrial relations system, but rather, there is a system with many "construction sites," in which the actors have a range of options for, and considerable interest in, developing the system and adapting it to new conditions. Trade unions in particular, but to some extent employers and the state as well, are trying to utilize these options, since they continue to see considerable advantages in maintaining collective bargaining at the industry level.

Plant- or company-level bargaining will play a considerably more important role in a reformed German system than it has in the past. What is much less clear is the role that will be played by the national level as a bargaining arena. National collective agreements, commonplace in Latin countries, are unknown in Germany. Instead, in Germany, pay bargaining policy has been coordinated through the lead role played by IG Metall, the metal and engineering workers' union. The agreements concluded by IG Metall in the metal and electrical engineering industries have generally acted as a reference point for pay increases in other industries. IG Metall has always been conscious of its lead role in pay bargaining and its negotiating policy always has been guided more by macroeconomic data rather than by economic conditions in the metal and electrical engineering industries alone.

Earlier attempts to coordinate pay bargaining at the national level were initiated by the government. For example, at the end of the 1960s, the federal government tried, through its so-called "concerted action," to combine expansionary Keynesian economic policy with an anti-inflationary incomes policy. Trade unions opposed this attempt to exert influence over collective bargaining and subsequent governments relied on monetary policy to control inflation. At the end of the 1990s, it was the trade unions that proposed a national alliance for work. The aim was to exchange restraint in pay bargaining for certain employment policy promises from employers and the government. In contrast to the decentralized level, an arena that can be utilized by powerful actors, principally by employers and works councils, a national-level forum for collective negotiations is lacking in Germany and all attempts to put one in place have failed so far.

The structure of collective bargaining in Germany is described in the following section of this chapter. Empirical data on the importance of industry-level collective agreements and firm-level bargaining is presented in the third section of this chapter. The various causes of the decentralization of collective bargaining are discussed in the fourth section. Following this, I analyze the reactions of the state and the social partners to the decentralization of bargaining, and in the final section I examine the experiences with the national Alliance for Work.

THE STRUCTURE OF COLLECTIVE BARGAINING

After the Weimar Republic, the state relinquished its rights to intervene in collective bargaining through mandatory arbitration. One of the basic rights enshrined in the German Constitution is the freedom of coalition. The freedom enjoyed by the social partners to engage in collective bargaining on behalf of their members without state intervention is one of the most important concrete manifestations of this basic right.

The legal regulations governing collective bargaining are deliberately few in number, their main objective being to strengthen the negotiating privileges of trade unions and employer associations and to allow for binding collective agreements. The basic legal instrument is the Collective Bargaining Act of 1949. The main points of the legislation are as follows:

- Only unions and employers or employers' associations can conclude a collective agreement.
- The agreed standards are binding on union members and members of employers' organizations.
- The social partners have certain obligations, such as refraining from industrial action, while the agreement is in force and enforcing the agreement by advising their members of it.
- The agreed standards cannot be undercut, but can only be improved at the plant level (the so-called "favorableness [*Günstigkeitsprinzip*] principle")
- The state can declare a collective agreement as generally binding if an agreement already covers 50 percent of the employees in the industry in question and if a collective bargaining committee (with six members, three from the employers' federation and three from the unions) agrees.
- If a company leaves the employers' association, the validity of the collective agreement is extended until a new agreement has been concluded. This extended validity makes it difficult for companies to opt out of industrywide collective agreements.

The right to negotiate collective agreements is a union privilege. Works councilors do not have the right to negotiate on issues that are regulated in collective agreements. Unions are responsible for collective bargaining, while works councilors represent employees' interests at the plant level, implement collective agreements, and negotiate the additional pay increases discussed above. The works councilors negotiate so-called plant agreements. In contrast to the trade unions, works councils are consensus-seeking bodies that do not have the right to call workers out on strike. If redundancies are threatened at a company, for example, the works council has the right to negotiate how those redundancies are implemented and the compensation received by workers, but cannot strike over these issues. This division of labor between trade unions and works councils, the so-called dual system of interest representation, is intended to take conflicts out of the workplace.

In practice, however, there is an increasing overlap between collective and plant agreements. For a long time works councils have not limited themselves to the mere implementation of collective agreements, but have been negotiating relatively independently on a growing number of topics (this issue is discussed further below). Moreover, works councils have become, de facto, grass-roots union organizations. Union shop stewards are active now in only a few workplaces. The existence of works councils is often the factor that determines whether a company joins the employers' associations and adheres to the terms of an industry-level collective agreement. In small and medium-sized firms in particular, it is difficult for unions and employees to set up works councils. Since the average size of companies is declining and work councils are less likely to be set up in small and medium-sized companies, the real impact of collective bargaining on working and employment conditions has diminished.

Prior to recent legal reforms, the establishment of a works council in what was often a hostile environment was not easy because bureaucratic election procedures provided in the old Works Constitution Act gave management many opportunities to put pressure on potential works council candidates and on the work force. The coalition government, the so-called Red-Green Alliance of SPD and Green party, that came into power in late 1998, amended the Works Constitution Act (see box 1). The main inten-

---

BOX 1: THE MAIN CHANGES IN THE WORKS
CONSTITUTION ACT OF 2001

- *Simplification of election procedures*: The election of works councilors in small- and medium-sized firms can take place at a meeting of all employees instead of in formal elections with election campaigns. There is only one week between the first proposal to set up a work council and this election meeting. Employees who propose the elections are better protected against dismissals.

- *Improvement of working conditions of work councilors in small- and medium-sized companies*: In companies with more than two hundred employees (previously three hundred), one works councilor is exempted from work; works councilors in smaller companies have more rights to take time off to attend to their duties as works councilor; works councilors have the right to use modern information technology for their work (e-mail, access to internet).

- *Better representation for peripheral workers*: Works councilors have the right to represent tele- and agency workers.

- *Gender mainstreaming*: Women have to be represented on the works council in the same proportion as in the work force; works councils have more consultative rights on the recruitment and promotion of women.

tion of the reform was to facilitate elections in small and medium-sized companies and to strengthen works councils in these companies.

The formal structure of collective bargaining is determined not only by this legal framework, but also by the structure of unions and employer associations. German unions are unitary industry unions. More than 85 percent of union members belong to one of the unions affiliated to the DGB (German Trade Union Federation). DGB member unions represent a total of around 7.7 million workers. Union density is around 27 percent (Bispinck et al. 2001, 244). One of the DGB's responsibilities is to reach agreement on the demarcation of industries represented by its member unions in order to avoid competition within an industry or a company. The structure of the employers' associations often mirrors that of the unions. The employers have formed special organizations, such as Gesamtmetall, for collective bargaining at the industry level.

Only DGB member unions have the right to sign collective agreements. They do not delegate this right to the DGB. The employers' associations are in most cases more decentralized. Generally, only the regional employers' organization has the right to bargain. In some cases this right has been transferred to the central employers' organization, but it may be withdrawn at any time (for example, in the construction industry). In other cases the central employer organization does not have the right to sign agreements and tries to coordinate the different regional negotiations (for example, in the metal industry). The dominant level of collective bargaining is therefore the industry, which in turn is often broken into regions. IG Metall plays the role of pacesetter in pay bargaining by means of a regional "benchmark" agreement; in recent decades this usually is the agreement concluded in Baden-Württemberg.

Neither the unions' nor the employers' federal organizations can give binding assent to national agreements. As described more fully below, such assent can only take the form of declarations of political intent or of moral obligations. Tripartite bargaining is, however, institutionalized in other areas. The social partners participate in decision-making in national age, health, and unemployment insurance schemes. Their influence is limited, since the state provides the framework for these decisions in its budget and in social insurance legislation. However, the social partners can influence the ways in which the legislation and the budget are implemented. Only in the dual system of vocational training do the social partners have an independent and decisive influence. They decide, for example, on the modernization of old and the creation of new occupational profiles. The state supports this by providing resources—mainly through the Federal Institute of Vocational Training (BiBB) (Bosch 2000).

STATISTICAL EVIDENCE ON COLLECTIVE BARGAINING

At the end of 2001, a total of 57,595 collective agreements were recorded in the National Register of Collective Agreements compiled by the Federal Ministry of Labor. About 60 percent are industry-level agreements and the rest are firm-level agreements. Pay rates and working hours differ substantially between industries. There is a low-wage sector covered by collective agreements, mainly in the service sector, such as in retail trade (Bispinck et al. 2001). The number of company-level agreements has risen substantially in the last decade (from 2,550 in 1990 to 6,802 in 2001). In some industries, such as the metal industry, there are many regional industry-level agreements, while in other industries, such as public services, construction, and insurance, agreements cover the whole (national) industry. A total of 534 agreements have been declared generally binding, thereby extending coverage to around 1 million employees not otherwise covered. The number of agreements declared to be generally binding has fallen by eighty-eight since 1991 (BMA 2001). In some sectors, such as retail trade, the employers' representatives on the industry collective bargaining committee no longer supports the application the union regularly makes to have the collective agreement generally binding.

Data on collective bargaining coverage, based on nine thousand surveyed enterprises, are available from the enterprise panel of the IAB (Institut für Arbeitsmarkt- und Berufsforschung) for 1995, 1998, and 2000. The main results are as follows (Kohaut and Schnabel 1999; Kohaut and Schnabel 2001):

- 70.1 percent of West German and 55.4 percent of East German employees were covered by an industry- or firm-level collective agreement in 2000.[2] The differences between industries are considerable, for example, 96.4 percent coverage in mining/energy and 40.7 percent coverage in business services in West Germany.
- Agreement coverage increases with the size of the enterprise. In the year 2000 it ranged from 36.6 percent (18.4 percent in East Germany) in enterprises with one to four employees to 93.9 percent (93.9 percent in East Germany) in enterprises with more than a thousand employees.
- New enterprises are less likely to be covered by collective agreements as compared to than older ones. In 1998, in West Germany, 39.4 percent of enterprises established after 1992 were covered, compared with 49.9 percent of older enterprises (in East Germany the comparable statistics are 22.5 percent and 27.5 percent).
- Coverage by industrywide agreements decreased between 1996 and 2000. The share of employees covered dropped in West Germany by 6.4 percent and in East Germany by 10.8 percent.

- Many companies not covered by collective agreements use the relevant agreement as a reference point. This applies to 15 percent of employees in West Germany and to 24 percent of employees in East Germany.
- Adding together coverage by industry- and company-level agreements and the use of collective agreements as reference points leaves 15 percent of employees in West Germany and 21 percent in East Germany without protection by collective agreements.
- A substantial number of firms have switched in recent years from an industry-level to a company-level agreement or to individual contracts or vice versa. The existence of a works council considerably reduces the rate of withdrawal from industrywide agreements. One reason for going back to an industry agreement might be because of the introduction of an authorizing clause (see the section below that describes these clauses). Another reason for opting back into an industry agreement might be because of unexpected difficulties or disappointments with company agreements (difficult negotiations with the unions without the protection afforded by membership in the employer association).

Statistical information on collective bargaining at the enterprise level is provided in the Works Council Panel of the WSI (Trade Union Research Institute) (Bispinck 2001). This survey, however, covers only firms with more than twenty employees and a works council (Seifert 2000). The main results of this survey (around twenty-five hundred works councils responded to the survey) are as follows:

- 87 percent of the firms are covered by a collective agreement (West 89 percent, East 81 percent)
- 42 percent of those not covered by a collective agreement respect the prevailing agreement in their respective industry (West, 46 percent; East, 30 percent)
- In 15 percent of the firms not all of the standards provided in the collective agreement are adhered to (West, 12 percent; East, 26 percent).
- In 20 percent of the firms, authorizing clauses (see below) were used in order to deviate from contractual standards (20 percent, West; 30 percent, East). The authorizing clauses were used primarily to increase working hours, of second highest frequency were clauses introducing temporary working time reductions, and of third highest frequency were clauses lowering pay rates for newly recruited workers.
- 25 percent of works councilors think that decentralized collective bargaining allows for better adaptation of regulations to firm

specific situations, 19 percent think it increases the influence of the works councilors, 72 percent think that it strengthens the position of the employer, and 30 percent think that it does not improve the works council's bargaining position.

The Works Council Panel also examined the extent and content of new types of company bargaining, the so-called "company alliances for work and the improvement of competitiveness." Many companies today are seeking to change their entire work organization system rather than just modify single work organization practices, such as pay or working hours. In the German system of industrial relations, with strong works councils at the firm level, any work organization change requires the negotiation of packages in which both sides see some advantage, and more and more these alliances are being concluded in order to negotiate such packages. Some of these packages are based on authorizing or hardship clauses contained in industry-level agreements. Other packages are the result of proactive coalitions formed between management and works councils and are intended to improve competitiveness in the long run even though the parties do not face severe immediate economic pressures (Mauer and Seifert 2001, 490).

The Works Council Panel shows that about 30 percent of all works councils have signed such agreements (Seifert 2000; Maurer and Seifert 2001). Only 6 percent of the agreements place no obligations on management. Case studies show, however, that the concessions made by work councils generally outweigh the new obligations placed on management. In 39 percent of the agreements signed after 1998, company profitability is regarded as good or very good, in 32 percent profitability is seen as satisfactory, in 20 percent it is perceived as poor, and in 7 percent profitability is seen as very poor. These figures show that the proactive approach is dominant. The packages differ depending on the economic situation of the company in question. In firms with poor or very poor profitability, temporary working time reductions and more internal flexibility (for example, concerning working time or multiskilling) are traded for a guarantee that workers will not be dismissed. The works councils often also accept wage cuts as part of packages in these firms. In more profitable companies, increases in machine operating hours and long-term job guarantees are important. Management is also more likely to agree to recruit new workers in these firms.

Company-level "work alliances" negotiated by labor and management are no longer exceptional, as they have become a standard instrument for promoting organizational change in the workplace. Both sides seem to

> **BOX 2: INTERNAL FLEXIBILITY IN GERMANY**
>
> Internal flexibility is more widely used in Germany than in many other European Union (EU) countries. In the manufacturing industry, 84 percent of firms react to changes in capacity utilization by changing working hours. The EU average is 70 percent. Only 35 percent of German firms adapt by changing the number of employees. The EU average is 40 percent (European Commission 2001: 155–56). A German manager described the concept of internal change in the following terms: "We dismiss hours not employees."

agree that employees will more readily accept modernization if it is negotiated, rather than imposed. At the same time, however, company-level work alliances, as well as authorizing clauses in collective agreements that allow temporary working time reductions and increase internal flexibility (see box 2) reinforce a core principle within the traditional German model of industrial relations, namely, the long-term nature of employment relationships. Many managers seem to hold this system in even higher esteem than in the past, since they are investing more in their employees' skills and do not want to lose these investments.

Industrywide bargaining is still the dominant form of collective bargaining in Germany, even though fewer employees today are covered by collective agreements than a few years ago and company-level agreements, negotiations involving works councils, and individual contracts have all increased in importance. Furthermore, even where decentralized collective bargaining is occurring, industrywide bargaining continues to function as the main reference point. The strong influence of industry-level collective agreements is reinforced by the fact that it is not possible to withdraw from industrywide agreements without costs because industry agreements remain in force until replaced by another arrangement and works councils are strengthened in their company-level negotiations by strong codetermination rights. Consequently, increasing decentralization of the structure of collective bargaining has not led to a substantial loss of power for unions and works councils.

REASONS FOR THE DECENTRALIZATION OF COLLECTIVE BARGAINING

Diverse forcers are causing the decentralization of collective bargaining in Germany. The most important of these forces are (1) the high unemployment caused by German unification, (2) the globalization of product and labor markets, (3) industrial restructuring, (4) the introduction of flexibile working time and new production systems, and (5) stagnation in the reform of the collective bargaining process. Unification and its consequences are a specifically German problem, while the challenges arising out of (2) to (4) are also being faced in other industrialized countries. Stagnation in the reform of the collective bargaining process is not solely a German problem, either. However, deciding whether we are dealing with specifically German or universal trends is less important than investigating how these developments are unfolding in the particular context of the German industrial relations system. Clearly, the ramifications of industrial restructuring in a country with industrywide collective agreements are completely different than those that occur in countries with predominantly national- or firm-level collective bargaining.

The High Unemployment Caused by German Unification

After German unification the social partners agreed to raise East German employment standards to the West German level as quickly as possible. Adjustment to West German standards has not yet been successfully completed, since productivity in the East German economy is considerably lower than it is in West Germany, partly because of low capacity utilization and technological and organizational lags in East Germany. The average collectively agreed wage rate in East Germany, which in 1990 was around 60 percent of the West German level, rose to 91.5 percent of the West German level by 2001.[3] However, actual earnings in East Germany are considerably lower than the collectively agreed rates; at the beginning of 2001, they were only around 75 percent of the West German level (BMA 2001). The lower level of actual wages in East Germany is a consequence of the higher share of firms not covered by collective agreements, the lower share of firms covered by collective agreements that pay above the agreed rates, and finally, nonadherence to collective agreements. In many firms in East Germany, the works councils agreed to wage rates below the collectively agreed rate in order to ensure the company's survival; in view of the high level of unemployment and the lower wages paid by firms not covered by collective agreements, they had no choice. Noncompliance with contractual standards became acceptable and was even supported publicly by important representatives of the employers' associations (Bispinck 1998, 13). In some firms, a lowering of wages and other employment terms came through the negotiation of so-called "hardship clauses." Hardship clauses (see box 3), which enable firms in difficult economic circumstances to undercut collectively agreed pay rates, were

BOX 3: AUTHORIZING OR HARDSHIP CLAUSES IN COLLECTIVE AGREEMENTS

Most industry agreements today contain authorization, or hardship, clauses, although these clauses differ substantially in content and procedures across industries (Bispinck and WSI Tarifarchiv 1999). Below are examples of differences in content:

- Working time differentiation: in the chemical industry, working hours can vary between thirty-five and forty hours.

- Temporary working time reductions to prevent dismissals: in banking from thirty-nine to thirty-one hours, in metal industry from thirty-five to thirty hours.

- Pay cuts: in East German construction industry and in West German chemical industry: 10 percent pay reduction to protect jobs and improve competitiveness.

- Exemption from agreed pay increases: East German metal industry, West German textile industry for enterprises in a difficult economic situation

- Differentiation of wage increases by size of firm: lower pay increases in East German retail trade for firms with up to fifteen employees

- Lower wages for new recruits: in the West German chemical industry the long-term unemployed receive 90 percent and other new recruits 95 percent of the agreed wages

Examples of differences in procedures:

- In East German metal industry, hardship clauses can be introduced only in proven difficult economic situation.

- In West German chemical industry, introduction requires union agreement.

- In West German textile industry, introduction dependent on job guarantees.

- In East German construction industry, introduction is negotiated at enterprise level.? Changes to standards are temporary in West German chemical industry and can be permanent in East German construction industry.

Two industries that made use of hardship clauses:

- East German construction industry: all the firms that had previously respected contractual rates took advantage of the opportunity to cut them by 10 percent. Other firms had not respected the collective agreement before and had already cut the wages. The pay reductions appear to be permanent (Bosch and Zühlke-Robinet 2000).

- West German chemical industry: the agreement covers sixteen hundred firms (with 600,000 employees). In thirty-seven companies (with 11,475 employees) working hours are above the weekly standard of 37.5 hours, in fourteen companies (with 3,455 employees) working hours are below the standard. Temporary working time reductions have been approved in order to avoid dismissals and working time increases have been approved in order to eliminate production bottlenecks. In thirty-one firms (with 9,576 employees), wages were cut below the contractual rate mainly in order to avoid outsourcing or investments outside the coverage of the agreement. All cuts in wages are temporary. If wage cuts are not extended in subsequent negotiations, contractual standards will be reestablished (Förster and Hausmann 2001).

Conclusion: authorizing clauses do not generally weaken industry-level collective bargaining. Concessions generally have been negotiated with the unions and may in fact stabilize industrywide bargaining by avoiding further corporate withdrawals from industry-level agreements.

accepted by unions in an effort to stem the flood of companies withdrawing from collective agreements.

The collapse of the East German economy, which led to the loss of around 3.5 million jobs out of a total 9.5 million German jobs, had major effects on the German labor market. The high level of migration from East Germany to West Germany spread unemployment across the entire country. More than 4 million workers, a postwar record, were unemployed. The deep recession of 1993–94 in West Germany that followed the postunification honeymoon changed the pattern of collective bargaining. For the first time since the Second World War unions had to accept pay reductions (for example, the extra "thirteenth month's salary" was cut for many workers). Hardship clauses we also accepted in some industries. "This made it abundantly clear that the underlying fabric of pay negotiations was undergoing fundamental change. The clear allocation of roles with the trade unions as the party making the demands, and the employers, who after stubborn resistance had to make smaller or larger concessions, was gone. Employers' associations increasingly developed their own package of demands, not only for tactical reasons in the negotiations, but with the actual aim of implementing them aggressively" (Bispinck 1998,

13–14). However, not all the authorizing clauses in collective agreements during the economic crisis involved union concessions. The unions in some cases demanded such clauses in order to protect jobs. In particular, they negotiated temporary working time reductions as a means of preventing dismissals. Their intention was to generalize the Volkswagen model, which had avoided thirty thousand dismissals by reducing working hours from 35 to 28.8 hours per week. Most German collective agreements now contain provisions allowing for temporary working time reductions.

The Globalization of Product and Labor Markets

The globalization of product and labor markets also has had significant impacts on collective bargaining. The globalization of markets actually is not a new phenomenon. Germany has long had a high rate of exports and since the late 1950s has had a significant amount of immigration. Due to these pressures, economic competitiveness had always been a central concern in industry-level collective bargaining. The continuing ability of the German economy to export successfully shows that union negotiators have been able to set their pay demands at an appropriate level. And once certain discriminatory provisions were abolished, foreign workers were paid the same as Germans. Collective agreements now apply to all workers in a region irrespective of nationality (territorial principle) (see table 4.1).

Today, however, the German system of industrywide collective agreements is being called into question by two new forms of globalization: international cost competition for investment projects and the so-called free supply of services. At the beginning of the 1990s, large German firms such as Daimler or BMW were mainly national players. They exported products, but produced mainly in Germany. German multinationals did not use their investment projects to renegotiate standards as did large U.S. multinationals such as General Motors (GM) or Ford. This changed substantially in the second half the 1990s. Major investment projects planned by German or foreign companies are now being used to extract concessions from labor. If the concessions offered are judged insufficient, then

TABLE 4.1. FORM AND REGULATION OF THE EMPLOYMENT OF FOREIGN WORKERS

Form	Regulation of working conditions
Permanent migration	Territorial principle
Temporary migration (seconded labor)	Principle of origin

Source: Bosch/Zühlke-Robinet 2000, 215.

the company in question threatens to invest abroad. Such threats appear to be very serious, since several production sites both in Germany and abroad are usually competing with each other for any given project. Using this technique Daimler has achieved substantial working time flexibility over the production cycle at its Rastatt plant, and BMW has done the same thing at its new plant in Leipzig.

The most prominent and far-reaching example of the use of an investment project to generate labor concessions is Volkswagen's 5000 × 5000 model (see box 4). The trade unions agreed to some of these exceptional arrangements, even though some of them infringe on collective agreements. It is not difficult to imagine other companies demanding similar concessions, which will inevitably lead to an increase in the number of downward deviations from collective agreements.

Since the beginning of the 1990s, companies (particularly in the construction industry) have increasingly been taking advantage of their right

---

BOX 4: VOLKSWAGEN 5000 × 5000

In 1999, Volkswagen declared it would produce its new minivan in Germany if labor costs were reduced below the level of the company agreement. The company wanted to hire five thousand unemployed people and pay them a monthly wage of DM 5,000 (2,556 EURO). This wage was to be paid not for a fixed number of hours but for a fixed output. If the target was not reached, workers would work up to 48 hours a week in order to deal with the backlog. No overtime, night, or weekend premia would be paid. The works council and the union (IG Metall) were ready to negotiate because they wanted this investment in Germany but said that they would not accept a 48-hour week, arguing that it would represent a step back from the 35-hour week that is the current standard in the German metal industry and from the 28.8-hour week that is the current standard in the VW company agreement.

Unions, works council, and VW negotiated for nearly two years. In May 2001 VW moderated its demand and proposed an upper limit on weekly working hours of 42.5 hours, which still was not acceptable for the union. The negotiations failed. In August 2001, an agreement was finally signed. The main points of the agreement are (IGM 2001):

- A new VW company will be set up (Auto 5000 GmbH).
- This company will hire five thousand unemployed workers.
- The weekly "value adding" working time is thirty-five hours.

- The monthly wage is 4,500 DM (2,301 EURO).

- The minimum annual bonus is 6,000 DM (3068 EURO); 2,000 DM (1,023 EURO) of this bonus will be used for night and Sunday premia. The bonus might be increased to reflect individual performance (including individual working time flexibility) and profits.

- The unemployed recruits will receive three months' training provided by the Employment Office before they join VW. They will also receive training in the first six months of their employment. For that initial period, the monthly wage will be 4,000 DM (2,045 EURO). After that period, the weekly training time will be three hours, half in the employee's time, half paid for by the employer. The skills acquired will be certified.

- The maximum weekly working hours will be forty-two hours (including Saturday morning). Each employee has to work ten Saturday afternoons a year. The additional hours will be registered on a working time account. Overtime will be recompensed with time off in lieu; otherwise overtime attracts a supplement of 25 percent per hour. Supplements for Sunday work are time and a half and for public holidays double time.? There will be flat hierarchies (three levels) and everybody will work in a team.

- The teams are responsible for producing the stipulated quotas to fixed quality standards. If they do not reach the target they have to work longer. If production is interrupted for reasons for which the employer is responsible or due to force majeure any additional hours worked will be paid for.

- Production targets will be agreed in negotiations between management and works councils. Criteria for fixing targets will be the agreed weekly working time and ergonomic standards. If they are not reasonable the works council has the right to object and to ask for revisions.

- Volkswagen AG has undertaken not to recruit workers from Auto 5000 GmbH.

Conclusion: this is the first time the term *value adding* working time has been included in a collective agreement. Some of the risk of not reaching production targets and quality standards has been shifted to employees. Management has committed itself to continuous training and to the introduction of modern forms of work organization. The unions' concession was to agree that all employees should invest 1.5 hours of their leisure time in training. Wage rates are below those paid by Volkswagen AG but equal to those stipulated by the regional agreement for the Lower Saxony metal and engineering industry.

under European Union (EU) legislation to provide services in another member state. The legislation stipulates that workers from all EU member states can be employed on service contracts to work in Germany. Moreover, under the terms of bilateral agreements between Germany and thirteen Central and Eastern European countries, construction workers from these countries can be "seconded" to (i.e., temporarily work in) Germany. The territorial principle that once governed the implementation of collective agreements no longer applies. Since workers seconded to Germany remain employees of the foreign company, they are employed on the terms and conditions prevailing in their home country (see table 4.1).

These seconded workers are mostly found in the construction industry and have the effect of undermining the generally binding collective agreement in this industry. The Seconded Workers Act of 1996 gave the social partners the power to negotiate minimum wages for seconded workers (see box 5) and thereby reestablish the territorial principle.

Industrial Restructuring

The considerable structural changes t hat took place in the economy in the postwar period did not call into question the importance of industry-wide collective agreements, although considerable shifts occurred in the power held by various unions. For example, the once very powerful trade unions in the textile and mining industries lost members and have now been absorbed into other unions. The notion of an industry union, which has long served as the basis for dividing up the spheres of influence of DGB-affiliated unions, is becoming increasingly fragile. There are several reasons for this.

While German companies have traditionally tended to be highly integrated, both vertically and horizontally, recently they have been seeking to reduce the degree of integration and increasing the outsourcing of activities.[4] One reason for this outsourcing is an increasing concentration on core competencies. Another motivation is to reduce wage bills. Companies compare the contractual pay rates in different industries and seek cost reductions through outsourcing. This leads to the sort of "beauty competitions" between industry agreements that the negotiation of industry-level collective bargaining agreements originally was intended to prevent. In particular, wages for low-skill services such as cleaning and catering can be reduced substantially by changing to another collective agreement or even to individual contracts. However, because the old agreements stay in force until new arrangements are put in place, companies do not always obtain the effects they are seeking immediately. In the works council panel survey, works councilors were asked about the consequences of out-

The Changing Nature of Collective Bargaining in Germany

BOX 5: SECONDED FOREIGN WORKERS: THE CASE OF THE GERMAN CONSTRUCTION INDUSTRY

- The German construction industry is a highly regulated industry. There is an agreement between the social partners on so-called social funds. Around 20 percent of gross wages are paid into the funds. The funds are used to finance paid holidays and supplementary pensions, to pay some of workers' wages in bad weather periods when no work is possible, and to finance vocational training. The agreement has been declared as generally binding for the whole industry.

- Since the beginning of the 1990s, the Federal Government has concluded bilateral agreements with thirteen Central and Eastern European countries regarding seconded workers. Each bilateral agreement lays down a different quota for the number of workers that can be employed in Germany. The agreements also stipulate that hourly rates of pay for these workers should take the collectively agreed German rate as a reference point, but that holiday entitlement, holiday pay, and sick pay are to be regulated in accordance with the law of the country of origin.

- The number of seconded workers employed in the German construction industry reached a peak of 188,000 (1992: 116,000 and 2000: 138,000). Since unemployment among construction workers was beginning to rise at the same time, the quotas for East European countries were reduced considerably. The use of seconded workers from EU member states could not, however, be restricted since the freedom to provide services is regarded as a basic right in the EU.

- The outsourcing of production has been considerably accelerated by the increased use of contract labor. Firms that continue to rely solely on German workers are no longer competitive and have to subcontract parts of their orders. The wages paid to seconded workers are much lower than those of German workers. In some cases, the workers are being paid considerably less than five Euros per hour when the "going rate" in the area is over ten Euros. Many German construction workers have been made redundant and replaced by contract or illegal workers.

- The Seconded Workers Act of 1996 allowed collectively bargained minimum wages for seconded construction workers to be declared generally binding. The social partners in the construction industry agreed to a minimum wage of 9.30 Euros in the West and 8.50 Euros in the East. However, the representatives of the German Employers' Associations (Bundesvereinigung Deutscher Arbeitgeberverbände, BDA) on the industry

> collective bargaining committee (mentioned earlier in this chapter) were unwilling to agree to minimum rates at such levels. The construction industry employers' federations threatened to resign from the BDA if no agreement was reached. After a lengthy debate, the BDA agreed to a minimum rate of 8.50 Euros, which was reduced in 1997 to 8 Euros (7.60 Euros in Eastern Germany). In September 1999, the minimum rate rose to 9.25 in the West and 8.10 in the East. This latest significant increase became possible only after the new SPD-Green coalition government had changed the process of declaring collective agreements generally binding in this industry. Now the Federal Ministry of Labor may determine by right of ordinance that a collective agreement on minimum wages shall be declared binding.
>
> - Unlike in Denmark, the agreement on minimum pay rates is often infringed. In Denmark, trade union density is much higher and the unions stop work if seconded workers are not paid the same rates. The German unions have lost this degree of control on construction sites.
>
> *Source:* Bosch/Zülke-Robinet 2000 and 2002

sourcing for collective agreements. In 32 percent of cases the old agreement is still valid, in 20 percent of cases it has been discontinued, in 27 percent of cases the old agreement has been replaced by a new agreement and in 24 percent of cases the works councils have no information on the matter (Bispinck 2001).[5] In a few cases unions have succeeded in negotiating new so-called service agreements with reasonable wages, as at Volkswagen (see box 6).

The European Commission has deregulated many public services such as telecommunications, transport, energy, and water. In cases were public monopolies were the sole providers, private competitors have been able to enter the market, for example, in telecommunications, railways, energy, water, and local transport. Where in the past the state subsidized public services such as local transport, bid tendering is now mandatory and the bid requiring the lowest level of subsidy is awarded a license and subsidies for five years. In Germany most basic public services used to be provided by federal or local monopoly providers.[6] Coverage by collective agreement in these cases traditionally was high, whether by federal agreement for government employment or by industry agreements in the post and telecommunications industries. With privatization, however, an increasingly diverse array of companies provides these services. Private companies may provide services that previously were provided exclusively

> **BOX 6: THE SERVICE AGREEMENT WITH VOLKSWAGEN 2000**
>
> In partnership with the city of Wolfsburg, Volkswagen has set up a new adventure service park in Wolfsburg with hotels, restaurants, and a car museum. Customers can collect their new car, and it is hoped that they will stay one or two days in the adventure park. Around twenty-eight hundred jobs will be created. IG Metall wanted to represent these employees and agreed to sign a service contract. The key elements of the contract are:
>
> - Weekly working time is thirty-eight hours and will be reduced to thirty-five hours in 2002.
> - Because the park is a tourist attraction, Saturday and Sunday are normal working days. No supplements are paid.
> - Hours can be distributed flexibly (maximum ten hours a day and forty-eight hours a week).
> - Monthly pay is between 2,250 and 7,000 DM (1,150 to 3,579 Euros). The average wage will be 4,000 DM (2,045 Euros).

TABLE 4.2. COLLECTIVE AGREEMENTS AND TRADE UNION SPHERES OF INFLUENCE IN THE TELEPHONE INDUSTRY

Firm	*Responsible trade union*	*Collective agreement*
TELEKOM D1	DPG (VER.DI)	Yes
VODAFONE D2	IGM	Yes
VIAG—INTERCOM	IGBCE	Yes
E-PLUS	IGM/DPG (Ver.di)	No
ARCOR	Transnet	Yes

Note: DPG (Deutsche Postgewerkschaft), Transnet (Gewerkschaft der Eisenbahner Deutschlands), IGBCE (Industriegewerkschaft Bergbau, Chemie, Energie), IGM (Industriegewerkschaft Metall), Ver.di (Vereinigte Dienstleistungsgewerkschaft).

by public agencies. In local transport, for example, public companies now compete with private companies who pay their workers around 30 percent less than these public companies. The public companies now outsource services, lease buses with drivers, or buy private companies to order to be able to pay less. To safeguard collective agreements in these services, unions have signed a new agreement covering local transport workers that establishes a two-tier pay system. Standards for those already employed are guaranteed, but wages for new recruits have been lowered.

Because of the universal nature of the technology, the activities spawned by new information and communication technologies frequently straddle more than one industry. Furthermore, companies in very different industries have outsourced their information (IT) departments or invested in new activities. Several trade unions have claimed jurisdiction in this area of activity (see box 7).

> BOX 7: THE CONCEPT OF AN INDUSTRY HAS BECOME BLURRED: THE CASE OF THE IT INDUSTRY
>
> The demarcation lines between the various trade union spheres of influence in the IT industry used to be clearly drawn. IG Metall, the metal workers' union, traditionally represented employees in the hardware manufacturers; IG Medien represented workers in the printed media and in radio and television; the Deutsche Postgewerkschaft (DPG, the German Postal Workers' Union) represented employees of the former telecommunications monopolist (Deutsche Telekom); and HBV, the distribution, banking, and insurance workers' union, represented employees in service-sector enterprises such as software developers and IT service providers. These clearly defined demarcation lines no longer exist, for two reasons.
>
> First, completely new activities that do not fit into any traditional industrial breakdown, such as mobile telephone services, are emerging. Second, the provision of software services crosses sectoral boundaries. Thus, for example, the departments that used to be responsible for internal data processing and software are being spun off from manufacturing firms and developing into independent software companies.
>
> The organizational principle of the German trade union confederation—"one trade union per industry"—no longer applies. In new activities and in software services, the origin principle has replaced the industry principle. If the software companies have been spun off from firms in the engineering industry, then IG Metall represents their employees; the same applies when the parent companies have invested in the new sector.
>
> The fragmentation of the trade unions can be clearly seen in the telephone industry (see table 4.2), where the origin principle led to employee representation by four DGB-affiliated unions. In two newly established companies (Mobilcom and Talkline), no trade union has been able to gain a foothold. To date, a collective agreement covering the whole industry has not been achieved; instead, a number of company agreements have been negotiated, which threatens to "Japanize" industrial relations in the sector.

Working Time Flexibility and New Production Systems

Reductions in working time over the 1980s and 1990s (from forty to thirty-seven hours for all employees and from forty to thirty-five hours in the metal industry) could only be achieved after unions granted firms more room to introduce working hours flexibility and differentiation (Bosch and Lallement 1991). Now one of the main issues in the decentralized of collective bargaining that involves management and works councils is the organization of working hours. Nearly all German collective agreements now allow for variations in working hours over a year or even longer periods and hours variations in response to fluctuations in demand (Bosch 1997). Some collective agreements allow individual differentiation of working hours. For example, up to 18 percent of the employees in the metal industry can work up to forty hours per week without payment of overtime supplements. Many agreements allow longer machine operating hours, including Saturday or Sunday work, or annual working hours accounts, both of which was restricted before. Furthermore, it has proved advantageous for companies to decentralize the management of complex working time systems.

Working time flexibility has prompted many firms to rethink their entire systems of work organization, since real working time flexibility requires workers to be able to fill-in for one another and that they have the necessary training to do so. The creation of greater flexibility in working time has been one of the most important reasons for the introduction of post-Taylorist forms of work organization in Germany (involving team-work, flat hierarchies, and more responsibility devolved to employees). The diverse functions served by these work organization changes have not been properly analyzed in previous research.

Firms are experimenting in their search for effective forms of work organization and this experimentation has not led to the demise of Taylorism in German workplaces. The share of firms using traditional Taylorist forms of work organization is increasing, as is the proportion of those that have introduced post-Taylorist forms. It is the middle group (hierarchical work organization based on skilled labor) that has become less common. If work organization patterns become more polarized, then industrywide bargaining will become more difficult. Interestingly, to date, the greatest pressure on industrywide collective agreements has not come from firms with post-Taylorist forms of work organization. Such firms tend to pay above the collectively agreed rates and therefore have had enough room to devise individual solutions to any problems. The firms that are the most keen to withdraw from industrywide collective agreements are those with Taylorist forms of work organization in the low-wage sector, as withdrawal gives these firms the opportunity to undercut contractual rates of pay.

Stagnation in the Process of Collective Bargaining Reform

Some of the job classifications and pay systems found in collective agreements date back to the early 1950s and reflect the work organization and worker mobility patterns of that time. Thus in the public sector wages still rise with age. This seniority principle made sense at a time when employees stayed in public service their whole working life and employers wanted to retain them. Today, mobility between the public and private sector is increasing and seniority wages have become a barrier to mobility, especially for older workers. Most agreements also still contain different job classifications for white and blue-collar workers and refer to the hierarchical types of work organization initiated in the 1950s. Yet, the distinction between white- and blue-collar work is becoming increasingly obsolete and flat hierarchies and teamwork have been spreading. If the collective agreements do not provide an adequate framework for modern work organization, companies find their own solutions outside of these agreements.

In a few industries, such as the chemical industry, joint white- and blue-collar agreements were negotiated as early as 1987. In other industries, including the metal industry, unions and employers have been negotiating for more than twenty years on this issue. Employers are tending to lose interest in these negotiations, since they are increasingly finding firm-specific solutions. In the meantime, the employer associations and the unions in some industries became aware that innovations are the only way to stabilize industrywide collective bargaining. In two regions (North-Rhine Westphalia and Baden Württemberg), for example, labor and management agreed on a new job classification system covering all categories of employees (see box 8). In other industries, however, the reform process has stagnated because the unions were weakened and power has been distributed unevenly between the negotiating parties. In the retail trade sector, the German trade unions are clinging on to collective agreements that they themselves regard as outdated, since they would have to accept significantly worse conditions if they were renegotiated.

Thus there are strong forces driving the actors into decentralized collective bargaining or at least a new division of labor between industry- and company-level negotiations. The very diversity of these forces makes stock responses impossible. The consequences of German unification may

BOX 8: THE JOINTLY NEGOTIATED JOB CLASSIFICATION SYSTEM IN THE METAL INDUSTRY OF BADEN-WÜRTTEMBERG AND NORTH-RHINE WESTPHALIA 2002

- Four job classifications exist in the collective agreements of the German metal industry: one for blue collar workers, one for masters, one for technical employees, and one for commercial employees

- These job classifications date back to the 1950s. They reflect the traditional distinction between blue- and white-collar workers and the hierarchical and rigid work organization of that time.

- This kind of job classification has become more and more a barrier to modern organization. Wage differentials of up to some hundred marks between equally qualified blue- and white-collar workers are not justified any longer. Both categories of workers are cooperating with similar responsibilities in projects. More and more blue-collar workers are operating expensive machinery and their increased skills are not rewarded. In addition, teamwork, flexible work behavior, and lifelong learning need to be encouraged.

- The new job classification system will be introduced in all firms until 2008. The additional costs of 2.79 percent will be set off with wage increases in the next years.

- In North-Rhine Westphalia the new job classifications are based on a point system. The job of each employee is evaluated. Five characteristics of the job will be evaluated: (1) Necessary skills (*Können*) (6 to 108 points), (2) Experience (*Berufserfahrung*) (6 to 12 points), (3) Scope for decisions and maneuver (*Handlungs- und Entscheidungsspielraum*) (2 to 40 points), (4) Cooperation (*Kooperation*) (2 to 20 points), (5) Management (*Führung*) (0 to 20 points).

- Work teams and flat hierarchies are encouraged by the new job characteristics (3) to (5). Blue-collar workers can move up the wage scale easier than in the past because the whole wage scale is open for them. Some employees will acquire lower-ranked classifications, especially those who do not have to cooperate with others, are not required to make critical decisions, and are not delegated management tasks. These losses will be mitigated because the new job classifications will be introduced over a period of six years, guaranteeing that the "losers" will not suffer wage cuts, but will only receive lower wage increases.

be felt for only a limited period, but the magnitude of these other forces makes them the factor with the greatest potential for bringing about fundamental and lasting change in the German collective bargaining system.

RESPONSES OF UNIONS, EMPLOYERS, AND THE STATE

A number of analysts, including Schroeder and Ruppert (1996) and others (Ettl and Heikenroth 1996; Schnabel and Wagner 1996) have found that the membership of employers' associations has declined in recent decades, particularly among small- and medium-sized firms. The state has responded by making it easier to establish works councils, particularly in small- and medium-size firms. This has strengthened not only works councils' bargaining power, but also the workplace bodies responsible for monitoring compliance with industrywide agreements. The interest of small- and medium-sized firms in joining the relevant employers' association may well be reawakened if those firms are required to follow the relevant industry agreement through legal extension of the terms of that agreement even if the firms do not belong to the respective industry association. Firms' loyalty to their employers' association, which was described by Schroeder and Ruppert (1996) as the "Achilles heel" of industrywide collective agreements, could be strengthened as a result.

The government considered legislation that had the purpose of strengthening the leverage of unions in firms that participate in public contracts. In 2001, the German Parliament, under strong pressure from the unions, passed legislation requiring compliance with collective agreements in the case of public contracts ("tenders"). Contractors responding to public requests for bids in the construction industry and public transport were to base their bids on established local rates of pay. The new legislation would have given unions an opportunity to create support for collective bargaining in an important privatized sector, local transport. Furthermore, the new legislation, combined with the agreement of generally binding minimum rates of pay (see box 5), would have helped stabilize industrywide collective agreements in the construction industry, where unions have been threatened by new service supply rights across EU member states. Yet, in 2002, the Bundesrat, the second chamber, in which the conservatives have the majority, blocked this legislation.

The opening up of industrywide collective agreements to negotiations at a more decentralized level through authorizing clauses (see box 3) has certainly helped to make these agreements more palatable to employers. The introduction of authorizing clauses has persuaded many companies not to withdraw from their respective employers' association, since the firms' wishes for greater freedom to organize matters as they see fit are accommodated by these clauses. Many employers and important association representatives loudly and clearly have declared their faith in collective agreements and have fought back against sometimes vehement criticism from within their own ranks. For Dieter Hundt, the chairman of the BDA (Bundesvereinigung deutscher Arbeitgeberverbände, or Federal Alliance of German Employers' Associations), the future lies in reformed industry-level collective agreements with authorizing clauses and a greater scope for firm-level negotiation. He points out that most firms covered by collective agreements have works councils whose pay policies would not differ much from the policies supported by the unions. If industrywide collective agreements were abolished, then these works councils would, under German law, inevitably acquire the right to call strikes. This would bring industrial disputes right into the workplace (Hundt 1998). Reflecting concern for these matters, the chief executive officer of the Federal Association of Chemical Industry Employers, K. Molitor, has called for controlled collective bargaining decentralization, along the lines that has already been introduced (Molitor 1998).

However, company membership in employers' associations depends on the strength of unions as well as on the quality of collective agreements. Companies still join employers' associations in large part in order to seek protection from trade unions. In manufacturing industries, the trade unions, particularly IG Metall, have been able to demonstrate their strength. Several times in recent years employers have sought open confrontation with IG Metall and have suffered bitter defeats. The strike in Bavaria in 1995, which the employers lost, led to a change of personnel at the top of Gesamtmetall, the metal industry employers' organization, with the "hawks" being replaced by advocates of social partnership (Turner 1998; Thelen 2000). I heard Mr. Hundt, at a conference of the Bertelsmann Foundation, defend his notion of a social partnership against neoliberal hardliners with the statement that "as long as I am active, I will not get past a strong IG Metall."

However, this argument cannot be applied to all industries. The unions' failure to gain strong footholds in new companies, the blurring of demarcations between industries due to privatization and outsourcing, and the increasingly debilitating competition for new members among DGB-affiliated unions have given fresh impetus to interunion cooperation. Working conditions, which used to be taken out of competition through industrywide collective agreements, have now become a crucial factor not only in interfirm competition, but also in competition between different collective agreements. In order to tackle these problems more effectively five service-sector unions agreed in 1997 to a plan to merge and form the Vereinigte Dienstleistungsgewerkschaft (United Service Workers Union), known as Ver.di. The new union has about 3 million members. The following unions are involved in the merger (membership numbers follow for each union): Öffentliche Dienste, Transport und Verkehr (ÖTV, the public service and transport union, 1.64 million), Handel Banken und Versicherungen (HBV, the commerce, banking, and insurance union, 0.49 million), Deutsche Postgewerkschaft (DPG, the postal workers' union, 0.49 million), Deutsche Angestellten Gewerkschaft (DAG, the white-collar union, 0.48 million) and Industrie Gewerkschaft Medien (the media union, 0.19 million). The DAG's involvement in Ver.di is particularly noteworthy; it was not previously affiliated with the DGB, but competed for members with other unions and was regarded as a politically conservative union. The merger formally occurred in 2001.

To make the new megaunion manageable thirteen specialist sections, incorporating hitherto overlapping activities, were created (see table 4.3). Thus, the new financial services section will include the banking and insurance section of the HBV and the publicly owned savings and cooperative banks section of the ÖTV. The aim of the merger is to reduce interunion competition, to make more efficient use of resources, and to increase the unions' ability to take effective political action.

In addition to this merger, the member unions of the DGB have agreed

TABLE 4.3. ORGANIZATION OF THE VER.DI MEGAUNION

Specialist sections of Ver.di
• Financial services
• Utilities and waste disposal
• Health, social services, charities and churches
• Social security
• Education, science and research
• Federal and state government
• Local authorities
• Art and culture, media, printing and paper, industrial services and manufacturing
• Telecommunications, information technology, data processing
• Logistics and postal services
• Transport
• Distribution
• Special services

to the following arrangement for the media and communications industry, in which interunion competition is particularly intense:

- when several unions have members in the same industry, then a working party will be established to coordinate membership and collective bargaining policy for that industry; one trade union will take the lead in organizing this working party;
- with the establishment of Ver.di, the five trade unions involved in the merger agreed not to recruit members outside their old spheres of influence;
- the DGB will mediate any disputes and will maintain a register of trade unions' jurisdictional rights.

This agreement is intended in the short term to reduce conflicts between the DGB-affiliated unions and in the longer term through industry-level deliberations the parties are supposed to coordinate recruitment and collective bargaining policies. The unions are particularly eager to recruit members in nonunion firms. The agreement is regarded as a test of the unions' ability to cooperate with each other and, if successful, may be extended to other industries (such as transport and logistics).

The employers' associations also have reorganized. In 2000, various specialist sections from a number of different employers' associations merged to form Bitkom (Bundesverband für Informationswirtschaft, Telekommunikation und neue Medien, or the Federal Association for IT, Telecommunications, and New Media), an association with a membership of around twelve hundred companies and employing 700,000. This association represents hardware and software producers. It does not have the right to engage in collective bargaining over pay, but already it has become involved in negotiations with unions on other issues, such as the development of occupational profiles and further training regulations. The employers' associations also have taken steps to improve communications with each other in other cases where industries have been reorganized. In local transport, for example, steps in this direction have involved the public transport and private bus operator associations. New industrywide collective agreements or new union alliances (or mergers) may follow in these industries.

Unions and employers' associations in established relationships are also aware that they have to modernize their collective agreements. Modernization requires that the parties respond to new needs among the work force (especially women and highly skilled employees) and to new types of work organization. The unions also want to increase individual rights and options for training and for leave. In some industries, unions have

> BOX 9: KEY ELEMENTS OF THE COLLECTIVE AGREEMENT
> ON TRAINING IN THE METAL INDUSTRY IN
> BADEN-WÜRTTEMBERG 2001
>
> - The social partners agree that lifelong learning is the key to the future competitiveness of companies and the employability of workers.
> - Each employee has the right to regular discussions with the employer on his/her individual training needs.
> - Employees on parental leave also have the right to such discussions.
> - If there are training needs, an individual training plan will be agreed on.
> - If there is no agreement, the employers and the works council, or in companies with more than three hundred employees, a joint committee (with parity in seats) should try to reach an agreement.
> - If they do not reach an agreement, a representative of the new Agency for the Promotion of Further Training will become a member of the committee with the right to vote.
> - The employer pays for the training.
> - After successful completion of the training, employees can request that their new skills be put to use.
> - The social partners are to establish an Agency for the Promotion of Further Training.
>   The agency should
>   - consult with companies,
>   - develop training programs for unskilled and semiskilled workers,
>   - monitor structural change in the industry and draw up training programs.?
> - Each employee with five years of job tenure is entitled to three years of unpaid leave for training.

succeeded in negotiating entitlements to unpaid parental leave. A pioneering agreement on supplemental training was signed in the metal industry in 2001 (see box 9).

German unions also have begun to develop links with unions in neighboring countries. In the so-called "Doorn Declaration," unions from Belgium, the Netherlands, Luxembourg, and Germany agreed to coordinate their collective bargaining. In order to avoid unfair competition and "beggar-thy-neighbor" policies, they agreed to use a formula for wage demands based on the inflation rate plus the increase in hourly labor productivity that was occurring in their respective countries. However, since the German unions are perceived as pacesetters in pay negotiations and the unions in the smaller neighboring countries tend to postpone their bargaining until the German bargaining round is completed, this declaration is unlikely to significantly influence actual wage bargaining in these countries. The declaration does, however, mark the beginning of closer transnational union cooperation.

Collective agreements in the construction industry do show, however, how far international cooperation can go. The construction unions and employer organizations concluded agreements involving the construction industry social funds in France, Belgium, and the Netherlands. If construction workers are seconded to these countries, they are exempt from paying contributions to the social funds in the host countries if they can prove that they are already paying contributions to their national funds. The funds exchange information on this.

Improved interunion cooperation will not in itself stabilize industry-level collective agreements. Political support at national and, increasingly, EU levels is also required. European minimum standards, such as limits on maximum working times or the introduction of a minimum holiday entitlement of four weeks under the terms of the Working Time Directive of 1993, could help to reduce the pressure on national labor standards arising out of globalization.

Unless there is an appropriate response, market deregulation and inadequate EU-level reregulation threaten to destroy the German model. However, future policies taken by the various nation states will matter, and there continues to be considerable scope for individual countries to determine their own path of economic and social development.

THE NATIONAL ALLIANCE FOR WORK: A NEW FORUM FOR TRIPARTITE NEGOTIATIONS

Until relatively recently, any initiative in favor of centralized pay bargaining in Germany always came from governments seeking to extend their economic policy by introducing an incomes policy. The industry unions typically refused to accept pay guidelines, which they regarded as infringing their right to free collective bargaining. It was all the more surprising, therefore, when the former president of the metal and engineering workers' union, Klaus Zwickel, came forward with a proposal to trade wage restraint for a guarantee of no job cuts and an increase in employment levels in the metal industry. The employers gave the proposal a rather cool reception, stating that they could not commit their members to specific personnel policy measures.

Shortly after it came to power in 1998, the SPD-Green coalition took up Zwickel's proposal and set up the national Alliance for Work.[7] The intention was to promote social dialogue after many years of confrontation between government, unions, and management. The Netherlands served as a model for this initiative, as there compacts on pay moderation and also agreements on a number of other topics, such as increasing working time flexibility and better protections for part-time workers, have been forged. Out of this in the Netherlands a new culture based on cooperation and a pragmatic approach to contentious issues emerged. The plans for Germany were similarly ambitious.

Employers eventually joined the alliance effort in Germany. A steering group now oversees the workings of the Alliance for Work and is made up of the presidents of the employers' associations and the industry unions and half of the German cabinet. Particular issues such as working time or vocational training are discussed in a number of subgroups. In the steering group, representatives of labor and management agreed to a declaration in support of an approach "to collective bargaining that emphasizes job creation."

The two sides, however, have different understandings of the goals of the alliance. The employers are seeking wage restraint and the unions favor work sharing. The unions say that collective bargaining itself cannot be a subject for discussion in the Alliance for Work. The employers do not see the point of such an alliance if it does not lead to wage moderation. The employers interpreted the low wage increases in the bargaining round of the year 2000 as a successful product of the alliance. The president of the employers' association said, "Collective bargaining can be enjoyable again" (Bispinck and Tarifarchiv 2001, 135). For the unions, the alliance's successes lie in other areas, such as the employers' commitment to offer more apprenticeships, an agreement on increased training for information technology (IT) specialists, and 2001 legislation on part-time work, which gives every full-time employee the right to work part-time (Lang 2001).

After an initial burst of enthusiasm and a few successes, the run-up to the 2002 parliamentary elections saw the alliance lose its impetus somewhat. The employers are playing a waiting game; their sole criterion for the success of the alliance is the establishment of a moderate wages policy. The government, in turn, does not want the alliance to tackle any controversial issues before the election, since it is worried that any objections from the employers' side would put it on the spot politically. Certain important political issues, such as the reform of labor market policy, were not made part of the alliance's agenda; the task of drafting proposals for reform was delegated to an expert committee on which the unions were only marginally involved. However, the government also has sought to use the alliance to commit the unions to a moderate wages policy. The government wanted to keep pay increases low in the public sector to help it achieve budget expenditure targets.

After several years of low wage increases, the unions came under pressure from their members and this led them to oppose any national wage compact. At the end of 2001, IG Metall cancelled a meeting of the alliance that had been called by the government because the wage demands for the 2002 bargaining round were being formulated at precisely the same time.

Since the middle of 2001, all those involved privately have expressed concerns regarding how the Alliance for Work should proceed in future. Some commentators (e.g., Hassel 2002) laid responsibility for the ensuing policy stagnation at the unions' door, since they are allegedly unwilling to enter into an agreement on pay. However, a number of factors make decisions regarding the future of the alliance complex, including the limited scope for national-level action by both employers and unions and flaws in the design of the alliance itself. The government, in fact, has been the party that has brought forward virtually all the topics discussed in the alliance. Union presidents have not been willing to enter into agreements on pay without consulting their respective industry-level collective bargaining committees and the employers have always stressed that they are not authorized at the national level to sign binding agreements.

Furthermore, labor and management have not put forward topics for discussion and developed proposals that could be addressed through the alliance as their Dutch counterparts have in their Stichting van der Arbet. A subgroup of the alliance, the so-called benchmarking group, made up largely of academics, was originally to have laid the intellectual foundations for the alliance's work by doing preliminary thinking and putting forward topics for discussion. However, the group's work resulted in divided opinions. Its academic members, including Wolfgang Streeck, who for two decades extolled the virtues of the "German model," no longer regards this model as a resource that can serve as a basis for renewal but rather, because of its egalitarian pay policy, now views the German industrial relations system as an obstacle to the expansion of service-sector employment. These academics argued in favor of the establishment of a low-wage sector in Germany and published their arguments, in extremely polemical terms, in the German weekly *Der Spiegel* (Streeck and Heinze

1999). There could have been no more glaring contrast with the procedure used in the Netherlands, where controversial subjects are first discussed behind closed doors and without any public apportioning of blame.

Nevertheless, the Alliance for Work has left untouched the many other well-functioning corporatist arrangements that operate at the national level in Germany. Thus, in recent years, labor and management have jointly modernized many occupational profiles and developed new supplemental training regimes, for example, in the sphere of information technology. In the process, there has been much adroit policy deliberation. When the actors judged that useful support for these endeavors might be obtained from the alliance, they brought proposals forward for discussion; when they saw no advantage to working within the alliance, they simply continued to work in other forums. However, the fear that involvement in the alliance, with its high political stakes and consequent instability, could lead to the loss of tried and tested cooperative arrangements caused the parties to proceed with great caution.

CONCLUSIONS

Collective bargaining in Germany still takes place largely at the industry level. A majority of employees are covered by industrywide collective agreements, although there is a downward trend in the structure of collective bargaining. A number of factors have led to a decline in the share of the work force covered by collective agreements, including globalization, German unification, the disintegration of traditional industries and development of new industries, the introduction of new production systems and increasingly flexible working times, and stagnation in the reform of collective bargaining policy.

Labor, management, and the state agree on some of the changes needed in the system and disagree over other change proposals. The reconstruction and redefinition of industries, for example, has been a source of much disagreement. Unions, in particular, are trying to adapt their internal organizational structures to new economic circumstances in order to retain influence. Crucial efforts include putting outsiders not previously bound by collective agreements within the scope of industrywide collective agreements. Inclusion is encouraged through the introduction of minimum wage rates for seconded workers and collective agreement compliance regulations in public bid processes.

The status of centralized collective agreements, which has been called into question by the wide economic differences that exist between East and West Germany and new production systems, has been improved through the introduction of authorizing clauses and the modernization of collective agreements. Some successful cases of stabilized industrywide collective agreements have emerged. The long-term effects of these measures are not easy to predict, since this depends on factors such as the evolution of the East German economy.

Labor, management, and the state want to preserve industrywide collective bargaining because they are familiar with the advantages of this system, because there is no viable alternative to this system, and because of the extent to which industrywide bargaining meshes with other public policy measures. The vocational training system that is so important to Germany, for example, is strongly rooted in a number of industries and is integrated with prevailing pay differentials and pay procedures (Bosch 2000). Many of the industry associations have discovered that industrywide collective agreements help them recruit highly qualified and motivated workers through the development of new occupations. Furthermore, the employers' associations are organized on an industry basis. Thus, the industry focus found within collective bargaining is socially embedded in a variety of ways. As a result, Thelen's (2000) prediction that the German system is not going to simply collapse, but rather will change gradually, seems to be more accurate than Streeck's (2001) more pessimistic forecast.

The reason why employers have not identified an alternative to the existing system, despite being much more critical of industrywide agreements than the unions, is to be found in the decentralizing mechanisms that are feasible within the German system. On the one hand, it is costly and procedurally difficult for firms to withdraw from industrywide collective agreements. In addition, withdrawal from an industrywide agreement likely would force an employer to confront a strong works council that could use prevailing industrywide collective agreements as a reference point for their demands. Furthermore, works councils have been strengthened recently by the changes made to the Works Constitution Act.

While employers are tempted to take advantage of the weakening of the works councils' bargaining power due to high unemployment, particularly in East Germany they are afraid that changes in the bargaining system would lead the works councils to acquire the right to strike or jeopardize trust-based relations at the workplace. Employers have acquired sufficient leeway to engage in company-level bargaining though the introduction of authorizing clauses. This of course has strengthened the company level within the German collective bargaining system, apparently permanently. Of course, industrywide standards have been weakened though this process. Many downward deviations can be negotiated at the plant level and in some cases these deviations, and not the contractual standard, have become the norm. Substantive standards, like weekly or yearly working hours or pay minima, are often accompanied by promotion standards, such as entitlements to further training, or by procedural standards that delineate the rights of unions or works councils to negotiating any downward deviations.[8] So, for example, IG Metall and the works council at Volkswagen are confident that through their codetermination rights concerning production targets and ergonomic standards they can insure that working time standards will not be undercut. Labor and management are still searching for a new equilibrium with a mix of substantial, promotion, and procedural standards. The unions will accept a shifting of weight from substantial to procedural standards and greater reliance on more individual promotion norms only if they have strong representation at the plant level.

The evolution of the national-level interaction between labor, management, and the state is unstable and dependent on political circumstances. Neither employers nor trade unions have a mandate to engage in collective bargaining at the national level, and this has led to the consultative nature and limited agenda of the national Alliance for Work. This contrasts with the contractual foundation of the two other (industry and firm) levels of the German industrial relations system.

Thus the German collective bargaining system resembles a large construction site. Work at the various parts of the site is progressing at varied rates. On one side of the site are splendid new buildings have already been completed, while on the other side of the site are old buildings that are being torn down, and it is not yet clear whether anything will take the place of these buildings or whether that part of the site will remain a wasteland. In other parts of the site there are buildings from the 1950s that are in good condition due to the fact that they were renovated on several past occasions. The buildings being put up today are different from those of the past: there are more small functional buildings and fewer splendid mansions. Despite the fact that is not clear exactly how the construction site will evolve, and the prevalence of much idling and pervasive coordination problems, and contrary to the pessimism expressed by some observers, there is no doubt that construction is progressing.

5 The Rise and Fall of Interunion Wage Coordination and Tripartite Dialogue in Japan

Akira Suzuki

Comparative industrial relations researchers have tended to characterize the structure of collective bargaining in Japan as being decentralized at the enterprise level (e.g., Crouch 1985). However, actual labor-management interactions are much more complex than suggested by a simple decentralization thesis. While the enterprise remains the focal point of industrial relations in Japan, enterprise unions have coordinated the process of collective bargaining in annual rounds of wage bargaining called *Shuntō* (spring offensive) at the industry level since the mid-1950s. Moreover, a form of tripartite dialogue developed in the mid-1970s as industry-level federations of enterprise unions and national-level union confederations increased their involvement in governmental policymaking. Thus enterprise-level collective bargaining has been embedded in a broader context of industry-level as well as national-level industrial relations. Recognizing this embedded process, some recent studies of comparative industrial relations do not regard Japanese industrial relations as a highly decentralized system and pay attention to the coordination that links industrial relations actors (Soskice 1990; Traxler 1994).

This chapter examines industrial relations in Japan with a focus on the structure of collective bargaining. I use the term *collective bargaining structure* in a broad manner, referring not only to collective bargaining between unions and management over the terms and conditions of employment, but also to any tripartite consultation that involves unions, management, and the government at the national level. I begin by outlining the characteristics of enterprise unions and the development of *Shuntō* wage bargaining. Then I examine the extent to which the structure of collective bargaining shifted to the national level in the mid-1970s and whether the national tripartite negotiations that began in this period were substantial or perfunctory. Third, I analyze the impact the severe economic recession in the 1990s had on those aspects of collective bargaining that were occurring above the enterprise level, such as industry-level *Shuntō* wage bargaining and national-level tripartite dialogue. I consider whether the economic recession has had a "redecentralizing" effect on the structure of collective bargaining and the roles played by power shifts. I then examine emerging industrial relations trends, focusing on new types of unions. Finally, I speculate on whether enterprise-based industrial relations has started to wither under the strains produced by prolonged economic recession.

THE GENERAL CHARACTERISTICS OF INDUSTRIAL RELATIONS IN POSTWAR JAPAN

The Predominant Position of Enterprise Unions

In the post–World War II period a core feature of the Japanese industrial relations system has been its decentralized structure, with enterprise unions constituting the predominant form of union organization.[1] The membership of enterprise unions is usually limited to regular (i.e., full-time) employees of a particular enterprise or plant, including both blue- and white-collar workers.[2] Nonregular workers such as part-time and dispatched workers are not allowed union membership. Enterprise unions enjoy full decision-making authority on issues such as their constitution, finances, collective bargaining policies and the election of officials (Shinoda 1989, 14–15; Shirai 1983, 119). Although enterprise unions are affiliated with industry-level federations, they retain the right to engage in collective bargaining and do not delegate this right to these federations.[3]

Enterprise unionism is not unique to Japan, as this form of union organization appears in a number of countries, including South Korea. However, in countries that include unions with an enterprise structure, the specific "scope" of union membership differs. For example, enterprise unions in South Korea mainly represent nonmanagerial blue-collar workers while those in Japan represent white-collar workers and lower-ranking managers in addition to blue-collar workers. This difference in the scope of membership affects union behavior. The presence of white-collar workers and lower-ranking managers contributes to the cooperative stance Japanese enterprise unions take toward higher management, especially in the area of productivity improvement. Blue-collar domination, on the other hand, contributes to the more militant behaviors Korean unions exhibit concerning wages, working conditions, and personnel policies (Jeong 1995, 267).

The functions of Japanese enterprise unions of large private-sector firms are predominantly economic, as unions are concerned with the market competitiveness of their firm. These unions typically actively cooperate with management in the rationalization of the shop floor production process (Gordon 1998). This policy orientation of cooperative economic unionism is reinforced by interlocking relationships between management and union officials. Union posts, especially those at the shop floor level, commonly are filled by lower-ranking managers. Even if occupied by regular workers, these union posts are widely regarded as a stepping-stone to lower managerial posts (Seifert 1988). Critics of enterprise unions see this relationship as an indication of the subordination of enterprise unions to management (Yamamoto 1981). Enterprise union advocates, on the other hand, see the relationship between union office and subsequent managerial promotion as an indication of an extent to which enterprise unions are able to participate in managerial decision-making (Inagami 1995). This latter interpretation is flawed as, although leaders of enterprise unions do share information with management through consultative processes, union leaders generally passively go along with management's wishes and information sharing is typically accompanied by limited union democracy. That is, union leaders tend to act on behalf of management in their relationship with rank-and-file union members rather than as true representatives of members' interests when those interests clash with management's wants.

Opinion surveys of union members reveal the passive tendency and the limited representational function of enterprise unions. According to a survey conducted by the Japanese Electrical, Electronic, and Information Union (the JEIU) in 1994, while 69 percent of respondents noted the contribution unions make to the improvement of their working conditions in general, 45 percent of the respondents thought that unions were not checking sufficiently aggressively the activities of management. To the question asking whether unions protected members' interests when management implemented rationalization programs, including personnel reductions, 54 percent of the respondents answered in the negative (Chōsa Jihō 1995, 136–37). Surveys of the JEIU also asked whether respondents' opinions were reflected in union activities. According to the 1982 JEIU survey, 46 percent of respondents answered that their opinions were either not reflected well or were not reflected at all in union activities, and another 11 percent answered that they never expected anything meaningful from their unions (Chōsa Jihō 1983, 141). In other words, 57 percent of respondents held either negative or indifferent views on the representation functions of unions.[4] Opinion surveys of members of the Japan Federation of Steel Workers' Unions (the JFSWU) similarly indicate the limited representation functions of enterprise unions. About two-thirds of respondents answered that their opinions were either not reflected well or not reflected at all in union activities (64 percent in 1984 and 66 percent in 1988) (Chōsa Jihō 1989, 146).

Shuntō Wage Bargaining

The decentralized structure of enterprise-level collective bargaining did not imply that there was no coordination among unions at a level above the enterprise. In fact, enterprise unions and their industry-level federations have actively coordinated their activities, particularly their wage demands, during *Shuntō* wage bargaining.

Shuntō wage bargaining started in 1955 at the initiative of five industry-level federations affiliated with the leftist national confederation Sōhyō (General Council of Trade Unions). These federations called for interindustry union coordination in springtime wage bargaining through a joint struggle committee in order to overcome the weak position held by unions in enterprise-level collective bargaining. In subsequent years, other industry-level federations, including those affiliated with the Federation of Independent Unions of Japan (Chūritsu Rōren, a loose national confederation of unions unaffiliated with Sōhyō or Dōmei), participated in *Shuntō* wage bargaining. Dōmei (the Japanese Confederation of Labor), a confederation that advocated moderate policies, initially was critical of *Shuntō* wage bargaining, but many of its member federations also engaged in wage negotiations in the springtime, thus informally participating in *Shuntō*.

Interunion wage coordination during *Shuntō* took place at two levels. First, each industry-level federation coordinated the activities of member unions so that member unions made a uniform wage demand during a similar schedule of collective bargaining under the threat of possible joint strike action. The joint struggle committee in turn oversaw the overall schedule of *Shuntō* bargaining by coordinating the wage campaigns of the various industry-level union federations (Hyōdō 1997, 126–29, 138; Sako 1997, 246). In response to intra- and interindustry coordination on the union side, the management side started to informally coordinate at the industry-level about the amount of wage increases during *Shuntō* (Lee 2000, 37).

By the mid-1960s, *Shuntō* had become an institutionalized feature of industrial relations, and a consistent pattern of wage bargaining and annual wage increases linked private- and public-sector industries. The wage settlement reached in the heavy chemical industries, especially the steel settlement, commonly set the pattern, and then other private-sector industries such as private railways subsequently reached pattern-following wage settlements. The annual wage increases received by workers in the public sector were then based on the private railway wage settlement (Hayakawa 1992, 246). *Shuntō* wage bargaining, in combination with the labor shortages that were common from the mid-1960s until the mid-1970s, also exerted leveling effects on the wage settlements of large firms within and across industries.[5] Thus, although wage negotiations were being conducted at the enterprise level, decisions about annual wage increases effectively were being made at the industry level (Hyōdō 1997, 144; Lee 2000, 35–36).

Until 1974, Sōhyō played a leading role in the annual wage negotiation rounds, and many unions, including those in the private sector, supported Sōhyō's militant stance. The unions demanded large wage increases and pressed their demands through strikes and mass meetings coordinated by the joint struggle committee dominated by Sōhyō. In the second half of the 1960s and the early 1970s, unions achieved annual nominal wage increases between 10 and 15 percent. The rampant inflation that occurred in the first half of the 1970s due to the first oil crisis led unions to make even higher wage demands in order to prevent their real wages from declining. The Sōhyō-led *Shuntō* reached its peak importance in 1974. In that year unions mobilized the largest number of members in support of strikes during the wage negotiation round and attained the highest wage increase (32.9 percent).

A turning point occurred in 1975 *Shuntō* wage bargaining. The wage increase in that year's *Shuntō* declined to 13.1 percent, less than half the previous year's increase. The decline in the annual wage increase in 1975 was so large because the government and the Japan Federation of Employers' Association (Nikkeiren), alarmed by the possibility of cost-push inflation, acted in an unusually coordinated manner. Furthermore, some union leaders supported wage restraint as a way to control inflation. These union leaders represented the moderate union movement in export-oriented industries such as steel and were critical of Sōhyō's wage campaign on the grounds that it did not take into account the competitive "reality" facing the Japanese economy (Hyōdō 1997, 292–93; Hayakawa 1992, 249–50).

In the 1975 *Shuntō* and thereafter, moderate private-sector unions, particularly those affiliated with the IMF-JC (the Japan Council of International Metalworkers Federation), played a leading role in the wage bargaining process instead of Sōhyō.[6] Annual wage increases after 1976 were less than 10 percent. The rate of inflation (CPI), which had peaked in 1974 at 20.9 percent, thereafter declined to 10.4 percent in 1975, to 9.5 percent in 1976, and to 4.8 percent in 1979. The low inflation rate was said to be one of the important factors for the quick recovery of the Japanese economy from the recession relative to other industrialized countries (Sako 1997, 247–48).

It should be noted that interunion coordination remained one of the important features of *Shuntō* wage bargaining even after 1975. The purpose of interunion coordination, however, shifted from that of winning a greater share of profits created by economic growth to that of helping management recover from economic recession by restraining wage demands.

INDUSTRIAL RELATIONS FROM THE MID-1970S TO THE LATE 1980S—A TREND TOWARD CENTRALIZATION?

The Development of Tripartite Dialogue at the National Level

As noted in the previous section, although formally collective bargaining took place at the enterprise level, interunion coordination at a level above the enterprise had developed since the mid-1950s as a result of *Shuntō* wage bargaining. In the mid-1970s, another above-the-enterprise level of interaction emerged in Japan as tripartite coordination and dialogue developed between unions, management, and the central government.

The development of tripartite dialogue was closely related to the wage restraint exercised by the IMF-JC and other private-sector unions in the 1975 *Shuntō*. In the bargaining process leading to the wage settlement in that year's *Shuntō*, union leaders engaged in "intensive consultation" with government officials and business leaders. Through this consultation, which was mostly informal, union leaders came to share a similar perspective on economic conditions with government officials and business leaders, and accepted a much lower rate of wage increase than that provided in the previous year's (1974) *Shuntō* (Sako 1997; Shimada 1983; Shinkawa 1993, 213–14).

In making concessions in the 1975 *Shuntō* and thereafter, top union leaders of the IMF-JC and Dōmei expressed the willingness to make a "social contract" with the government so that union wage restraint would be reciprocated by the government's promise to contain inflation. This union policy was modeled on the social contract involving the Trade Union Congress (TUC) and the Labor government in Britain, and in Japan was referred to as a "social contract union movement" (Hayakawa 1992, 249–50; Lee 2000, 45). The Japanese government, in fact, never ended up making a public promise to control inflation in exchange for union-promised wage restraint, and consequently, the social contract proposed by union leaders was often referred to as "a contract without the other party" (Matsuzaki 1982, 251).

However, the intensive informal consultation that occurred between top union leaders, business leaders, and government officials during the 1975 *Shuntō* paved the way for the formalization of tripartite dialogue on a more regular basis. The Round Table Discussion Meeting of Industrial Labor Problem (Sanrōkon) subsequently developed as a tripartite forum in which representatives of labor unions, management, and "men of learning" exchanged opinions with the government on labor and industrial issues. Sanrōkon, modeled on German "concerted action committees" (Shinoda 1997, 203), had been established in 1970 as one among a number of committees that advised the Minister of Labor. Sanrōkon, however, had drawn little attention until the 1975 *Shuntō*, when it played an important coordinating role in wage restraint (Tsujinaka 1987, 67).

After the 1975 *Shuntō*, Sanrōkon came to be widely recognized as a key forum for tripartite discussions. Sanrōkon was held eight to eleven times a year in the second half of the 1970s and first half of the 1980s. Top government officials, such as the prime minister and other cabinet members, frequently attended the committee meetings. The fact that either the prime minister or the vice prime minister attended seven out of the eight meetings held in 1975 indicated that the government accorded much importance to Sanrōkon. The attendance of these top government officials, however, declined in 1976 and thereafter (see table 5.1). Union leaders originally regarded Sanrōkon as an important place where they could press their policy demands to the government. Union leaders requested that the function of Sanrōkon be strengthened in such a way that the prime minister's cabinet would respect the committee's decisions. This request was partly granted, as policy recommendations made in Sanrōkon meetings started to be reported to the cabinet.

Researchers are divided in their assessment of the extent to which Sanrōkon signified the development of a macrocorporatist institutional arrangement in Japan. Some researchers regard the policy participation of union leaders through Sanrōkon and other advisory committees (*Shingikai*) as an indication of the development of a type of macrocorporatism even in the face of enterprise-based industrial relations. These researchers argue that as a result, "Corporatism without Labor" (Pempel and Tsunekawa 1979) became an inadequate description of Japanese industrial relations. These analysts also claim that labor unions, through participation in governmental policy making, gained the enactment of public policies that protected the real income of workers and their employment security in the second half of the 1970s (Inagami 1996; Kume 1998; Lee 2000).

Other researchers are skeptical of the macrocorporatism claim, arguing instead that the development of tripartism was not accompanied by any increased influence of organized labor in national politics. Toshimitsu Shinkawa, for example, argues that Sanrōkon remained one of the minister of labor's informal advisory committees and "did not have the authority to influence national policies in any sense." He further argues that the organizational strength of labor unions, widely seen as one of the preconditions for tripartite corporatist arrangements, remained weak and even declined because of decreases occurring in the rate of union density from 34.4 percent in 1975 to 30.8 percent in 1980 (Shinkawa 1993, 222, 230).

Similarly, Ronald Dore (1990) notes the increased opportunities for union leaders to be represented in consultation committees attached to government ministries, such as Sanrōkon, but suggests that the participation of union leaders in these bodies was largely symbolic. Unions neither pressed "distinctive policies," nor engaged in any "overt bargaining" with the "ruling establishment" (i.e., the government, the ruling party, and business) through these bodies. In addition, Dore claims that the ruling establishment did not need the support of unions to implement their policies, except for union support for wage restraint in the 1975 *Shuntō*. As Dore (1990, 55) writes, "what they (labor unions) gained is recognition, honour, respect—accorded more particularly to trade union leaders than to the union collectively."

In my view the presence of organized labor in national politics at this point in time was rather formal and perfunctory (thus I side with the second group of researchers). As Dore posits, although Sanrōkon was perceived to have attained upgraded status, the committee seemed to function primarily as a forum for the exchange of opinions among representatives, rather than as a place for substantive bargaining or for the making of economic decisions.

The increased involvement of organized labor in the policy-making process did occur at a time when some legislation and policies beneficial to the interests of workers were being adopted. For example, the government passed three laws designed to maintain employment security of workers in private-sector firms in 1974 and 1977. These laws provided subsidies to employers of several structurally depressed industries to reduce the layoff of redundant workers and increased the amount of unemployment benefits to laid-off workers in these industries (Kume

1998). However, it is difficult to attribute the passage of this legislation to the increased influence of organized labor in national politics. The government seemed to be persuaded to adopt these policies primarily because employers, as well as organized labor, believed these policies would support the continuation of stable union-management relations at the enterprise level. The passage of this legislation also was helped by a shift in the balance of power between the ruling party and opposition parties in the Diet that occurred in the mid-1970s as a result of other factors.[7]

The Development of Union Movements from the Mid-1970s to the Late 1980s

From the mid-1970s to the late 1980s, union consolidation led by moderate private-sector unions took place, paving the way for the formation of a dominant united union confederation. In 1976, sixteen industry-level federations of private-sector unions formed the Trade Union Council for Policy Promotion (Seisui Kaigi) as a forum for coordinating their efforts to make policy demands on the government and as a preparatory step for the possible unification of union confederations (Hyodō 1997, 417). In 1982, the Japan Private Sector Trade Union Council (Zenmin Rōkyō), a loose confederation consisting of forty-one industry-level private-sector union federations, succeeded the Trade Union Council for Policy Promotion. In 1987, all national-level union confederations, except Sōhyō, were dissolved, and the Japanese Trade Union Confederation (Rengō) was formed as a formal confederation consisting of sixty-two industry-level private-sector union federations. Sōhyō continued to exist as a confederation of public-sector unions, but was dissolved in 1989 when these unions joined Rengō.

The creation of Rengō, however, did not completely unify the labor movement. A minority of leftist unions opposed the moderate policy line of Rengō and formed two rival confederations, the National Confederation of Trade Unions (Zenrōren) and the National Trade Union Council (Zenrōkyō).

The formation of Rengō was widely regarded as contributing to a centralization tendency within the structure of collective bargaining, as the confederation represented a majority of organized labor (about 62 percent in 1990) and was well positioned to engage in "political exchanges" with the government and management in tripartite bargaining. In fact, senior leaders of Rengō gave high priority to a "demand for policy changes and institutional reform" (*seisaku seido yōkyō*). Rengō sent representatives to government ministry advisory committees and held "policy talks" with government ministries, the cabinet, and the ruling party (Shinoda 1997; Igarashi 1998, 360–63). Moreover, Rengō and its member unions were the only unions that had a channel for discussions with the government, since representatives from the two smaller confederations were not included in advisory committees and policy talks.[8] Whether this in fact led to a meaningful increase in Rengō's influence in national politics and allowed Rengō to realize its policy goals is examined in the next section.

INDUSTRIAL RELATIONS IN THE 1990S—THE REEMERGENCE OF DECENTRALIZED COLLECTIVE BARGAINING?

The Impact of the Heisei Recession on Labor Markets and Industrial Relations

The Japanese economy went into severe recession after the "bubble economy" collapsed in 1990 (the so-called *Heisei Fukyō* or Heisei recession). The five-year average rate of GDP growth (in real terms) declined from 4.6 percent (1985–89), to 2.2 percent (1990–94), and to 1.2 percent (1995–99). The poor economic conditions after 1990 adversely effected labor markets. While the unemployment rate was less than 3 percent in the first half of the 1990s, it started to rise rapidly in 1995. The unemployment rate then rose from 3.2 percent in 1995, to 5.0 percent in 2001, the highest rate since the unemployment rate was first measured with modern methods in 1953. The number of unemployed people rose from 1.3 million in 1990, to 2.1 million in 1995, and to 3.4 million in 2001. Among unemployed people, the number who had left their previous jobs involuntarily rose after 1997 and approached the number of people who previously had left jobs voluntarily.

Another important change occurring in the labor market was an increase in the number of workers in "nonregular employment," such as part-time workers and "dispatched" workers in the second half of the 1990s.[9] The number of nonregular workers increased by 36 percent from 1995 to 2001, and their share of all employees (except executives) rose from 21 percent in 1995 to 27 percent in 2001. Of the 13.6 million nonregular workers in 2001, 73 percent were female (Sōmushō 2001).

These data indicate that employment security, widely regarded as one of the basic principles of Japanese industrial relations, has become less certain for many workers, including regular male workers employed in large private-sector firms. Since the mid-1990s, many large corporations have implemented reductions in the number of regular employees by transferring redundant workers to other companies, or by introducing voluntary or early retirement schemes. This has led to decreases in the number of "core" workers (i.e., male full-time workers working for enterprises with more than 999 employees). From 1995 to 2001, the number of core workers decreased by 680,000 (from 6,620,000 to 5,940,000) (OISR 2000, 45–49; Sōmuchō 1995; Sōmushō 2001).

Reflecting the weak state of the labor market, wage increases moderated. The wage increases paid by major corporations averaged 5.9 percent in the 1990 *Shuntō*, and declined to 2.8 percent in 1995, to 2.1 percent in 2000, and fell to 1.7 percent in 2002 (see table 5.2). Wage increases in Japan include two components: an increase in the basic wage rate and an annual seniority pay increase. The first pay component involves an upward-shift in firms' wage curves and represents "real" increases in wages. The latter pay component represents a moving-up by one step in firms' seniority wage ladders (and are generally expected to amount to 2 percent a year), and this pay increase is supposed to cover expected increases in the living expenses of workers as they age (Weathers 1999, 966; Fujita 1996, 18). The amount of "real" wage increases (the rate of wage increase minus 2 percent) has drastically declined since the late 1990s: while the rate was 0.66 percent in 1998, it declined to 0.06 percent in 2000 and to 0.01 percent in 2001. In the 2002 *Shuntō*, the rate of wage increase decreased to 1.66 percent, smaller than the usual annual seniority raise.

The "Reform" of *Shuntō*—A Decline in Interunion Coordination?

By the mid-1990s management and unions generally began to favor reform of the *Shuntō* process. Nikkeiren, representing the management side, started to criticize *Shuntō* for creating a high-cost structure in the Japanese economy. According to Nikkeiren, *Shuntō*'s pattern bargaining increased wages in domestic-oriented industries, such as telecommunications, electric power, and private railways, more than the amounts warranted by the productivity increases that were occurring in these industries. Nikkeiren stressed that wage determination should be based strictly on productivity growth and "the capacity of each company to pay" (Shimamura 1995; OISR 1996, 120).[10]

Industry-level union federations within Rengō also started to discuss the reform of *Shuntō* in the mid-1990s. Motivating these discussions was the realization by some union leaders that unions were no longer able to achieve across-the-board wage increases through *Shuntō* wage bargaining. Moreover, some union federations such as the JFSWU (Japan Federation of Steelworkers' Unions) came to share management's critical perspective on the pattern bargaining role of *Shuntō*, agreeing that wage increases in an industry or an enterprise should reflect productivity increases in the industry or enterprise (Hyōdō 1997, 523). In addition, union federations became concerned about the administrative cost of *Shuntō*. Although unions devoted a lot of organizational resources to *Shuntō*-related activities every year, they had not been able to achieve significant results (in terms of wage increases) since the start of the Heisei recession and union members began to question the value of participating in the process.

The content of proposed reforms varied across union federations, with many federations advocating greater autonomy for industry-level federations in *Shuntō* wage negotiations. Along these lines some union federations proposed limiting the role of Rengō during *Shuntō* to setting the minimum standard for wage demands and giving more autonomy to industry-level union federations in deciding the specific level of wage settlements. Some union federations went even further, arguing that the discretion to reach a wage settlement should be given to enterprise unions, with an industry-level federation playing only a supporting role by setting a minimum wage demand (Shikata 1999).

The decline of interunion coordination became evident as Rengō and its member unions prepared for the 2002 *Shuntō*. Rengō decided not to set a unified standard for the basic wage increase being demanded during the 2002 *Shuntō*. This was because many labor unions, facing pressure from the severe recession and the increasing unemployment rate, accorded more importance to the protection of union members' employment than to wage increases. Rengō even was prepared to accept wage cuts in industries and enterprises if such concessions were required for the maintenance of union members' employment. This policy effectively left it to each industry-level federation to decide whether or not to demand a wage increase on the basis of each industry's economic conditions (SRN 2001a). Some federations, such as the JFSWU and the JEIU (Japanese Electrical, Electronic and Information Union), did not demand an increase in the basic wage rate in the 2002 *Shuntō* and instead demanded employment security for union members (SRN 2001b, 2001c).

Rengō leadership plans not to set a unified standard for wage increases in the 2003 *Shuntō* and to let each industry-level federation set an industry-specific wage increase target (if it decides to do so) (SRN 2002). If Rengō and its industry-level federations do not make national or industry-level standards for wage increases in the 2003 *Shuntō* and thereafter, then the interunion coordination function served by *Shuntō* will weaken considerably, and the focal point of wage bargaining will move even further to the enterprise level. This shift will go a long way to meeting the demands of the employers' association.[11]

The Development of Tripartite Dialogue—A Marginalization of Labor?

Macrolevel tripartite dialogue was revived in the 1990s in countries such as Italy and South Korea, when these countries experienced serious economic troubles that led to major reforms in their industrial relations and social security systems. In Japan, the Heisei recession brought about an unprecedented degree of employment insecurity, and the government established macrolevel tripartite bodies besides Sanrōkon to promote social-level dialogue on employment issues. These bodies, however, did not have any meaningful influence on policy formation and implementation.

The Japanese government established a new tripartite committee specializing in employment issues in 1998. The group, called the Tripartite Council on Employment Policy, included top leaders of Nikkeiren, Rengō, and key cabinet members. The Tripartite Council held six meetings from September 1998 to November 1999, where the government's 1-trillion-yen program to create 1 million jobs through spending on welfare, education, house construction, and the environment was discussed. In these meetings, Rengō and Nikkeiren presented a joint proposal for the creation of specific numbers of jobs in each expenditure category area and asked the government to formally develop this proposal (SRN 1998; Weekly Rengō 1999). However, the government was slow to formalize and implement the recommended program, and the unemployment rate continued to rise (SRN 1999a, 1999b). Moreover, the government suspended the Tripartite Council for a year and a half after the council's sixth meeting in reaction to Rengō's strong opposition to pension reform expressed in a major protest campaign against the government and the ruling party (discussed further below).

The government resumed the Tripartite Council in June 2001, but the council mainly served as a forum where opinions were exchanged. In order to propose a more concrete policy to cope with the rising unemployment rate, the government established another tripartite council for discussing work-sharing schemes in December 2001. The new council aimed to establish a guideline for work-sharing schemes so that employers would not lay off workers and, rather, would create new employment opportunities based on shorter working hours. The government, Nikkeiren, and Rengō reached a basic agreement on two types of work-sharing schemes in March

2002 (one scheme is based on the creation of various working styles and another one is based on reductions in the wages of currently employed workers in accordance with shorter working hours). However, these principles proposed only the general terms of work-sharing schemes and left the working out of the specific arrangements in these schemes to negotiations between employers and unions at the enterprise level. Moreover, employers were rather indifferent to the discussion of work-sharing schemes. According to a survey of employers, 85 percent of them had not introduced, or did not have any plans to introduce, work-sharing schemes (Ogino 2002).

The Heisei recession also produced pressures that encouraged the deregulation of labor standards and employment relations as well as reforms in the pension system that led to reductions in government expenditures. Rengō, in addition to participating in the macrolevel tripartite bodies, regularly sent representatives to advisory committees that were attached to various government ministries (*Shingikai*) with the goal of influencing the policy-making process in favor of the interests of organized labor in the midst of trends toward deregulation. However, the influence of Rengō in the policy-making process became marginalized in the course of the 1990s.

Rengō and its affiliated unions sent approximately 290 delegates to seventy advisory committees in 1997. These committees covered various policy areas, such as labor, social security, education, environmental, economic, and gender equality issues (Rengō 1997). Among these policy areas, Rengō accorded particular importance to the participation of union representatives in the policy-making process concerned with labor policies. There were ten advisory committees attached to the Ministry of Labor, and most of them were tripartite bodies. These advisory committees consisted of representatives on the union side (monopolized by Rengō and its member unions), representatives on the management side, and those who represented the "public interest" (*Kōeki gawa Iin*). Of these committees, the Central Labor Standards Committee (Chūkishin, the CLSC) and the Central Employment Stability Committee (Chūshokushin, the CESC) discussed policy proposals related to labor standards and employment relations, respectively.

Until the early 1990s, these advisory committees deliberated and then submitted reports to the ministry through a consensus-based process. When the union and management sides opposed each other on a certain issue, representatives of the public acted as mediators by proposing their own draft report, and typically the two sides then reached a compromise that was based on this report (Miura 2001, 1; Kume 2000, 5).

In the second half of the 1990s, however, the government shifted to more strongly endorse a "neoliberal" policy orientation in an effort to revive the stagnant economy. In 1995, the government established a powerful committee attached to the prime minister's office for the purpose of promoting administrative reform and market deregulation. One of the key goals adopted by this committee was labor market deregulation (JTUC-RIALS 2001, 396). Since the positions of the union and management sides were often irreconcilable on the issue of labor market deregulation, it became difficult for the advisory committees to maintain a consensual approach. In cases where consensus was not reached, the CLSC and the CESC submitted reports to the Ministry of Labor that did not incorporate the opinions held by union representatives, and this made it clear that organized labor had become marginalized in the policy-making process.

In 1998 and 1999, the government successively revised the Labor Standards Law and the Worker Dispatching Law as part of its deregulation policy and enacted the Pension Reform Act in 2000. The revision of the Labor Standards Law, among other things, expanded the occupational categories eligible for discretionary work arrangements so as to include white-collar workers.[12] The revision of the Worker Dispatching Law liberalized the use of dispatched workers, "with only a few exceptions in port, transport, construction, guard services and others designated by the Cabinet Order as prohibited types of dispatched work" (Japan Labor Bulletin 1999). The Pension Reform Act aims at reducing the level of pension benefit payments by 20 percent in twenty years. Measures to reduce benefits include a 5 percent reduction in "the salary-linked portion of payments," a gradual increase in the age at which individuals become eligible for pensions (from sixty to sixty-five, from 2013), and an end to the sliding scale that had tied pension benefit levels to wage levels for those recipients aged sixty-five and over (OISR 2001, 371; Japan Labor Bulletin 2000).

The CLSC and the CESC debated the proposed revisions to the Labor Standards Law and the Worker Dispatching Law under strong pressure to conform to the government's policy preferences. In these debates union representatives strongly opposed the expansion of the discretionary work scheme to white-collar workers as well as liberalization of the use of dispatched workers. Concerning the former, unions argued that many white collar jobs are not suitable for the discretionary work scheme, as application of this scheme to white-collar workers would lead to increases in working hours without overtime pay. Concerning the latter, unions feared that the more liberalized use of dispatched workers would promote the replacement of regular workers by dispatched workers, thus undermining long-term employment (JTUC-RIALS 2001, 421–62, 502).

Representatives on the management side, on the other hand, strongly supported these deregulation measures, and they had the support of the public representatives. Thus, the CLSC and the CESC did not adhere to a consensual process and in the end reports were submitted (in December 1997 and May 1998) that supported the policy changes favored by the Ministry of Labor without incorporating the contrary opinions held by union representatives (JTUC-RIALS 2001, 477–78, 512–15).

The government also carried out reforms of the pension system despite strong protests from the labor movement. The Pension Committee (Nenkin Shingikai) attached to the Ministry of Health and Welfare submitted a report that gave its assent to pension reforms in March 1999 after only three days' of deliberation. On the last day of deliberation, all three union representatives walked out from the committee, arguing that they did not want to take responsibility for the report. Moreover, the union representatives formally resigned from the committee, because the ministry refused to consider Rengō's request for repeal of the report. This was the first time since the establishment of Rengō that its representatives had resigned from a governmental advisory committee (OISR 2000, 203, 240).

Because of the marginalization of its influence on policy advisory committees, Rengō shifted the focus of its policy-related activities to the National Diet. In an effort to influence the Diet, Rengō worked closely with opposition parties, trying to modify various government bills (Miura 2001). Moreover, Rengō began to mobilize union members for various protest meetings and demonstrations. In some cases, Rengō coordinated the schedule of meetings and demonstrations with Zenrōren and Zenrōkyō so that union members of the three confederations could act jointly (OISR 1999, 209; OISR 2000, 214). Because of these activities, particularly Rengō's lobbying activities during Diet sessions, the original bills concerning revisions in the Labor Standards Law and the Workers Dispatching Law were modified to a certain extent in favor of organized labors' interests.

The modified bills were passed with the support of the ruling and opposition parties except for the Japan Communist party. In the case of the revision of the Labor Standards Law, Rengō did not accomplish its goal of passing a counterproposal to the original bill that deleted the whole section dealing with the expansion of the occupational categories eligible for discretionary work. However, the ruling and opposition parties did agree to Rengo's desire for three important modifications to the original bill. First, the expansion of the discretionary work scheme was postponed for one year. Second, specific guidelines for implementing the expansion of the discretionary work scheme would be decided based on the opinions held by the CLSC. And third, a section was added to the original bill requiring that employers get the consent of workers when a discretionary work scheme is introduced and also prohibits "disadvantageous treatment" when workers refuse to work under such a scheme (JTUC-RIALS 2001, 490–95; OISR 1999, 197).

With regard to the Worker Dispatching Law, modifications were made to the original bill in line with Rengō's desires so as to make the conditions under which dispatched workers could be hired more stringent, and protections of dispatched workers' rights were improved (JTUC-RIALS 2001, 531–37). With the Pension Reform Act, in contrast, the government and the ruling parties made no concessions to the labor movement or to opposition parties and pushed the unmodified bill through the Diet.

The decline of Rengō's influence in the advisory committees of the government suggests a decline in the influence of tripartite activities in the second half of the 1990s. However, through lobbying activities in the Diet and member mobilization, Rengō and other union confederations achieved some of their objectives as meaningful modifications were made to pending labor-related legislation.

In light of these events, researchers have arrived at a mixed assessment of Rengō's influence in the political arena. On the one hand, researchers note that Rengō did obtain certain results, in particular, by modifying bills pending in the Diet. The capacity of Rengō's policy participation also improved over time as Rengō mobilized its organizational and political resources. On the other hand, however, Rengō's efforts ended up either "bringing a big minus closer to zero" or "reducing the size of a big minus" (JTUC-RIALS 2001, 541–42).

Some observers argue that Rengō is effectively acquiescing to the deregulation drive promoted by the government and employers. For example, Onomichi (1998, 13), commenting on the modifications made to the Labor Standards Law, claims that the requirement for the consent of workers and the prohibition on disadvantageous treatment by management will not deter the arbitrary application of the discretionary work scheme by employers because individual workers do not exert much power at the enterprise level.

In my view Rengō has been influential enough to set some meaningful restrictions on the deregulation of labor markets in the legal framework, but Rengō is not powerful enough to make sure that enterprise unions will enforce these restrictions and effectively regulate working conditions and employment relations. This follows not only from the fact that Rengō does not exert real authority over enterprise unions, but also because enterprise unions are not generally active in representing individual members' interests to management at the workplace.

The Development of Region-based Unions—A Trend Toward the "Individualization" of Industrial Relations?

While an overwhelming majority of Japanese unions are organized at the enterprise level, a few unions have a regional representation structure with members drawn from a number of firms. These regional unions (often referred to as "community unions") generally cover "peripheral" workers. These workers include part-time and dispatched workers (i.e., nonregular workers), workers in small firms, middle-aged workers targeted for layoff or early retirement as part of corporate restructuring, female workers discriminated against in wages and promotion, and foreign workers. The number of regional unions has increased since the mid-1980s because of the growth in the number of these peripheral workers.

A loose nationwide federation of regional unions was established in 1989. In the late 1990s, seventy-five unions, with about fourteen thousand members, belonged to the federation, and on average they each had two hundred members (Takai 1997; Takagi 1999a, 1999b).[13] Some observers argue that regional unions are likely to grow in the future in part due to the fact that enterprise unions are limited in their ability to organize peripheral workers and because a regional structure is well suited to serving the diverse interests of peripheral workers (Takai 1997; Takagi 1999a, 1999b).

The style of bargaining used by regional unions contrasts with that common to enterprise unions. Enterprise unions set general rules governing industrial relations, but are usually not involved in the specific problems that arise between individual workers and management. Regional unions, in contrast, typically address the complaints that individual workers have with their employers and any ensuing disputes. Regional unions usually organize new members by offering counseling services on labor issues to workers having disputes with employers.[14] After these workers become union members, the unions engage in collective bargaining on members' behalf to resolve disputes concerning dismissals, overdue wages, poor working conditions, and harassment and discrimination at the workplace (Takagi 1999a, 1999b; Obata 1996). By focusing more on individual rather than group-related issues, the bargaining style of regional unions represents an individualization of collective bargaining.

The regional unions also exhibit certain aspects of social movement unionism. For one thing, they deal not only with economic issues, but also with social issues, such as gender-based discrimination in pay and job assignments and the poor working conditions of foreign workers (many of them are overstaying visas and are not covered by health and accident compensation insurance). In fact, some regional unions, such as those representing the interests of female workers, grew out of social movements (Takagi 1999a). Second, in contrast to the bureaucratized organizational structures typical of enterprise unions, regional unions have high levels of rank-and-file participation. Union members participate, for example, by volunteering as labor-issue counselors for other workers and as union representatives in other members' collective bargaining with employers (Kotani 1999, 2001).

Although labor market conditions, namely an increase in part-time and dispatched workers, seem to favor the growth of regional unions, to date the growth in regional unions has not kept up with increases in the number of nonregular workers. For example, the proportion of part-time workers among the total number of union members was only 2.7 percent in 2002. The growth of regional unions, it seems, depends on the extent to which Rengō and other union confederations or federations mobilize resources targeted on organizing nonregular workers into regional unions.[15]

AN EXPLANATION FOR CHANGES IN THE STRUCTURE OF COLLECTIVE BARGAINING—A SHIFT IN THE BALANCE OF POWER IN FAVOR OF MANAGEMENT?

Even in the face of all the developments discussed in this chapter, decentralized enterprise-level collective bargaining continued to serve as the dominant form of labor-management interactions in Japan. The influence of enterprise bargaining was embedded in the informal and formal bargaining arrangements that operated above the enterprise level. *Shuntō* wage bargaining since the mid-1950s, based on interunion coordination within and across industries, for example, established a wage-setting pattern that was followed very closely across industries and had leveling effects on wage settlements between firms, particularly among the large firms in an industry.

The formal structure of labor-management interactions was somewhat centralized from the mid-1970s until the mid-1990s through the emergence of national-level tripartite dialogue. This centralization trend in Japan contrasts with the decentralization trend common to other industrialized countries during the same period, as reported in other chapters in this volume. The structure of collective bargaining in these other countries generally shifted from the national or industry level to the enterprise level, as unions and management, particularly the latter, sought labor market flexibility in response to intensified international competition. The decentralization of collective bargaining also was being promoted in these other countries as a vehicle through which unions and management could deal with production issues and worker skill-formation. Since the latter issues tended to be enterprise-specific, the shift in the focus of industrial relations to those issues naturally led to decentralization in the structure of collective bargaining (e.g., Turner 1991; Katz 1993).

The union movement in postwar Japan, in contrast, was generally interested in production-related issues as early as the immediate postwar period (Shinoda et al. 1989, 32). Collective bargaining at the enterprise level on production-related issues had often been adversarial until the end of the 1950s, as many enterprise unions engaged in intense shop floor struggles against the rationalization of production process that entailed the intensification of labor as well as possible dismissals of workers. However, by the early 1960s, unions and management at large private-sector firms worked out a sort of class compromise in which workers were to cooperate with management's rationalization efforts and in return workers received seniority-based wage increases and employment security. As this system evolved, management consulted with union officials about rationalization plans, and unions usually accepted these plans as the best way to ensure the market competitiveness of their firms and employment security. At the workplace level, shop floor struggles gave way to small group activities such as quality circles where workers discussed problems associated with their work tasks and suggested ways to solve these problems to management. With a few exceptions enterprise unions did not attempt to regulate the pace of rationalization.[16] In this way, production-related issues were virtually a managerial prerogative.

The centralization tendency that appeared in the structure of collective bargaining in Japan from the mid-1970s on was spurred by the shift in the main focus of industrial relations away from production-related issues and to wage issues. Since the wage issue was less enterprise-specific in nature, enterprise unions needed a device to coordinate wage bargaining within and across industries, which they did through *Shuntō* wage bargaining. When the first oil shock hit the Japanese economy in the early 1970s and caused a high inflation rate and ensuing militancy within unions, the government as well as management became concerned about wage issues. The government, management, and some union leaders worried that union efforts to address wage issues might negatively affect Japan's macroeconomic performance. Thus industrial relations actors developed coordinating activities among themselves that operated above the enterprise level in order to restrain wage increases, and the government supported these coordination efforts by providing a forum for tripartite consultation (i.e., Sanrōkon). Although there were important differences in the macrolevel concertation that occurred in Japan and the macrocorporatism found in many European countries, a key commonality in these activities was their concern with the relationship between wage increases and macroeconomic performance and their common efforts to contain cost-push inflation.

Then, why did interunion coordination during *Shuntō* and macrolevel tripartite dialogue decline in the late 1990s in Japan, thereby "redecentralizing" the structure of collective bargaining? The most important factor driving this shift in bargaining structure was the severe Heisei recession. The recession put so much market pressure on employers that they began to withdraw their support for the various core features of "Japanese-style management," particularly the employment security received by regular workers and seniority-based wages, as employers called for increasing labor market flexibility.[17] The recession shifted bargaining power in favor of management and put unions on the defensive.[18]

The shift in the balance of power thesis suggests two further reasons for the "redecentralization" of bargaining structure in Japan. First, interunion wage coordination and tripartite dialogue had taken place in the context of a decentralized (enterprise-based) structure of collective bargaining and were not accompanied by a strengthening in the authority of industry-level union federations or national confederations. Thus, industrial relations arrangements above the enterprise level rested on a fragile basis and, as a result, were not able to withstand the shift in the balance of power in management's favor that occurred with the Heisei recession. Second, the major focus of industrial relations shifted back from wage-related to production-related issues, and management became less motivated to engage in bargaining with unions at a level above the enterprise.

Management largely got what it wanted in recent *Shuntō* wage bargaining, as indicated by the decline in wage increases in the second half of the 1990s and early 2000s (see table 5.2). Consequently, management became less concerned with wage-related issues and more concerned with enterprise-specific production issues. These production issues included reductions in production capacity to be accomplished by the outsourcing of production and the relocation of plants overseas and increases in numerical work force flexibility through reductions in the number of full-time workers and increasing use of part-time and dispatched workers.

Moreover, a shift in power relations in labor politics reinforced the decline of tripartite dialogue. As discussed above, the government set up a powerful committee attached to the prime minister's office for promoting administrative policy reforms and market deregulation. The government, through this committee, put strong pressure on the tripartite advisory committees. As a result, the advisory committees affirmed the deregulation of labor standards and employment relations as well as the reform of the pension system, despite strong opposition from union representatives. Although the advisory committees played an important role in the policy-making process by mediating the various interests of the concerned parties, the government began to critically evaluate the role of advisory committees and consider reducing their number (Kume 2000, 3, 6). These changes in the policy-making process indicate that a new framework of labor politics has begun to emerge, in which the power of the cabinet is being strengthened while the influence of organized labor is becoming marginalized.

CONCLUSIONS

This chapter shows that tendencies developed that ran counter to the traditional Japanese enterprise-based structure of collective bargaining, including interunion coordination from the mid-1950s on and a form of tripartite bargaining from the mid-1970s on. The shift in the main focus of industrial relations from production-related to wage issues in the first

TABLE 5.1. THE FREQUENCY OF SANRŌKON (A) AND THE NUMBER OF MEETINGS ATTENDED BY THE PRIME MINISTER OR VICE PRIME MINISTER (B)

	From 1970 to 1974	1975	1976	1977	1978	1979	1980	1981
A	46	8	8	11	10	9	9	9
B	n.a.	7	2	2	1	1	2	0

	1982	1983	1984	1985	1986	1987	1988	1989	1990
A	7	9	9	9	8	8	6	6	7
B	1	1	1	1	1	1	1	1	1

	1991	1992	1993	1994	1995	1996	1997
A	8	8	5	5	5	4	4
B	2	0	2	0	1	1	1

Source: Rōdōshō (the Ministry of Labor). Shiryō Rōdō Undō Shi (Documentation on the history of the labor movement).

TABLE 5.2. THE SETTLEMENT AMOUNT AND THE RATE OF *SHUNTŌ* WAGE INCREASES IN MAJOR CORPORATIONS*

Year	Settlement (yen)	Rate (%)	Quartile Variance
1989	12,747	5.17	0.11
1990	15,026	5.94	0.08
1991	14,911	5.65	0.08
1992	13,662	4.95	0.11
1993	11,077	3.89	0.12
1994	9,118	3.13	0.12
1995	8,376	2.83	0.10
1996	8,712	2.86	0.10
1997	8,927	2.90	0.11
1998	8,323	2.66	0.12
1999	7,005	2.21	0.15
2000	6,499	2.06	0.14
2001	6,328	2.01	0.15
2002	5,265	1.66	0.15

* Major corporations: with capital of at least 2 billion yen and more than 999 employees.
Source: http://www.mhlw.go.jp/houdou/2002/08/h0829-2.html

half of the 1970s spurred the development of tripartite dialogue between unions, management, and the government. However, the shift in the balance of power in favor of management due to the Heisei recession, as well as a shift in the focus of industrial relations back to production-related issues, promoted a redecentralization of the structure of collective bargaining in the 1990s. In addition, the shift in the balance of power in labor politics, particularly the strong commitment of the government to labor market deregulation, marginalized the position of organized labor in the policy-making process.

Analysis of the evolution of the structure of collective bargaining suggests that the mid-1990s may be a major turning point for industrial relations in Japan as labor market conditions surrounding industrial relations radically changed. Management withdrew their support for Japanese-style employment relations and started to adapt employment systems to global standards by seeking numerical flexibility through the replacement of full-time workers with nonregular workers.

The gradual crumbling of traditional industrial relations arrangements also is being prompted by two other sources. First, enterprise unions face a crisis of representation because they do not adequately protect the interests of core workers (male full-time workers employed by large firms). While many enterprise unions insist on employment security of union members in their formal slogans, they have come to accept personnel reductions if such reductions are accomplished through "voluntary" retirements or transfers to other firms. Second, an increase in the proportion of part-time, dispatched, and other peripheral workers may intensify conflicts over differences in the treatment of these workers and full-time workers, particularly over the issue of whether the principle of equal pay for equal work is being violated (many part-time and dispatched workers have almost the same responsibility in their jobs as full-time workers, but their wages are much lower than those of full-time workers).[19] Concerns about these issues among nonregular workers may promote a new type of union movement that bypasses existing enterprise unions and creates a sense of solidarity among nonregular workers across enterprises, as in the case of regional unions. Whether change in industrial relations in Japan actually follows along these lines is a subject for future research.

6 Will the Model of Uncoordinated Decentralization Persist?

Changes in Korean Industrial Relations After the Financial Crisis

Wonduck Lee and Joohee Lee

The decentralized Korean industrial relations system was to a certain degree predetermined by the industrial strategy of former authoritarian regimes. Export-led industrialization (hereafter ELI) maintained international competitiveness at any cost and developed an industrial structure that divided workers far before democratic transition opened the political sphere in 1987.

The major goal of the first stage of ELI was to pursue outward-looking industrialization by establishing a foundation of labor-intensive light industries based on cheap and abundant labor. It was well known that the Korean government virtually *disciplined* businesses using a variety of incentives, including export targets, subsidies, and preferential interest rates. As a result, the state became an arena in which the interests of business were critically dependent. Labor-intensive light manufacturing industries were usually based on a number of very small firms with few economies of scale and simple technology. Since these small firms were too compctitive with one another to mount a collective action of putting their interests to the authoritarian state, the state did not face a united business group despite rapid economic growth (Shafer 1990, 133). These characteristics also obstructed labor's organizational power, which had been crushed since the late 1940s.[1]

The second stage of ELI, heavy and chemical industrialization, was born of security concern and global recession. Nixon's opening to China and his doctrine demanding that Asian governments be largely self-reliant in national security, as well as the strategy of industrialization based on the exports of manufacturers to developed countries, began to expose many problems during the 1970s. As a result, the government has promoted heavy and chemical industries since 1973, emphasizing greater economic balance and independence as well as military build-up. To achieve these goals, the government encouraged monopolistic production, reduced tariffs on capital equipment, raised tariffs to protect infant industries, and established national investment funds. Between 1977 and 1979, 80 percent of the total investment in manufacturing went to the heavy industry. In contrast to the light industrialization period, heavy and chemical industrialization brought about a business concentration in large export-led enterprises. By 1985, the top ten large conglomerates (hereafter *chaebols*) dominated the economy, accounting for 30.2 percent of total shipments. In the late 1980s, more industrial wage earners were employed in heavy and chemical industries than in the light-manufacturing sector, which had employed about 60 percent of the country's total wage earners in 1963. Despite high labor productivity, real wages were kept low by repressive labor policies.

The democratic transition in 1987 occurred within this socioeconomic context. When massive and violent antigovernment demonstrations by a large segment of the urban population seriously weakened the repressive state machinery, long suppressed conflicts between labor and management began to emerge. Unions became much more politicized and radical during the transition period. During the summer of 1987, some three thousand violent strikes swept over Korea, which led to the doubling of wages in the subsequent two or three years.[2] Despite initial success, however, the labor movement largely failed to become a significant political force. One of the most distinguishing characteristics of the labor movement following democratization in 1987 was a massive growth in trade union activity by skilled male workers employed in the large enterprises of the heavy and chemical industrial sector. The core workers did not have enough time to develop their incipient trade union activities into a concrete political power. Instead, their militant activities were focused on improving wage rates and working conditions within individual enterprises. The industrial relations system based on the strong bargaining power of trade unions at the workplace level, lifetime employment, and seniority-based allocation rules was created during the transition period and continued without interruption until the financial crisis of 1997.

The legal framework of industrial relations in Korea during the two stages of ELI contributed much to the decentralized bargaining structure in Korea. The amendment of the labor laws in 1963 prohibited political activities by labor unions and forbade a second union (union pluralism) on both the plant and national level. The Special Act on National Security in 1971 severely restricted the right to collective bargaining and the right to act collectively, and provided the state with almost unlimited emergency power. However, the most significant blow to union activity came from the changed labor laws in late 1980, which decentralized union organization and made industrial action virtually impossible. The law reorganized industry-based unions into enterprise unions. The law also made union shops illegal and stipulated many complicated requirements for enterprise-union formation. Furthermore, the controversial Article 13 of the Labor Dispute Adjustment Law that prohibits third-party engagement in collective bargaining and other labor disputes has been successful in obstructing linkages among local unions, between union federations and local unions, and between progressive social forces and the trade union movement as a whole. As a result, most trade unions are organized on an enterprise basis, and collective bargaining is conducted generally at the enterprise level.

Despite the subsequent amendments of labor laws that eliminated such authoritarian legacies, the decentralized bargaining structure has remained more or less intact. Both enterprise unions and employers were responsible for this. During the authoritarian era, trade unions were not only organized on an enterprise basis, but also under the influence of *oyong* (pro-management) labor leaders. Most unions won union autonomy and democracy after Korea made a significant breakthrough in democratization. Trade union leadership operating on the basis of democratic procedure, however, must satisfy rank-and-file members' interests in order to get reelected, and some union leaders in large firms were reluctant to move toward industry-level bargaining for fear of losing their own influence and power (Wilkinson 1994). Employers who preferred enterprise-level bargaining actively sought to satisfy organized workers' short-term material interests within individual enterprises. These employers were able to pass on higher labor costs via market power through industrial concentration.

The Asian financial crisis, however, has brought about a sea of changes in the industrial relations model set up with the ensuing democratic transition.[3] The social impact of the financial crisis has been more distressing than expected. Growing employment insecurity among managerial/white collar workers and core production workers in large manufacturing companies revealed the weakening of the lifetime employment system that traditionally existed in these sectors of the economy. This chapter describes the sweeping changes in the Korean labor market that have occurred since the financial crisis and then critically assesses current developments in the Korean system of industrial relations. We argue that flexibility in the labor market in Korea has certainly weakened the enterprise-based labor movement, but at the same time, the current crisis has rekindled attempts to reregulate at the industry and central levels. Many industry or occupational associations are transforming themselves into industrial unions. However as limited as its role may be, the Tripartite Commission denotes the mechanism of consensus politics at the national level. In order to place these changes in the proper context, this chapter begins with a brief discussion of Korean labor reform before the crisis, followed by an overview of the labor market outcomes of the crisis and changes in labor relations. The conclusion will discuss major findings and their implications.

PRECRISIS LABOR REFORM

Facing competitive market pressures abroad, the Korean government attempted to institute a flexible labor market and industrial relations system in the early 1990s. The Korean economy at the time was more tightly integrated into the globalizing world economy. The pace of trade liberalization had been accelerated since the late 1980s, when Korea began to generate current account surpluses. In addition to import liberalization and tariff reductions, foreign direct investment (FDI) notification procedures were simplified, and sectors eligible for FDI were expanded. In this context, employers were increasingly constrained by volatile competition in the product market, and thus were burdened by the rigid rules and high wages of internal labor markets.

An inflexible internal labor market in core sectors of the economy was the outcome of the democratic labor movement in the late 1980s. Democratization in 1987 brought about changes in labor law that abolished the minimum membership requirement for union organization, thus providing more favorable conditions for workers to organize and bargain collectively. As a result, the number of legally recognized unions and union membership grew rapidly: the number of local enterprise unions almost tripled and the number of union members doubled during 1987–89. More than two-thirds of the workers in large firms with more than five hundred employees were organized when the overall organizational rate reached its peak in 1989. The unionization rate of firms employing less than three hundred workers also tripled during the same period, but only one-tenth of these workers were members of trade unions. Highly organized core workers substantially reduced the discretionary power of management by requiring that some of the institutional rules be jointly decided by union and management.

The Korean economy is composed of a very small number of gigantic firms and a huge number of small- and medium-sized firms. Only large firms were able to afford costly concessions such as stable employment and high wages. In addition, workers in small- and medium-sized firms possessed too little organization and bargaining power to enjoy the kinds of working conditions that core workers in large firms enjoyed. Because of the fragmented bargaining structure, vigorous enterprise union activities that pushed for stable employment and greater wage gains for their own members inevitably brought about dualist tendencies in the economy. Core workers in large firms were thus able to improve their material welfare and reduced the intrafirm welfare gap between production workers and managerial employees. Meanwhile, however, this process increased the interfirm welfare gap, as most unorganized workers in small- and medium-sized firms were not able to do the same. National labor organizations, especially the Korean Confederation of Trade Unions (KCTU), became dissatisfied with the growing wage and welfare gap between large and smaller firms, which impeded a unified political labor movement. The KCTU aimed to restructure enterprise-based unions into industry-based ones that could go beyond the confines of enterprise unionism and strengthen the political power of labor.

The revision of the labor law in December 1996 reflects a compromise between labor and management that was not immune to the impacts of globalization (Lee and Lee, 2001a).[4] Employers wanted to eliminate rigid rules and regulations governing the internal labor markets in core sectors of the economy in order to flexibly contract and deploy their labor force in response to volatile market pressures. A new macroeconomic environment that could jeopardize job opportunities also threatened the labor movement, so labor aimed to strengthen the autonomy of unions and to reduce the level of state intervention. The revised individual labor law legalized corporate layoffs for business reasons with a two-year grace period, introduced a flexible work hour system, and provided legal provisions for activating part-time work. The collective labor law promoted labor rights by eliminating authoritarian labor codes designed to discourage concerted collective action by workers. More specifically, the law legalized multiple trade unions (immediately for industrial or national level unions, and for enterprise-level unions, by the year 2002), allowed political activities of trade unions, and removed the provision that prohibited third-party engagement in collective bargaining and other disputes. The labor movement refused to accept the new labor law and launched general strikes during the winter of 1996. The government made a few concessions in the final round of labor law reform in March 1997, as it strove to mitigate growing discontent among workers. As a result, conditions for corporate layoffs became more restrictive.

Precisely because the new labor law was designed to serve the demands of both labor and management, the law pleased neither party.[5] For employers, the revised law failed to bring about the flexibility employers needed. With a union present at the workplace, it was still hard to lay off workers. For workers, the law provided provisions that could undermine their job security and did not fully extend teachers' and public servants' rights to organize and bargain collectively. The institutional configuration of the new law, however, significantly shaped labor market outcomes and changes in industrial relations after the financial crisis. On the one hand, the new institutional environment certainly improved labor market flexibility. Facing a mild economic recession in early 1997, employers extensively used part-time and temporary workers while reducing the number of regular workers. On the other hand, the new law recognized the formerly illegal national labor organization, the KCTU, allowing the organization to participate in the Tripartite Commission after the crisis.

LABOR MARKET AFTER THE CRISIS

The financial crisis brought about a sharp economic slowdown and financial and corporate sector restructuring that drove many firms to bankruptcy or temporary closing. In the financial sector, more than four hundred insolvent institutions had been either closed or suspended from operating by early 2000. Since most banks were forced to meet the Bank for International Settlements (BIS) capital adequacy ratio of 8 percent, they were hesitant to issue new loans even to solvent firms. This credit squeeze closed down a large number of small- and medium-sized firms, and several *chaebols* (Korean industrial conglomerates) also filed for bankruptcy protection. Due to high debt-to-equity ratios, Korean *chaebols* were especially vulnerable to cyclical downturns and changes in debt servicing costs (IMF 1998). *Chaebols* thus had to reduce their debt leverage, which inevitably led to massive layoffs and other measures of employment adjustment. As a result, fundamental changes in labor market institutions began to take place.

Thanks to impressive economic performance leading up to the financial crisis, Korea was accustomed to near full employment for several decades. Compressed industrial transformation in Korea constantly created new jobs in nonagricultural sectors of the economy. After a period of relative stability during the early 1980s, the demand for labor increasingly outstripped supply (OECD 1994b). The unemployment rate thus fell to 2.5 percent in 1988, and remained near or below that level through 1997. This employment trend, however, was radically reversed by the severe economic recession in 1998. When the unemployment rate soared to 6.8 percent in 1998, it was an enormous shock to Korea, particularly since its so-called natural rate of unemployment had been substantially lower than that estimated for other OECD countries.

A remarkable change occurred in the manufacturing sector in 1998, which shed 590,000 jobs in just a year. Although its employment share has fallen slightly since 1989, the manufacturing sector experienced the fastest growth in demand for labor over several decades. An equally important change was the decrease of employment in the construction sector. With 346,000 jobs lost, employment in the construction sector fell below the level of 1992. These two sectors accounted for almost 1 million job losses in 1998. At the same time, jobs in the personal and public sector increased slightly, reflecting the effect of the massive public works programs. In sum, the financial crisis accelerated the decline of employment in those sectors of the economy that had played a major role in sustaining Korea's rapid economic growth.

The unemployment rate gradually decreased to 3.7 percent in 2001, but the decline in unemployment was accompanied by a worsening employment structure. The proportion of temporary and daily workers in the total employed increased from 41.9 percent in 1995 to 51.3 percent in 2001.[6] The growth of nonstandard employment was most conspicuous in the banking sector, traditionally known for providing the most "secure" jobs in Korea. In just two years after the financial crisis, Korean banks reduced 35 percent of their regular work force. As a result, the proportion of temporary/part-time workers grew rapidly, from 11.8 percent in 1997 to 21.8 percent in 1999. Irregular workers in the banking sector attracted public and media attention, as some of them were previously employees of the same banks who were laid off due to the financial crisis. Despite their temporary/part-time status, their job descriptions and working hours were not vastly different from those of regular workers. The increasing size of the nonstandard work force has raised concern because these jobs pay low wages, provide few benefits and social insurance, and do not have implicit guarantees of long-term employment. Labor laws governing social protection for workers often do not apply to those in nonstandard arrangements. Furthermore, even if laws provided such protection, employers often violated them.

Tight labor market conditions combined with strong union power during the past decade substantially increased real wages. The government tried to restrain wage growth using target guidelines, which unexpectedly complicated the compensation structure with various allowances. Employee compensation in Korea is composed of regular earnings, bonuses, and overtime payments. Although cumbersome to implement, the compensation structure allowed for wage flexibility, which made it easy for firms to adjust. Bonus and overtime payments have been more sensitive than regular wages to fluctuations in economic conditions (OECD 1998). These payments shrunk by more than 15 percent right after the financial crisis, but immediately bounced back to normal increase rates when the economy later resumed growth. After the financial crisis, nominal wages grew more slowly than labor productivity. The wage gap between production workers and managerial/white collar employees has also begun to widen since 1998 because production workers suffered more severe pay cuts due to the drastic reduction in overtime working hours.

DECLINE OF ENTERPRISE UNIONISM

Ever since the financial crisis, the Korean government has consistently implemented market-based economic reforms. With structural adjustment a top priority, the government firmly believed that the most fundamental labor reform was one that aimed to improve labor market flexibility, which would in turn create both efficiency and employment.[7] This approach naturally led to intensifying industrial conflicts. Hence, the established Korean industrial relations system experienced a major crisis and, at the same time, was given an opportunity to rise above the usual enterprise unionism.

The scope of unionization is one of the most general indicators of trade union strength, as higher union density diminishes free-rider problems and thus facilitates concerted collective action. After reaching the highest rate of 18.6 percent in 1989, union density has steadily declined since 1990, when economic growth began to slow and the trade surplus turned into a deficit. The financial crisis in 1997 temporarily deepened the decline of union membership, which represented only 11.2 percent of the total work force. Employers who could no longer absorb wage increases because of fierce domestic and international product market competition became much less tolerant of the costs of unionization, and thus workers had to pay more attention to employment security than union organization. The falling ratio of union organization reflected job losses in heavily unionized sectors of the economy. In 2000, union membership stabilized at 12 percent, but the representation gap between large firms and small- and medium-sized firms remained significant. Whereas the unionization rate of firms with more than three hundred employees reached a record high of 70.9 percent, only 1.1 percent of workers in firms employing less than a hundred workers were organized.

Falling unionization does not necessarily diminish labor disputes. Many cross-national quantitative and case studies have argued similarly, specifying the mechanisms by which highly organized labor or some labor presence in government fosters cooperation between industrial actors in wage bargaining. The Korean case after the financial crisis confirms that decentralized and weak labor unions during the period of structural adjustment are more susceptible to industrial conflicts. The number of annual labor disputes, which had averaged about one hundred during the mid-1990s, more than doubled, increasing to 198 in 1999 and 250 in 2000. Not surprisingly, most strikes were provoked by layoffs and other measures of employment adjustment. In response to unfair labor practices such as delaying wage payments and discharging trade union leaders, unlawful labor disputes were widespread. Labor relations in large manufacturing firms, where internal labor markets and enterprise welfarism previously protected workers, became particularly confrontational as these firms implemented structural reforms and employment adjustment.

Industrial conflict at Hyundai Motor Company (HMC) is a case in point.[8] In May 1998, management announced that it had to lay off 8,189 workers due to a plunge in domestic demand and a 40 percent fall in production. Conflicts between labor and management deepened when management actually notified 1,538 employees that they would be discharged. Because HMC was the symbol of Korean economic success and Korea's leading export firm, prolonged confrontations brought about increasing pressure from the government. With intensive mediation efforts by the minister of labor and representatives of the ruling National Congress for New Politics, labor and management forged a compromise in August. Management laid off 277 workers and offered long-term unpaid leaves for the remaining 1,261 workers. Labor relations at HMC, however, did not stabilize afterward. Management was displeased with the union's interference in the legally approved layoffs. Rank-and-file workers were angered by the HMC union leadership's decision to accept layoffs in addition to 13.8 percent pay cuts. The union was frustrated by management's reluctance to accept the union's work-sharing plan, as well as by diminishing support from its workers.

If the enterprise can be thought of as a single economy, an enterprise union is an encompassing organization in microcosm. The membership of enterprise unions typically includes all regular production workers, as most large companies usually adopt a union-shop policy. The enterprise union usually pays exclusive attention to the affairs of the enterprise without concern for national policy issues, as the goal of the union is to win concrete economic gains for regular workers via high profitability of the firm. The lifetime employment system was one of the most central mechanisms by which enterprise unions could secure rank-and-file support and contain dissent. The introduction of layoffs severely damaged the precarious balance between pragmatic enterprise unionism and industrial peace. Some enterprise unions have tried to prevent massive layoffs by allowing firms to utilize a growing number of temporary workers. However, as those workers with temporary contracts established their own unions, the conflicts between regular enterprise unions and temporary workers' unions surfaced more frequently, and many temporary workers devalued the enterprise unions' capacity for interest representation.[9]

The weakening power of enterprise unions at the workplace is well reflected in the growing "individualization" of employment relationships. After the financial crisis, Korean employers became much more aggressive in benchmarking American management strategies. They experimented with various personnel procedures that linked pay to individual performance, which was very different from the traditional seniority-based wage system. According to a survey of 543 firms employing more than a hundred workers (Lee 2001), about 33.5 percent of firms have implemented the merit-based pay system. It should be noted, however, introduction of a new pay system did not necessarily mean the abolishment of the seniority element in the total pay. Enterprise unions were also adversely affected by the industrial relations and human resource administrations of foreign-based multinational companies (MNCs). MNCs usually did not understand Korean employers' practice of paying full-time enterprise union officers and refused to follow the practice.[10] Because of limited enterprise union funds at small- and medium-sized firms, these unions generally could not survive without employers' financial support. One viable way of solving this problem would be to establish encompassing industrial unions.

PRESSURE TOWARD CENTRALIZATION

The two national-level labor organizations, the Federation of Korean Trade Unions (FKTU) and especially the militant KCTU, have long attempted to improve the organizational power of the labor movement by promoting industrial unionism. Both organizations, facing financial problems because of reduced union dues, grew keenly aware of the weakness of enterprise unionism. Furthermore, employers were eager to reduce labor costs and, on the grounds that cheaper labor was necessary for economic survival, demanded concessions from their unions after the financial crisis. During a moment of concession bargaining, one possible compromise was for union workers to give up future earnings in exchange for employment security. However, even those firms that officially promised unions that they would guarantee job security failed to come through on their word, provoking strikes and protests. In addition, management demanded a wide variety of concessions, such as greater flexibility in job assignments, work rules, and wages.

It was in this process that the limitations of enterprise unionism loomed large. The banking sector, which experienced one of the most severe employment adjustments, best illustrates how the loosely connected enterprise unions were led to form an industrial union that could represent the interests of workers across all banks. There were clear divisions between those enterprise unions that faced the danger of structural and employment adjustments and those unions that did not. For example, employees in such strong banks as Korea Exchange Bank and Shinhan Bank had little incentive to participate in strikes against structural adjustment, as their banks were growing even faster than before, partly because of the dismal performance of insolvent banks such as Seoul Bank and Korea First Bank. In this situation, the establishment of an industrial union was the best way to coordinate conflicting interests and to improve the welfare of workers as a whole in this industry.

The banking sector displayed one of the most contentious examples of labor relations. The forced merger between the five weakest and strongest banks in June 1998 prompted the employees of the liquidated banks to worry about job losses.[11] The five banks to be closed included four provincial banks—Daedong, Dongnam, Kyungki, and Chungchong—plus Dongwha, which was established by North Korean émigrés. The five strongest banks were Shinhan, Boram, Kookmin, Hana, and Korea Housing Bank. The trade unions in the weak banks refused to cooperate with the new owners and violently protested by demanding reemployment guarantees. Conflicts between labor and management were no less significant at other banks. After intensive negotiations with their trade unions, nine commercial banks barely reached an agreement to reduce 32 percent of the labor force by the end of 1998. To avoid a repeat of such concession bargaining that brought about massive layoffs, unions in the banking sector formed the Korea Financial Industry Union in March 2000.

When the second phase of the financial restructuring plan was made known to the public in 2000, the Korea Financial Industry Union vehemently protested against the establishment of financial holding companies, which again would lead to another round of employment adjustments. As sixty-five thousand bank unionists threatened to walk off their jobs, the government finally reached an agreement with the union. Although the union had to accept the plan to launch financial holding companies, the government pledged not to initiate forced mergers of banks and to honor the collective bargaining agreements between labor and management regarding work force reduction and downsizing branch offices. However, the ongoing mergers between banks made it hard for the government to keep this promise, and labor relations in the industry have not stabilized.

The Korea Financial Industry Union accomplished the first "unified" collective bargaining agreement between twenty-four bank presidents and twenty-four union branch office presidents in 2001. As the employers in the banking sector were not organized, all forty-eight representatives participated in the bargaining process. Through coordinated bargaining, management and union negotiators decided on a 5.5 percent wage increase rate and forged a new "skill training" agreement. The branch offices of the union were delegated to deal with the remaining bargaining issues such as fringe benefits and other company welfare provisions. In Korea, very few industry unions were able to conduct industry-level collective bargaining. Despite the lack of employers' associations, the Korea Financial Industry Union has made more progress in coordinating bargaining activities.

Table 6.1 demonstrates that enterprise-based collective bargaining has been slowly evolving into industry-level bargaining. Table 6.2 shows that a large number of industrial/occupational federations are taking steps to

TABLE 6.1. CHANGES IN COLLECTIVE BARGAINING STRUCTURE, 1995–1999

	Company-level bargaining	Associational bargaining*	Not relevant
1995	88.1	11.6	0.3
1996	87.4	12.2	0.4
1997	84.5	14.9	0.6
1998	84.7	14.6	0.7
1999	84.1	15.2	0.7

* Associational bargaining includes industry-level bargaining as well as the most popular form of bargaining arrangements between company-level unions or their umbrella union organizations and individual employers.

Source: Ministry of Labor, Organizational Characteristics of National Labor Unions, 1995 to 1999.

TABLE 6.2. INDUSTRIAL UNIONS UNDER TWO NATIONAL CENTERS, THE FKTU VS. KCTU

	Federation of Korean Trade Unions	Korean Confederation of Trade Unions
Number of Unions	4,501	1,341
Number of Union Members	888,503	586,809
Industrial Federations	**Bank and Finance** (Mar. 2000) **Taxi** (April 2000) *Electrical* *Railway* *Post* *Tobacco and Ginseng* *Art* *Teachers and School Workers* *Chemical *Metal *Textile Communications Port and Transport Automobile Rubber State-Invested Industry Foreign Organization Tourist Industry Public Construction Apartment Urban Railway Seafarer Mine Printing Food Industry Public Service Medical	**Hospital** (Feb. 1998) **University Workers** (Nov. 1998) **Teachers** (1989) **Cargo Transport** (Feb. 1999) **Construction** (Dec. 1999) **Metal** (Feb. 2001) **Press** (Sept. 2000) *Clerical and Financial Workers *Public Transportation Service *Commercial *Tourist *Chemical-Textile (2005) Women Workers Taxi Facility Management University Lecturers Bus

Note: Industrial Federations written in **Bold** indicate that they have already evolved into industrial unions. Those written in *Italics* indicate that they are occupational trade unions classified as small-size industrial unions. Those denoted by * indicate that they are about to become industrial unions.

upgrade or merge with other federations. The KCTU, which is ahead of the FKTU in establishing industrial unions, is planning to reorganize its industrial federations into eight industrial unions by the year 2005. The prospects for coordination at the industry level are, however, still not very promising. Most of all, Korean employers are poorly organized. Except for the Korea Employers Federation (KEF), which is organized at the national level and specializes in labor-management relations, employers are not in a position to engage in industry bargaining. Even with comparable occupational organizations, they have usually refused to bargain with industrial unions.

This attitude of employers was the major obstacle to the establishment of an industry-level bargaining structure by the Korean Health and Medical Workers Union. Established in 1998, the Korean Health and Medical Workers Union comprises 170 local unions and more than forty thousand members. The union has continuously asked the Korean Hospital Association to participate in industry-level negotiations, but the association has consistently refused to do so. With more than six hundred member hospitals, the association is certainly capable of playing the role of representative bargaining partner. One of the major barriers to industry bargaining in this sector was tremendous heterogeneity among members of the association. The KCTU, with which the Korean Health and Medical Workers Union is affiliated, is strongly demanding that the government devise institutional preconditions that can bolster sound industry bargaining.

The lack of support on the part of enterprise unions is another formidable barrier that delays coordination and centralization of the bargaining structure. Some enterprise union leaders have been quite hesitant about relinquishing their bargaining rights to industrial unions. This problem is more obvious in those sectors of the economy where firms are heterogeneous in terms of their size and bargaining power. The Korean Metal Workers Union, formed in February 2001, best illustrates this point. Large metal sector enterprise unions, especially those that would contribute to the union's transition to industrial unionism, that is, HMC, Hyundai Heavy Industries, and Daewoo Heavy Industries, have not yet joined the union. As a result, only one-fifth of total metal sector workers were members of the union, and the Metal Workers Union still coexists with the Korean Metal Workers Federation.

EXPERIMENTS WITH TRIPARTISM

It has been a longtime priority of the Korean government to replace confrontational labor-management relations with more cooperative systems.

During the past one or two decades, the Korean government has made a great deal of effort to spawn several tripartite initiatives at the national level that could bring about wage restraints and industrial peace. Most of them, however, have been unsatisfactory. Underlying these initiatives was usually a political agenda more than economic motives. The first attempt was made by the Economic Planning Board (EPB), which proposed the National Wage Council in 1989.[12] Because of strong resistance by the FKTU, this proposal did not materialize. The FKTU suspected the council would just be another attempt to disguise and impose the same "wage guidelines" of the past and did not want to be seen as a willing participant. As an alternative, the FKTU proposed the National Economic and Social Council in 1990. This new council, composed of representatives of labor, business, and public interests, dealt with a wide range of industrial and welfare policies. Since the council excluded wage policy from its agenda, however, its role in economic policy-making was fairly limited.

As the economic downturn in the early 1990s provoked a sense of crisis, the FKTU and KEF reached agreements on wage increase rates in April 1993 and again in March 1994. However, these agreements discontinued afterward. Rank-and file members of trade unions were extremely critical of their leadership's decision to participate in the government's wage stabilization policies. The Presidential Commission on Industrial Relations Reform in 1996 broadened the scope of the tripartite process in Korea by inviting representatives of the then-illegal KCTU. The commission extensively discussed the pending issues of labor law reform, but the government revised the labor law as it saw fit without considering the recommendations of the commission in December 1996. This labor law reform process triggered nationwide strikes and protests, as well as the decline of the commission in the eyes of the general public.

Despite the government's strong desire to institute corporatist policy-making concertation, sheltered microcorporatism dominated the most strategically important sectors of the economy, and the national industrial relations system in general was extremely adversarial (Lee 1998). It was only after the financial crisis that the government was able to forge a rather stable tripartite institution at the national level.

The pivotal political problem of economic reform after the financial crisis had to do with the significant transitional costs involved in structural adjustment. As the IMF imposed far-reaching structural reforms alongside austerity policies, the government had to follow suggestions attached to the IMF's lending program, which required comprehensive restructuring of the financial sector, increasing transparency in corporate governance, and flexibility in the labor market. This dilemma deepened when sudden economic downturns accompanied intensive reform efforts and, as a result, coordination of the conflicting interests and diverging views of major producer groups was urgently required. The Tripartite Commission was established to smooth out the process of economic restructuring in January 1998. The proclaimed goal of this tripartite institution thus was to strengthen national competitiveness and cohesion, via "fair burden-sharing" among social partners.

The Tripartite Commission, created as a presidential advisory body, was composed of representatives from the government, the two trade union confederations—the FKTU and the KCTU—and the national-level employers' associations, the FKI (Federation of Korean Industries) and the KEF. After releasing the "Tripartite Joint Statement on Fair Burden-Sharing in the Process of Overcoming the Economic Crisis" on January 20, 1998, the commission forged a detailed social pact on February 9, 1998, which encompassed ninety items and twenty-one additional issues to be discussed. The foremost concern of the commission was to advance labor market flexibility, for which labor's cooperation was vital.

Table 6.3 summarizes the core contents of a social pact agreed on by social partners in February 1998. The most significant "political exchange" in the pact was the consent by the labor sector to accept employment adjustment, in return for the government's promise to expand public expenditure for the social safety net and improve basic labor rights. The commission agreed on the revision of the Labor Standards Act to ease the procedures for laying off workers due to urgent managerial reasons and introduced a draft act for employment of dispatched workers to replace temporary vacancies.[13] At the same time, a total of 5 trillion won was allocated for various unemployment measures, and freedom of association and political activities of trade unions were more extensively guaranteed. *Chaebols* were also obliged to improve corporate financial structure and transparency and establish a responsible management system. Wage restraint was not a critical issue in the pact of 1998 because trade unions had already engaged in pervasive concession bargaining that entailed pay freezes and reduction of welfare allowances. Furthermore, the complicated employee compensation structure composed of regular earnings, bonuses, allowances, and overtime payments allowed for wage flexibility that made it easy for firms to adjust.[14]

Capital market integration in general has constrained the capacity of governments to run deficits and pursue inflationary monetary policies (Iversen 2000), but the Korean government at the time had the added problem of being under the vigilant scrutiny of international financial institutions. The government was mostly deprived of policy means to

TABLE 6.3. TRIPARTITE AGREEMENT OF 1998: CORE CONTENTS OF "POLITICAL EXCHANGE"

Labor	State	Capital
PROMOTE LABOR MARKET FLEXIBILITY Ease the procedures for laying off workers Legalize temporary work agencies	STRENGTHEN SOCIAL SAFETY NETS Allocate 5 trillion won for unemployment measures Reform the health insurance system and expand coverage	INITIATE CORPORATE RESTRUCTURING AND *Establish a Responsible Management System* Develop workers' participation schemes
	IMPROVE BASIC LABOR RIGHTS Legalize trade unions' right to engage in political activities Legalize the Teachers' Union Establish work councils for government officials	
PROMOTE LABOR-MANAGEMENT COOPERATION	PROMOTE LABOR-MANAGEMENT COOPERATION Establish labor-management cooperation center Guarantee and support free collective bargaining between labor and management	PROMOTE LABOR-MANAGEMENT COOPERATION Invest more in workers' training programs

satisfy social partners, especially labor. Instead, the state provided labor with some opportunities to coregulate postcrisis labor market outcomes and employment relations. Several special committees established to discuss these matters usually comprised members of labor unions and employers' associations, government officials, academics, and labor experts who represented "public interests." For example, the second Tripartite Commission was launched in June 1998 with four committees specialized in the following areas: economic reform, employment, labor relations, and social welfare. In the third Tripartite Commission inaugurated in September 1999, four special committees that deal with public sector and financial sector restructuring, unfair labor practices, and working hour reduction were added to its structure.

The government's efforts to institute cooperative labor management relationships at the national level, however, have met with many obstacles. The temporary accord began to show signs of disintegration when massive layoffs and wage cuts aggravated worker discontent. Although it is true no social accord could endure such pervasive layoffs and concession bargaining, a more fundamental reason for the currently stymied Tripartite Commission lies in the fact that Korea lacks institutional preconditions for neocorporatist policy-making. Neither of the two labor confederations in Korea was an encompassing organization with direct decision-making power over its members. More important, policy-making concertation also requires a system of formal politics that inspires confidence in both parties that the terms of bargaining can be enforced. Because of a long history of confrontational industrial relations, the institutional setting for the necessary reciprocity and trust to develop was not available.

Relatively well-organized trade unions with the capacity to coordinate the diverging interests of their members are one of the most important prerequisites of new corporatism. Unfortunately, because of the legacy of authoritarian labor law that reinforced the division and decentralization of the labor movement, this crucial element of corporatist coordination has always been absent in Korea. In addition, national union leadership was split into two federations, the FKTU and the more militant KCTU. The FKTU, which was at one time a political supporter of past authoritarian regimes, was able to rebuild its tainted public image after 1987 when dissident labor leaders seriously challenged its leadership. For some workers, however, reform efforts by the FKTU were not considered significant enough to bring about an improvement in workers' political power (Kim 1994). Labor activists who aimed to create an alternative national federation that could eventually replace the FKTU and its business unionism established the KCTU. Both federations participated in the Tripartite Commission at the beginning, but the KCTU eventually withdrew from the commission as its members strongly denounced the leadership's decision to reach an agreement that made it easier to lay off workers. The tripartite agreement of 1998 thus became defective, and the Tripartite Commission has been critically impaired by the absence of the KCTU.

The institutional features of the trade union movement also made it hard to represent the interests of labor as a whole in joint policy-making processes. Labor could not articulate its core demands with national trade union leadership divided and each federation suffering from internal conflicts. Due to low union density and its skewed concentration in the large-firm sector, there were no formal channels through which the interests of marginal workers could be voiced. Protection for the irregular work force is a case in point. After the financial crisis, nonstandard forms of work and employment significantly expanded. While enterprise unions in general did not accept workers with a temporary status, some enterprise unions tried to prevent layoffs of regular workers by allowing firms to utilize a growing number of temporary workers. Meanwhile, in February 2001, the Tripartite Commission agreed to an additional five-year grace period before introducing multiple trade unions at the enterprise level. Because of this decision, the right of irregular workers to organize their own unions at the enterprise level was not fully guaranteed until the year 2007.

It is obvious that labor is not entirely responsible for the problems and stalemates in the Tripartite Commission. Above all, the government and social partners were inundated with too many detailed items that required immediate settlements. It was an understandable situation, considering the fact that Korea lacked the mesolevel bargaining arrangements to which some of the issues to be discussed could have been delegated. There were times when the social partners were able to agree on reform proposals, but the ruling party could not submit the bill to the National Assembly. In some cases the government also lacked proper administrative capacity to implement the agreed labor reforms, mostly because of interdepartmental conflicts. Considering that Korea has strong statist roots and limited collective action capacity of labor, and the fact that the tripartite arrangement was initiated by the government, state leadership is a much more critical factor in determining the outcome of corporatist policies.

In the Tripartite Commission, business was more a reluctant participant than an active leader, despite the fact that the two powerful national-level employers' associations—the FKI and the KEF—were involved.[15] Of these two, the FKI was the most influential employers' organization, representing the interests of powerful *chaebols*. It was the FKI that organized the KEF, which specialized in labor-management relations. Business was passive in the commission partly because employers had advantages over workers in many dimensions, and thus they were not solely dependent on the tripartite arrangement to achieve their policy goals.

After the social pact was forged in 1998, Korea made a spectacular comeback in terms of macroeconomic performance. Macroeconomic indicators have substantially improved, although no direct causal relationship could be assumed between the social pact and economic recovery. Because of the financial crisis, Korea's GDP shrank 6.8 percent in 1998, but it immediately bounced back to its normal growth rate of 10.9 percent the following year. The exchange rate has also stabilized with usable foreign reserves already surpassing $45 billion in October 1998. As promised in the social pact, the government also increased public spending on social safety net programs.

Public expenditure on labor market programs was almost negligible in Korea before the financial crisis. Throughout the 1990s, Korea spent less than 0.1 percent of GDP on these programs, one of the lowest rates in the OECD area. The small amount of spending during this period reflects the low level of unemployment and its relatively short average duration (OECD 1998, 148). But this picture significantly changed after the crisis. Although slightly lower than the OECD average, Korean public expenditure on unemployment measures expanded to 1.87 percent of GDP in 1999. One notable feature of public spending on unemployment measures by Korea was that more was spent on active measures than on passive income support. Except for Sweden, Norway, Portugal, and Italy, the share of spending on passive measures was far greater than on active measures in most OECD countries. On the one hand, it is a promising sign that Korea is in line with the general principle of shifting public resources from income support to active labor market policies, a strategy that has been endorsed by many labor ministers in developed countries (Martin 1998). On the other hand, social assistance programs in Korea are generally underdeveloped with numerous cutoff levels for eligibility and restrictions on entitlement. Under such conditions, the proportion of public spending on passive income support should be increased.

The tripartite experiment in Korea, however, did not pay enough attention to the widening income gap among socioeconomic groups. In 1999, about 6.8 percent of all urban households suffered extreme poverty, with their income falling far short of the minimum cost of living (KLI 1999). The public assistance program at the time only covered about 3 to 4 percent of the population. The impact of the economic crisis and social policies on various socioeconomic groups differed. Although the middle class or regular workers employed in the core manufacturing sector may have suffered relatively large drops in living standards, the very poor were more severely affected when left unsupported.

What the government eventually aimed to achieve in the tripartite arrangement was to replace chronic antagonism between labor, capital, and the state with institutionalized cooperative relations. In this regard, the social pact was not successful. The number of labor disputes continued to grow after the financial crisis. Throughout the process of implementing tripartism, conflicts and divisions within the trade union movement added to existing confrontations between labor and capital. After the KCTU left the commission and protested against the government's structural adjustment policies on the streets, the relationship between the KCTU and the government irrevocably worsened. At the enterprise level, conflicts between regular workers protected by enterprise unions and irregular workers who enjoyed no such protection began to surface more frequently. In addition, due to the government's inability to follow and activate what was agreed on at the national level, labor groups increasingly regarded the government and its policies with deep distrust.

While tripartism at the national level remained at a stalemate, a regional tripartite commission was first established in 2000. This regional effort was known as the Seoul model, as this commission involved public firms that belonged to Seoul Metropolitan City, as well as union leaders at these enterprises. Among them, it was the president of the Seoul Subway Labor Union (SSLU) who actually suggested the formation of a regional tripartism in Seoul. The regional commission debated issues such as wage levels and working conditions, social policies that affect workers' job security, workers' participation schemes in managerial affairs, and methods to prevent labor disputes (Lee and Lee 2001b). However, the Seoul model has not been free from the deficient institutional preconditions that also adversely affected the National Tripartite Commission. The Seoul model was initiated without the support of rank-and-file members. Quite a few union members even labeled the president of SSLU's leadership a sellout. Furthermore, excluding the SSLU and the Seoul Metropolitan Subway Labor Union (SMSLU), participation by other enterprise unions has been disappointing.

CONCLUSIONS

Since the economic crisis at the end of 1997, the Korean labor market experienced tremendous shocks and surprises. The unemployment rate skyrocketed, and increased flexibility put more and more workers in precarious employment situations. The thorniest issue in implementing the IMF structural adjustment program was the significant social cost, which was not evenly distributed among different socioeconomic groups. The crucial policy dilemma here was that it was extremely difficult for a country like Korea, which had only recently attained a state of basic welfare, to simultaneously achieve flexibility in labor markets and social protection for workers.[16] Naturally, conflicts and confrontations dominated labor relations, and the Korean industrial relations system was in a state of transition. This study points to the following three findings of practical implications.

First, the economic crisis and the ensuing labor market environment have placed enterprise unions on the defensive. With rapidly declining union bargaining power, concession bargaining continued for a while. The results of such bargaining made industrial relations more rigid and confrontational, instead of creating a cooperative and "flexible" industrial environment. The labor movement, however, has not unilaterally weakened. Whereas labor unions, during times of economic prosperity, paid most of their attention to setting wage rates high and improving company-provided benefits, current union leadership is now concentrating on issues that are more broadly related to employment, welfare, and working conditions for all workers. The KCTU and FKTU's decision to focus on improving social welfare and its renewed attempt to increase minimum wage rates for marginal workers well indicate the changes in the policy direction of national union leadership.

The second finding is related to the first. Since the enterprise union system did not appropriately represent the interests of all workers, especially those workers in nonstandard arrangements, union leadership strove to develop industrial unionism. Some collective bargaining agreements in individual enterprises do not cover atypical workers, which provide employers with incentives to replace regular workers. In addition, as the case of the banking sector labor movement demonstrates, individual enterprise unions can be divided over the issue of employment adjustments. The fear of massive layoffs drove the effort to organize at the industry level. However, it is still too early to assess the sustainability and future of industrial unionism in Korea. There is also the possibility that only a few industrial unions will survive, while other enterprise unions remain divided. Furthermore, collective bargaining is still predominantly taking place at the enterprise level even after many of these enterprise unions were transformed into branch offices of an industrial union.

Third, it is therefore necessary to bring some "coordination" into the industrial relations system, by encouraging social dialogue between labor and management. The lack of coordination in the Korean industrial relations system has aggravated labor disputes and conflicts on distributional issues at the workplace, which again led to increasing wages and welfare gaps between the organized and the unorganized, and between regular and nonstandard workers. The Tripartite Commission in Korea was the result of President Kim Dae Jung's conviction that the country needed a consensus-building mechanism to overcome financial crisis and restore national competitiveness. The attempt by the government to create a tripartite body had initially received positive reviews from international labor specialists and domestic policy makers, but criticism of the tripartite body grew quickly as the commission's activities failed to meet the expectations of labor and the general public.[17] As the social pact drafted by the Tripartite Commission was forged during the period when neoliberal market reforms were strongly advocated by international financial institutions such as the IMF, the pact was bound to include some variants of policies that promoted labor market flexibility.

In order to broaden the social base that the national-level tripartite body critically lacks, the government should consider encouraging various forms of social compromise at the sector and enterprise level, where coordination of conflicting interests can be more easily realized. The development of mesolevel social dialogue institutions would also support and coordinate the pressures toward bargaining centralization by burgeoning industrial unions in Korea. Tripartism can produce a variety of favorable attributes that improve workplace labor-management relations when effectively implemented with innovative institutional design. New corporatist arrangements developed during the 1990s were capable of introducing workplace changes and various partnership arrangements. Korea needs not be constrained by the rigid national agenda set by the existing tripartite arrangements, and instead should try to explore opportunities to promote social partnership and workplace innovation by broadening the scope of the pact. Social partnership is essential in achieving the triple goal of labor market flexibility, social protection, and cooperative labor relations, which would allow postcrisis Korea to cope with challenges posed by the new competitive economic environment.

7 The Changing Structure of Collective Bargaining in Australia

Marian Baird and Russell D. Lansbury

The past two decades in Australia have been characterized by significant changes in industrial relations institutions and practices. For much of the past century, Australian industrial relations, because of its unique system of conciliation and arbitration, was considered to be among the most centralized of the industrialized market economies. When the Commonwealth of Australia was created in 1901, the constitution empowered the federal government to settle interstate disputes by means of conciliation and arbitration while giving it only limited power to directly enact legislation relating to industrial relations and employment matters (McIntyre and Mitchell 1989). The Commonwealth Court of Conciliation and Arbitration was established in 1904 (later to become the Australian Industrial Relations Commission, AIRC) with the power to conciliate between employers and unions and, if this was not possible, to unilaterally determine the terms and conditions of employment by "equitable awards."

Throughout most of the twentieth century the arbitration tribunals at both federal and state levels operated as quasi-judicial bodies and were to some extent independent of the governments of the day. This system provided the main institutional framework for determining employment conditions. Until the late 1980s, federal and state awards covered around 85 percent of all wage and salary earners, although these tended to set only minimum rates of pay and conditions and permitted the parties to establish supplementary rates by collective bargaining.

Hence, the OECD has referred to the Australian system as one of the "most highly centralized and highly coordinated of wage determination systems" (OECD 2000). The Australian system of conciliation and arbitration was, for many years, supported by all the major political parties as providing benefits for both workers and employers. Business accepted the arbitration system in exchange for tariff protection and industrial stability, while unions gained legitimacy and increased membership as part of the established, state-sanctioned industrial relations system.

In comparison with some other bargaining systems, in theory, the Australian tribunals provided procedures for the orderly settlement of industrial disputes and limited recourse to industrial action. The arbitration system also offered a mechanism whereby broader economic and social concerns (such as equity) could be brought to bear on industrial relations outcomes. Yet critics identified a number of deficiencies in the system, which included failure of the centralized award system to take into account the particular needs of workplaces and enterprises; frequent appeals to tribunals to settle disputes, which undermined efforts at negotiation and bargaining; fragmentation of bargaining through multiunionism at the workplace; and failure of the award system to reduce the number of strikes. Another issue that attracted widespread criticism was the existence of separate federal and state industrial relations jurisdictions, although this is a reflection of the particular division of power in Australia between the federal and state legislatures.

Since the 1980s, the Australian system of industrial relations has undergone several phases of reform as the long-established system of centralized wage determination has been displaced by a period of coordinated, or managed, decentralism (1987–90), followed by coordinated flexibility (1991–96) and the current phase of "fragmented flexibility" (since 1997).

From an international perspective, one of the most interesting aspects of Australian industrial relations has been the transition from a centralized system based on compulsory arbitration administered by the federal (and state) tribunals to a more decentralized approach of bargaining at the enterprise level. The tribunals, the Australian Industrial Relations Commission (AIRC) being the principal one, are quasi-legal courts that regulate and scrutinize employment conditions, assist in resolving industrial disputes, and regulate trade unions and employer associations. A president, vice presidents, deputy presidents, and commissioners who are drawn from industry, unions, and the public service make up the AIRC. Although the government appoints them, their role is theoretically separate from government policy. Traditionally, the role of the commission was to operate as an independent "umpire" in disputes between unions and employers.

During the initial years of the Labor government, led by Bob Hawke (from 1983 to 1986), there was a brief return to centralized wage determination as part of the initial accord. The accord was a bipartite agreement on wages and other matters between the Australian Labor Party (ALP) and the main union body, the Australian Council of Trade Unions (ACTU). Indeed, it was argued by the Hawke government during this period that the breakdown of the centralized wage system during the previous Liberal-National party coalition government (1975–83) had exacerbated economic problems. The Hawke government wanted to avoid the possibility of a renewed wage/price spiral that had characterized earlier periods of more decentralized bargaining. Furthermore, the government commissioned a review of the industrial relations system, chaired by Professor Keith Hancock. The Hancock Report (1985) recommended the retention and consolidation of the centralized system, with the continuation of a major role for the AIRC. This was on the grounds that a centralized system facilitated the enforcement of income policies and thereby helped to contain levels of unemployment and inflation.

However, following a balance of payment crisis and other economic problems in the mid-1980s, the Hawke Labor government abandoned its centralized approach and adopted a policy of coordinated or managed decentralism. In response to worsening economic conditions, the accord partners and the AIRC agreed to abandon full wage indexation in 1986 (Dabscheck 1995).

Subsequently, in 1987 a two-tier wage system was introduced that not only took account of productivity increases at the industry and enterprise levels, but also maintained a system of national wage adjustments. The AIRC retained an important role whereby the National Wage Cases set the framework for enterprise bargaining between unions and employers. The 1988 National Wage Case decision by the AIRC established a "structural efficiency principle" designed to encourage the parties to reach collective agreements, for example, on the introduction of multiskilling, broad-based work classifications, and a reduction of demarcation barriers. This period ushered in greater labor market flexibility while retaining the broad institutional framework.

The seeds of coordinated flexibility were sown in early 1990 when the government, employers, and unions submitted arguments to the AIRC in the National Wage Case that "enterprise bargaining" should become the main process for achieving wage increases. The change of policy by the Labor government and the unions (which had both previously resisted pressure from employers for such reforms) came amid continuing economic uncertainty and a campaign by opposition parties for enterprise-based bargaining. The ACTU and some elements of the union movement now supported managed decentralism because they believed the centralized system had compressed real wages, limited shop floor unionism, and overloaded unions and workers with demands for workplace change (Briggs 2001).

The AIRC initially rejected calls for enterprise bargaining on the grounds that the various parties had different (and contradictory) views on what the new system involved and, furthermore, that they were not ready or "mature" enough to negotiate independently of the tribunal. After intense debate, the AIRC eventually endorsed a more decentralized approach in October 1991. The AIRC retained the capacity to scrutinize agreements to ensure that they met "public interest" criteria. Under pressure from employers, who complained that it was too difficult to achieve enterprise agreements under this system, the government introduced further amendments to the Industrial Relations Act 1986, which reduced the power of the AIRC to veto agreements and widened opportunities for employers to opt out of the traditional award system. However, the AIRC continued to administer a national "safety net" of minimum wages and conditions for lowest paid workers by updating awards and conditions and conducting National Wage Case hearings.

After its surprise election victory in March 1993, the Labor government (under the leadership of Paul Keating) introduced further legal reforms to extend enterprise bargaining with the Industrial Relations Reform Act 1993. Although parts of the act were based on International Labor Organization (ILO) conventions and recommendations, which strengthened employment protection and granted a wider range of minimum entitlements, it also included provisions that facilitated employers making agreements with their employees without involving unions.

Enterprise Flexibility Agreements (EFAs), introduced under the 1993 Reform Act, did not require an eligible union to be involved. Unions opposed EFAs on the grounds that they encouraged employers to avoid unions and facilitated a move toward individual contracts of employment. Such fears were realized in a major dispute during 1995 between a large mining company, Rio Tinto (formerly CRA), and unions at Weipa in the remote north of Australia. This set the pattern for further disputes in the mining and maritime industries during the 1990s, which were designed to break the unions' bargaining strength by persuading workers to accept individual contracts. Hence the period from 1991 to 1996 was one of transition from the collective to more individualized forms of industrial relations, as some employers sought to take full advantage of the more flexible bargaining arrangements that were permitted under the new legislation and the role of the AIRC was significantly diminished.

The most recent phase of industrial relations reform, which has fostered a system of fragmented flexibility, began with the election of the Liberal-National party coalition government led by John Howard in 1996. The Workplace Relations Act 1996 signaled a more radical decentralization of industrial relations to the enterprise level, with broader scope for nonunion agreements, individualized arrangements, and further diminution in the role of the AIRC. A key element of the Workplace Relations Act 1996, embodied in the new Australian Workplace Agreements (AWAs), sought to enable (and encourage) employers to enter into individual (nonunion) contracts with their employees.

To date AWAs have played only a minor role in regulating wages and conditions, and cover only 1.9 percent of employees (ABS 2001, Table 6). AWAs are most attractive to small business (less than one hundred employees), whereas large employers are least likely to use AWAs (Office of the Employee Advocate 2001). The more significant pattern of individualization emerging in Australian industrial relations is the steady increase in the number of employees covered by individual common law contracts of employment, which are neither registered nor necessarily formalized. Employers may prefer these contracts as they are simpler to adopt and, in contrast to AWAs, they do not have to be vetted by a government agent. It is estimated that up to 38 percent of employees have their pay set by such contracts, and they are employed overwhelmingly in the private sector (ABS 2000). Despite their low incidence, the significance of AWAs is arguably in their use by employers as a bargaining lever or threat. For example, in a number of lockouts employers have used AWAs (or the similar Western Australian agreements) as a threat to force concessions from employees and unions during the bargaining process (Ellem 2001).

Under the Workplace Relations Act 1996, the role of the AIRC underwent further significant change. The AIRC's award determinations were restricted to a list of "twenty allowable matters," although it could arbitrate on "exceptional matters." As a result of the legislative and institutional changes, the current arrangements for determining wages and conditions of work in Australia are therefore quite complex and fragmented. There are four main streams of regulation:

1. Awards determined by the commission, which typically also involve a period of negotiations by the employers and unions. These are generally of an industry- (or sector-) wide nature.
2. Enterprise bargaining agreements (EBAs), which are negotiated between a single employer and the union. These are specific to the

company or enterprise, and supplement the award for that industry. In most cases they are negotiated with a union, but there is provision for nonunion collective agreements.
3. Australian Workplace Agreements (AWAs), which are contracts negotiated with an individual employee or a group of employees. Each contract must be signed individually and registered with the Office of the Employment Advocate.
4. Individualized nonregistered agreements, which operate outside the formal industrial relations framework and rely on the common law contract of employment.

Although it is difficult to obtain precise figures, it is currently estimated that approximately 20–23 percent of all employees have their wages and conditions entirely regulated by awards, while 35 percent of employees rely on a combination of awards and collective agreements. The remaining 40 percent of the labor force has their wages and conditions determined mainly by individual arrangements (ABS 2000). This latter change marks an important shift over the past decade or so away from Australia's traditional dependence on awards.

Hence, while there has continued to be a trend toward enterprise-based, single employer, and single union bargaining, this has led neither to a total abandonment of awards nor to the elimination of the AIRC. In addition to different bargaining arrangements, the bargaining agenda has also changed. Over the past five years, for instance, issues such as hours of work, training, health and safety, employee representation, redundancy, and family leave have all become more prevalent in collective bargaining (Buchanan 2002).

THE NATURE, ROLE, AND CONSEQUENCES OF RECENT TRIPARTITE AGREEMENTS OR INTERACTIONS

The Changing Roles of the Industrial Tribunals

It may be argued the traditional forms of conciliation and arbitration in Australia, as exercised by the AIRC and state tribunals, have provided the main vehicle for tripartite interaction and agreements. While the tribunals are not tripartite institutions in the conventional European sense, they have provided opportunities for unions, employers, and governments to discuss and negotiate issues of mutual concern such as national wage levels, wage equity, and leave provisions. Furthermore, the arbitral system has fostered centralization of industrial relations in Australia through National Wage Cases in which all parties are represented.

The system of state-sponsored conciliation and arbitration has not always enjoyed the support of the industrial relations parties. Employers were initially hostile to the establishment of the (then) Commonwealth Court of Conciliation and Arbitration (the forerunner to the AIRC) because it forced them to recognize unions registered under the act and empowered these unions to make claims on behalf of all employers within an industry. Having initially rejected the notion of compulsory arbitration, the unions changed their stance after some disastrous defeats during the strikes of the 1890s. The new federal government (at the turn of the century) was attracted to compulsory arbitration because strikes were becoming a problem as they spread across state borders (McIntyre and Mitchell 1989).

The establishment of systems of conciliation and arbitration at both federal and state levels marked an important departure from the British-style of industrial relations that had characterized colonial Australia in the late nineteenth century. While collective bargaining was supported by many British trade unions as the main channel for achieving agreements with management, and government generally took a passive role, the arbitration model prevailed in Australia. However, the arbitral system did not end the "barbarous expedient of strike action," as H. B. Higgins (an early president of the Arbitration Court) had hoped (Higgins 1915). Industrial relations remained a largely adversarial activity within the tribunals, with each party seeking to convince the arbitrator about the justice of their claims. Indeed, critics of the system have agreed that it enabled the parties to escape responsibilities for their actions as they blamed the arbitrator for breakdowns in negotiations and failures to achieve settlement (Howard 1987).

The Impact of the Accord

The negotiations of an accord between the Australian Labor party (ALP) and the Australian Council of Trade Unions (ACTU) prior to the national elections in 1983, paved the way for a fourteen-year bipartite agreement between successive Labor governments and the trade union movement. Although the accord underwent a number of permeations (known as Mark I to VIII) it was essentially an agreement under which the unions agreed to moderate wage demands (in order to reduce inflation) while the government pledged to retard prices under control (as far as it could), promote employment growth, and increase social welfare provisions. Using the accord framework, Labor governments also began a process of reform that had the effect of decentralizing the industrial relations system and introducing more flexibility in the labor market.

While the accord did not result in the type of corporatism of the kind found in parts of Europe, the close involvement of the unions in the government's economy policy formulation constituted a form of quasi-corporatism. Critics of union leadership argued that the interests of union members were sacrificed for the electoral survival of the Labor government. Certainly, real wages declined in relative terms during the accord period while levels of unemployment rose and the share of GDP accruing to the interests of capital exceeded the share to labor (Davis and Lansbury 1998).

Building on the momentum of the accord, the Labor government established various tripartite committees and councils at national and industry levels. Some, like the Economic Planning and Advisory Council (EPAC), proved to be influential in the determination of government policy. The accord also supported workers' involvement in decision-making and stressed that consultation was necessary to bring about changes at industry, company, and workplace levels (ALP-ACTU 1983, 9). In 1986, the Labor government published *Policy Discussion Paper on Industrial Democracy and Employee Participation.* This paper stated that "employee participation is now a major government priority and the government sees it as essential to a successful response to the significant challenges of the present time" (Department of Employment and Industrial Relations 1986).

The *Policy Discussion Paper* pointed to various alternatives that the government might take in support of industrial democracy, including the enactment of legislation, financial incentives, and assistance; and provision of resources, education, training, and information. However, the government stopped short of passing any legislation but urged employers and unions to directly negotiate arrangements on how participative arrangements should be introduced. The ACTU and the Confederation of Australian Industry (CAI) issued the *Joint Statement on Participative Practices* in 1988 that acknowledged the need to develop more effective employee participation based on information sharing and consultation, but there was no widespread support from either the unions or the employers for legislation or industrial democracy. Hence, at the national level there was no decisive action taken to establish tripartite bodies or mechanisms to achieve fundamental reforms in favor of industrial democracy such as codetermination or works council arrangements, although there has recently been some revival of interest in these issues (McCallum 2001).

The Rise and Decline of Microcorporatism

While there was little progress toward macrocorporatism involving all of the industrial relations parties during the period of Labor government, there were examples of "microcorporatism" undertaken at the industry and company levels. Such microcorporatism refers to government endorsed and formalized tripartite arrangements. Two outstanding cases were the auto manufacturing and steel industries, which were the subject of "strategic plans" developed by the then minister for industry, Senator John Button. These are two important strategic industries that play a major role in the Australian economy and employ large numbers of workers. Both industries received high levels of tariff protection for decades but became inefficient and plagued by poor industrial relations. The government implemented plans to gradually reduce tariffs while modernizing the two industries and introducing major structural changes. In both industries, this involved a high level of cooperation between the government, employers, and unions.

In the steel industry, where there was one major producer, BHP Ltd., the company was guaranteed a minimum of 80 percent of the domestic market for four years in return for a commitment of major capital investment by the company (Kelly and Underhill 1997). For its part, the union agreed to changes in work practices, adherence to dispute procedures, and voluntary redundancies. Management provided extensive training to the workers and a high level of consultation with all concerned parties. Under the Steel Industry Plan, workers were guaranteed there would be no forced redundancies and that any work force reductions would be achieved through voluntary early retirement schemes and labor turnover. BHP established an offsite training center and involved employees and their unions in the process of identifying new skills and job classifications that were related to new pay scales.

Under the Steel Industry Plan there was major investment in new technology that resulted not only in higher productivity and quality, and in a reduction of jobs. The industry was streamlined to make it internationally more competitive, but BHP found it difficult to keep the steel part of its activities operating on a profitable basis. Nevertheless, in collaboration with the unions, new forms of work organization were introduced, which included multiskilled teams and competency-based payment systems. Old distinctions between trades- and nontrades-related work became less relevant with the advent of broader-based job classifications.

Similar reforms have occurred in the automotive manufacturing industry since the mid-1980s (Lansbury and Bamber 1998). There are four assembly plants in Australia owned by Ford, General Motors (Holden), Toyota, and Mitsubishi. As in steel, the government agreed to lower tariff protection gradually in return for the companies upgrading their plant and equipment so that the auto industry in Australia would become more internationally competitive. In cooperation with the unions, the auto companies embarked on a major program of skills development through the establishment of a Vehicle Industry Certificate (VIC). This meant that pay rates became increasingly based on acquired skills and demonstrated levels of competence. Although there has been variation in the pace of change, all the auto companies have embraced the concept of skills-related pay (Bamber and Lansbury 1997).

After the defeat of the Labor government in 1996, not only did the accord between the labor movement and government cease, but also the coalition government abandoned attempts at "microcorporatism," as illustrated by the auto and steel plans. It is unlikely that there will be a return to any forms of tripartite agreements or interaction while the coalition government remains in office. Indeed, the union movement is focused on ensuring its own future survival by developing organizing strategies rather than seeking to develop partnerships or collaboration with employers under whichever political party is in government.

STRATEGIES AND RESPONSES OF UNIONS, EMPLOYERS, AND GOVERNMENT IN REGARD TO RECENT CHANGES IN BARGAINING STRUCTURES

The Federal Government

The strategies adopted by the coalition government since its election have been to reduce the role and power of the trade unions and to strengthen the rights of employers. As noted previously, the Workplace Relations Act 1996 hastened decentralization of bargaining to the enterprise level, reduced scope for award-making by the AIRC, and encouraged individual nonunion agreements. Unlike the previous Labor government that encouraged various forms of tripartism, albeit without legislative changes to foster such developments, the coalition government has emphasized employer-employee arrangements at the enterprise level without union involvement. The Workplace Relations Act 1996 also made it more difficult for unions to organize at the workplace level. Union officials only have access to work sites where they have members and only after they have given notice of their intention to visit. This makes it difficult to organize nonunion sites. It is illegal to have agreements that require employees to belong to unions, which is to say, the closed shop is unlawful.

The 1996 act also permits formal nonunion individual and collective bargaining for the first time. Both of these provisions have the effect of reducing the rights to recognition previously enjoyed by trade unions in Australia.

The 1996 act also impacts on union activity indirectly by privileging a system of single employer bargaining over multiemployer bargaining and arbitration. Unions may use industrial action to support their claims, but the conditions under which they can do so are prescribed, and there have been attempts by the coalition government to further amend the act to limit such action to a single work site. Hence, the Workplace Relations Act 1996 reflects the strategy of the coalition government to circumscribe and limit the role of unions in the workplace. The government has also reduced the formal opportunities for consultation with senior union officials by abandoning the National Labor Consultative Council (NLCC), which was established by the previous Labor government and facilitated dialogue between the Labor government and unions.

Employers

As a result of the negative political and legal climate created by the government toward trade union involvement, there has been a growth in confrontation between some militant employers and unions over the issue of union recognition for bargaining purposes. In Australia there is no legal requirement for employers to bargain "in good faith" with relevant unions. There has been an increase in the use of employer-initiated industrial action to support nonunion agreements among private-sector employers (Ellem 2001). Employers have initiated several high-profile disputes to introduce nonunion agreements in areas such as mining and the maritime industries, which were traditionally strongly unionized. These employers have been actively seeking to eliminate trade unions from their operations and activities.

One of the most extreme attempts to achieve radical workplace change by excluding unions was undertaken on the waterfront by Patrick Stevedores, one of two key companies in the industry (Dabscheck 2000). The publicly stated view of the company was that dockworkers (or stevedores) and their union, the Maritime Union of Australia (MUA), enjoyed a monopoly of labor supply on the waterfront and that the union fostered restrictive practices that resulted in inefficient container handling, making the industry unproductive by world standards. In April 1998, following a series of disputes with the union, Patrick decided to appoint an administrator and withdraw financial support from its newly formed subsidiary labor hire companies. Patrick thereby hoped to avoid its debts and lay off its fourteen hundred employees. New companies were contracted to replace former Patrick employees with nonunion labor. The government had been encouraging Patrick to take a strong line against the MUA and announced a levy on the movement of cargo at the docks in order to raise $161 million to fund Patrick's redundancies.

The union argued that the workers were not overpaid in view of their working conditions. Productivity had increased but was still lower than some overseas ports because in Australia there was a proliferation of relatively small ports. The Labor party also held that Patrick was trying to smash union power and to generate an issue to help the coalition government win the next federal election. The union had long maintained 100 percent membership among dockers.

The AIRC was restricted by the Workplace Relations Act 1996 from becoming involved in attempting to resolve the dispute by conciliation or arbitration because technically it was not a lockout (or industrial dispute) and the issue did not come under the jurisdiction of the commission. The dispute was publicly adjudicated in the media, on the docks, and streets themselves through community alliances and protests and in political debate. It was eventually settled in the legal arena. Ironically, although the intention of the federal coalition government's Workplace Relations Act 1996 was to remove the role of "third parties" such as unions and the AIRC, the waterfront dispute involved greater use of the civil courts (also third parties) than had usually been the case previously. This may also have reflected, in part, the parties' lack of experience in settling disputes autonomously—but also reflected the increasingly judicial nature of disputes with emphasis on the interpretation of the law rather than the root causes of disputes.

The coalition government and Patrick found themselves facing the likelihood of massive financial and even criminal penalties for allegedly conspiring to dismiss unlawfully the work force because they were union members. On the condition that the union would not proceed with further legal action, Patrick agreed to reinstate about half the unionized workforce and stop using nonunion replacement labor. The union also agreed to accept changes to work practices designed to raise productivity.

All of the parties to the dispute claimed to have achieved their objectives, but there were no clear winners. The government and Patrick both pointed to reduced numbers of employees on the waterfront and the likelihood of increased productivity, but this was gained at great economic and political cost. The union claimed that it had maintained the rights of waterfront workers to remain unionized and had retained a union shop.

Yet the level of employment on the waterfront was significantly reduced after the dispute.

While Patrick Stevedores was attempting to introduce workplace reform by discharging all of its workers (and hoping to avoid any financial liabilities in the process), the other stevedoring company, P&O, sought to introduce changes through negotiation with its employees and the union, and thereby achieve reforms in a more collaborative fashion. P&O was also concerned at what they felt was low productivity on the waterfront and argued that significant reforms were needed. Such responses show that not all employers have supported the coalition government's adversarial approach to industrial relations reform, and indeed some employers have supported company-level participatory schemes, though these are not often of a formal tripartite nature.

Evidence from the Australian Workplace Industrial Relations Surveys (AWIRS) of 1990 and 1995 reveal that there has been a growth of interest by employers in developing greater participation and involvement by employees in decisions at the workplace level (Morehead, et al. 1997). Some of these activities have focused on individual employees only, but others have involved unions. The most common forms of direct participation tend to be oriented around on employees' tasks and are designed to improve the performance of individuals or work groups, such as team building, group work, and total quality management. The majority of managers reported that direct forms of participation led to improvements in workplace performance, the introduction of change, and improved product or service quality. Most delegates in unionized workplaces believed that such schemes gave employees increased say at the workplace level. Yet when managers were asked whether they had consulted staff about important changes that had affected their workplaces during the pervious year, only 29 percent responded positively and only 18 percent said that employees had a significant input into decisions. This appears to indicate that while there has been an increase in degree of participation by employees, there continue to be important issues on which they were not consulted.

Managers were also asked by AWIRS if they had joint consultative committees, task forces, ad hoc committees, or other forms of indirect participation by employees as representatives on decision-making bodies. The proportion of workplaces with joint consultative committees increased between 1990 and 1995 from 14 to 33 percent. The increase in representation by employees on task forces or ad hoc committees was even greater, from 25 to 36 percent. However, these types of bodies are usually established to deal with particular issues as they arise and are generally limited in their scope and influence. The proportion of workplaces with employee representations on the boards of directors also increased during this time from 7 to 16 percent. But there is no legislated basis for employee representation on company boards, thus the functions of these boards vary considerably and are usually at the discretion of management. Not surprisingly, consultative committees were more prevalent in large workplaces (five hundred or more employees) than in small workplaces with less than fifty employees. Hence although formal systems of indirect employee participation have become more widespread, the degree of influence that employees are able to exert through such bodies appears to be minimal. While direct forms of participation have increased, employers do not appear to regard these as vital to the enterprise (Poole et al. 2001).

The past decade has thus seen a movement away from a collectivist approach, which favored participation by employees in decision-making within formal bodies (mostly through unions) to a more individualistic approach that excludes or minimizes union involvement. Not surprisingly, support among employees for formal participation or partnership arrangements with management has waned, while employers have extolled the virtues of directly involving employees in decision-making at the enterprise level. The evidence suggests that as employers have gained dominance and union power has declined, most managers have introduced change with minimal consultation and have shown little enthusiasm for either bipartite or tripartite approaches to joint decision-making. Unions have thus become disenchanted with most forms of partnership or collaboration with management in participative practices.

Union Movement

Union membership in Australia has steadily declined over the past decade. Union coverage or density fell from 49 percent in 1990 to 25 percent in 2000. A number of strategies aimed at reversing the tide of membership decline have been put in place by Australian unions in recent years. Australian trade unions were historically organized on a craft and occupational basis, but during the 1980s they focused on organizational restructuring, principally through amalgamations, which resulted in the merger of 360 unions into around 20 union conglomerates, many of which were based on one or more industry groups. The rationale for the creation of these unions was that it would release resources for improved provision of services to members. While the strategy was successful in changing the structure of Australian unions and reducing their number, it did not halt the decline of membership.

The reasons for the decline of union membership are complex and varied and relate not only to the decentralism that was occurring. These include changes in the structure of the economy, which has seen contraction of employment in manufacturing in which unions have traditionally been well organized, and the growth of the service sector, in which unions have been weaker. A major study by Peetz (1998, 82) concluded that "a reasonable estimate is that around half of the decline in union density in the decade to 1992 can be explained by these [structural] factors." Yet these phenomena have also characterized most advanced industrialized countries, not all of which have experienced as much decline in membership as Australian unions. Another important contributing factor in Australia include institutional arrangements, enshrined under the centralized system of arbitration (such as de facto compulsory unionism), which artificially inflated past union membership numbers.

Some analysts have also blamed membership decline on the union movement's participation in the accord with the Labor government. While it can be argued that union members benefited from the Labor government's provision of nonwage benefits (referred to as the "social wage") as well as increased government expenditure on health, education, and welfare, many unionists failed to attribute these benefits to the efforts of their unions. On the contrary, many have blamed the accord for a decline in real wages and feel that the unions sacrificed the interests of their members in order to enhance the electoral fortunes of the Labor government.

The strategies adopted by the union movement since the election of the coalition government in 1996, and the demise of the accord, have been focused on the principles of "organizing." Unions have been encouraged to build workplace activism, build alliances with the broader community, and develop capacities for strategic campaigning. The objective is that unions should redefine themselves as more autonomous and less dependent on the state. In 1994, the ACTU initiated an "organizing works" program, based partly on the experience of U.S. unions, in order to build their organizing skills and capacities of the Australian union movement and to give effect to an "organizing model." At the ACTU Congress 2000, a new strategy was launched known as Unions@Work that emphasized the central role of the organizing model in building a more inclusive social movement approach to unionism and thereby increasing membership (Cooper 2000).

During 2001, the ACTU mounted various campaigns aimed at the broader work force, rather than exclusively at union members, which were focused on issues of equity and fairness. A policy document entitled *Our Future at Work* was launched by the ACTU in 2001, based on evidence of a national survey that highlighted workers' concerns about work and family issues. The campaign focused on problems caused by increased casualization of the work force, inequality of wealth, job insecurity, and perceived unfairness in the industrial relations system. While under the Labor government the union movement had pursued the ideal of improved social conditions through the accord process, the new strategies adopted by the ACTU marked a more independent approach in which the unions are pursuing their own agenda for social reform regardless of which government is in power.

The union movement has therefore moved away from policies that emphasized cooperation with the government, and unions have eschewed any discussion of a new accord or social pact should Labor be returned to power. Although the unions retain a formal relationship with the ALP, there is a strong desire for the union movement to maintain an independent role so that it does not find its interests subordinated to that of a Labor government.

THE ECONOMIC AND SOCIAL CONSEQUENCES OF CHANGE IN THE BARGAINING STRUCTURE AND TRIPARTISM

Measuring the Consequences of Change

The Australian experience of the past fifteen to twenty years offers an opportunity to examine the consequences of labor market reform that has favored a more decentralized approach to bargaining and has increasingly emphasized both enterprise-based and individualized approaches to the determination of wages and working conditions. Although elements of the former centralized, collective approaches still remain, and the industrial tribunals still play an important role in award-making and certification of collective agreements, their importance has been significantly diminished. Australia has gradually moved away from the "coordinated market" economies of Western Europe toward the more "neoliberal market" economies that are typified by the United States, Canada, and the United Kingdom.

The consequences of these contrasting approaches remain the subject of debate. Some empirical evidence has confirmed the original Calmfors and Driffill (1988) hypothesis of a statistical relationship between countries' systems of collective bargaining (whether centralized or decentralized) and performance indicators relating to levels of employment and unemployment. However, recent OECD research has failed to establish any significant relationship, with the exception of earnings inequality, which is more pronounced in decentralized systems (OECD 2000, 1997). The consequences of changes in the bargaining structure in Australia toward a more decentralized system, and the decline of tripartism under the coalition government, can be analyzed in terms of industrial disputation, labor productivity, and earnings dispersion.

Industrial Disputes

While it is difficult (if not impossible) to determine the causes of changes in strike activity for a given country at any particular period of time, the strike rate in Australia has declined over the past two decades (ILO 2000; OECD 2000). The strike rate in Australia remains above the OECD average, yet the rate of reduction in strike activity has been slightly higher than the OECD average. The Australian strike rate in 2000 was much lower than a decade previously and almost ten times lower than in 1980. The number of disputes and the number of workers involved also declined between the early 1980s and the late 1990s by a factor of four and three, respectively. However, it is doubtful whether the reduction in industrial disputation in Australia can be ascribed solely to legislative changes introduced by the coalition government, as the major part of decline in strike activity occurred before the Workplace Relations Act 1996. Strike rates have been relatively stable since 1997 but are still among the highest in OECD countries.

The 1998 waterfront dispute was exceptionally severe, but for various technical reasons was not recorded as an industrial dispute in the official statistics (as the workers had been made redundant). The effects of the new legal compliance framework, introduced by the coalition government, with its distinction between "protected" and "unprotected" (that is lawful and unlawful) industrial action and its prohibition of strike pay by employers and secondary boycotts, may further reduce the incidence of industrial disputation, but it does not appear to have a significant impact thus far. Most industrial disputes in Australia continue to be of short duration, with strikes of two days or less accounting for half of all working days lost, and more than half of all strikes occur in manufacturing and construction, although mining and stevedoring also have a high strike rate. Among the major causes of disputes, "managerial policy" and "physical working conditions" account for over two-thirds of the total. Thus, although the strike rate has declined, the general pattern of industrial disputation has not changed radically in the past decade or so.

Labor Productivity

Proponents of decentralized bargaining tend to argue that a centralized and adversarial system of industrial relations imposes restrictions on firms' abilities to adjust to changes in the environment and to develop "high performance" workplaces. Labor productivity in Australia increased markedly in the 1990s (ahead of real wages) so that unit labor costs remained stable over the decade. The Australian Productivity Commission (1999) reported that productivity was above average during the 1990s compared with sluggish performance in the 1980s. The growth in labor productivity was particularly strong in mining, electricity, gas and water, finance, and insurance and communication services. These industries were characterized by restructuring and work force reductions during the past decade, which contributed to increased productivity.

It is not clear to what degree productivity improvements can be attributed to enterprise bargaining. As noted by Wooden (2000), the rise in productivity during the 1990s implied that Australians are working harder, smarter, or both. However, Wooden also concedes that working hours have substantially increased for some workers and while this has contributed to higher productivity, it may have adverse effects on health and family life.

The Dispersion of Wages and Earnings

An analysis of possible linkages between bargaining structures and economic performance by the OECD (2000) revealed a robust relation between the degree of centralization and earnings dispersion. According to a study based on data generated by employer surveys (Hancock 2002), there was a steady growth in pay dispersion between 1975 and 1998. Males fared better than females during the latter part of the period, so that the advances in minimizing pay differentials between men and women made under the centralized system have moderated since the introduction of enterprise bargaining. However, the increase in wage dispersion was modest in comparison with the trend in the more decentralized labor markets of the United States, United Kingdom, and New Zealand. During the past fifteen years, wages dispersion in Australia was more pronounced and increased at a faster rate than in most continental European members of the OECD, particularly Germany and the Nordic countries (OECD 2001).

An important difference in wage dispersion in Australia between the 1980s and 1990s is accounted for by strong real wage growth. During the 1980s the accord between the unions and the government had a restraining influence on wage growth so that by 1990 the median real wage was similar to fifteen years earlier. During the 1990s, real wages increased across the earnings distribution, although at a lower rate for workers at the bottom decile (Hancock 2003, 16–17).

It is difficult to determine the factors behind the increase in earnings dispersion in Australia, but the trend began during the period of more centralized wage determination and has not shown a substantial increase as the system has become more decentralized. However, using AWIRS 1995 data, Wooden (2000) argues that changes in bargaining structure has been associated with rising wage differentials, particularly within occupations. Furthermore, the growing dispersion in rates of wage increases agreed through enterprise agreements appears to reflect a stronger link between remuneration and enterprise performance (OECD 2000).

Despite the weaker role played by the AIRC as a result of legislative changes, it has tended to agree to flat-rate increases of minimum wage rates during the annual Living Wage Cases when the "safety-net," or minimum wages, are reviewed. In these cases, the ACTU has tried to offset the trend toward rising wage dispersion. In 1997, the AIRC established federal minimum wages across industries and occupations that were set at the lowest level of the Metal Industries Award. However, minima have continued to fall behind average weekly earnings, and in 2000 the basic federal minimum weekly rate for adult male full-time workers was 46 percent of average weekly earnings compared with 58 percent for females (ABS 2001). Although the minimum rates have been declining, these rates remain higher than in other OECD countries with minimum wage legislation, with the possible exception of France (OECD 2000).

THE IMPACT OF ECONOMIC GLOBALIZATION ON THE STRUCTURE OF COLLECTIVE BARGAINING

The Emergence of Globalization

From the time of federation in 1901 until the 1970s, the major political parties agreed to a broad consensus on the importance of trade protectionism (through tariff policies to support Australian industry), centralized wage determination (through the arbitration system), and a welfare state (to assist the economically disadvantaged). Yet these three "pillars" of this "Australian settlement" have been undermined by both the Labor and coalition governments in recent decades as they embraced neoliberal economic policies designed to make Australia more "internationally competitive" (Kelly 1992). Until the Labor government, led by Gough

Whitlam, reduced tariffs by 25 percent in 1973, successive governments had maintained high tariff barriers to "defend" manufacturing industries from foreign competition. Tariff protection was strongly supported by the trade union movement as a large proportion of its membership worked in manufacturing and wage increases could be absorbed, to some extent, by raising tariffs levels. The Whitlam Labor government justified tariff reduction as part of the internationalization of the Australian economy, even though this action resulted in increased unemployment. The Hawke Labor government took the decision in 1983 to float the Australian dollar and abolish exchange-rate controls as the first step toward financial deregulation. The government also permitted the entry of foreign banks into Australia. According to Kelly (1992) "the move to financial deregulation was a decisive break made by the Hawke-Keating government with Labor dogma and Australian practice (and)... it harnessed the Australian economy to the international marketplace."

Federal Labor governments in the 1980s and 1990s also embarked on programs of privatization and commercialization of public-sector activities, such as banking, transport, and telecommunications. This was justified on the basis of opening up these sectors to global competition. It was accompanied by public-sector expenditure cuts and reductions in grants to the states, which had deleterious effects on the provision of social welfare. The stated aim of Labor's competition policy, which underpinned privatization of the public sector, was to create a positive climate for private-sector investment, especially from overseas. Yet as large sums of money were borrowed from abroad, Australia's net foreign debt rose from $6.9 billion in 1979/80 to $180.5 billion in 1995/96, which represented a sevenfold increase in foreign debt as a percentage of GDP. Much of the foreign investment was directed into speculative activities and assets such as tourist resorts, hotels, and office blocks.

The rising debt levels and volatility of deregulated exchange rates limited the Labor government's ability to pursue its social agenda. However, the coalition government, led by John Howard, pursued an even more aggressive program of privatization and deregulation after its election in 1996. Although a number of its programs were blocked by opposition parties in the Senate, the Howard government continued the process of dismantling the centralized industrial relations system by expanding enterprise bargaining and widening the scope for nonunion agreements. A more decentralized and deregulated system of bargaining was presented as being more in harmony with global competitiveness according to the director of the Business Council of Australia (BCA), which had a strong influence on persuading both the Labor and coalition parties to adopt a policy of enterprise bargaining: "Australian businesses need to be internationally competitive to succeed . . . and their employees need to be innovative, efficient, and able to respond rapidly to changing customer demands" (Salmon 1996).

The corporate sector strongly advocated economic globalization as the only choice available to Australia, particularly companies in the agribusiness and mining industries on which the Australian economy is heavily dependent. According to the chief executive of Mount Isa Mining Company "there is only one direction for us all and that is increased internationalization, increased strategic partnerships, and increased participation in the market place" (Watson 1996). Many of Australia's largest and most influential enterprises are partially or fully foreign-controlled. Some key industries are almost entirely foreign owned: 90 percent of auto manufacturing and 75 percent of pharmaceuticals and aluminum. The decisions of the largest two hundred corporations greatly affect the Australian economy because the employ about half of the work force in manufacturing and account for around 60 percent of fixed capital expenditure.

Australia's largest company, BHP Ltd. (which merged with the British-based Billiton in 2001), provides an illustration of a globalization strategy followed by large Australian-based firms in recent years, and its implications for collective bargaining. BHP's major operations are in steel production and mining, and the primary focus of BHP until the late 1960s was domestic production and domestic markets. During the 1970s, however, BHP began to expand its export production and acquired steel mills and mines overseas. It also became active in oil exploration and production in various parts of the world. By the mid-1970s, as a result of its strategy to become a global company, the proportion of BHP's work force employed outside Australia grew to 25 percent, the share of overseas sales rose to 65 percent, and the proportion of shares held in foreign ownership increased to 21 percent. BHP adopted a more aggressive approach in dealing with the unions and indicated that its strategies were based on global rather than domestic considerations. The BHP case, according to Brett, shows that "as Australian-owned companies pursue their economic interests on a world rather than national stage, the circle of mutual benefit is decisively broken" (Brett 1997).

Implications of Globalization for Industrial Relations

It is difficult to assess the impact of economic globalization on industrial unions. In part, this is because the process of globalization is superimposed on other fundamental cyclical and structural changes (Kyloh 1998, 18). However, globalization has encouraged some employers and governments to oppose unions more vigorously, particularly in regard to bargaining rights and bargaining structures. In a number of countries, governments have decentralized collective bargaining (as in Australia), restricted the coverage of collective agreements, and weakened minimum wage legislation.

The enhanced role played by multinational enterprises has also exacerbated the imbalance of power between labor and capital. In industries such as steel, textiles, and clothing, competition from low-cost producers is intense and exerts a downward pressure on wages and employment. These industries have traditionally constituted the "backbone" of the union movement, particularly in countries like Australia where high tariffs protected them from external competition. It is increasingly difficult for unions to limit the extent of competition over wages and employment conditions. This is because the world economy is much more interdependent and international financial markets demand that enterprises adopt continuous cost-cutting measures in order to remain competitive (Wiseman 1998).

Nevertheless, Australian unions are active at the international level through membership of organizations such as the International Labor Organization (ILO) that seek to maintain and enforce fundamental labor standards. The ACTU has been an active participant in the ILO and has raised complaints against the Australian government concerning breaches of Conventions 87 and 98 that guarantee rights to freedom of association and to bargain collectively. However, the coalition government has lessened Australia's role at the ILO and reacted in a hostile manner to the ILO's view that the Workplace Relations Act 1996 was in breach of the right to strike over social and economic issues.

Many Australian unions are also actively involved in various international trade secretariats. During the waterfront dispute of 1998, the Maritime Union of Australia (MUA) mobilized worldwide support for their cause through the International Transport Workers Federation, which threatened to block unloading in other parts of the world of ships that had unloaded in nonunion ports in Australia. The Miners Union in Australia (CFMEU) has also used its membership of the International Federation of Chemical, Energy, Mine, and General Workers' Union to successfully lobby the shareholders and board of Rio Tinto and forced the company to engage in collective bargaining and adhere to basic social, health, and safety standards. However, the success of Australian unions in cross-national collective bargaining has been very limited, and it has only been during major conflicts, such as the waterfront dispute, that

Australian unions have been able to utilize support from unions in other countries in order to enhance their bargaining power.

POLICY IMPLICATIONS

Winners and Losers from Recent Changes

The most significant change in the structure of collective bargaining in Australia over the past decade has been the movement away from a coordinated system, in which the industrial tribunals retained a significant role, toward a fragmented approach dominated by employers.

The decline in the role and authority of the AIRC has been deleterious for the unions and those members of the work force whose bargaining power is weak. Unions, in general, have failed to rebuild their membership and bargaining power under a decentralized system in which the AIRC plays a less significant role. While employers have generally welcomed the movement toward a more decentralized system, they do not appear to place as high a priority on the need for industrial relations reform. Some have expressed concern about the reduction in the role and authority of the AIRC, particularly in relation to its reduced capacity to effectively settle industrial disputes.

The Role of Government in Relation to Deficiencies of the Prevailing Structure of Collective Bargaining

The AIRC acquired considerable influence over industrial relations matters because the constitution compelled the federal government to delegate its powers of conciliation and arbitration to the tribunal. Although, the Nationalist government led by S. M. Bruce tried unsuccessfully to abolish the commission in 1929, successive Australian governments have complied with the decisions of the AIRC, even when these were not to their liking. The current coalition government, however, has raised the possibility of using the Commonwealth's corporation's power in the constitution to bypass and downgrade the role of the AIRC. So far, the government has been unwilling to do this because it raises a number of possible difficulties and is opposed by the opposition parties, which hold the balance of power in the Senate. The government has also raised the possibility of the states ceding their industrial relations power to the Commonwealth but, with the exception of Victoria, this has been opposed by most of the state governments, including those controlled by the coalition parties.

While the role of the federal government in resolving perceived deficiencies of the prevailing structure of collective bargaining is limited by the constitution, it can nevertheless make significant operational adjustments to the system through legislative change. This has been the main mechanism by which change has been introduced in the last decade. Hence, the government's strategy of reducing the arbitral powers of the AIRC has diminished the authority of the tribunal. The government has also created a new regulatory agency, the Office of the Employment Advocate (OEA), to process Australian Workplace Agreements (AWAs) and investigate contraventions of the freedom of association provisions of the act. The effect of the government's action has been to provide the AIRC with a potential, if not actual, competitor as well as facilitating the growth of individual rather than collective contracts and promoting an acceptance of individual rather than collective employment relations.

With the reelection of the conservative government in November 2002, further change is on the agenda. In particular, the coalition wishes to ease restrictions on dismissals for small businesses, make pattern bargaining unlawful, and introduce more stringent strike rules. In all, the reregulation of Australian industrial relations has weakened the capacity of trade unions to represent workers, placed undue restrictions on the arbitral powers of the AIRC, and left the weakest members of the work force with inadequate protection.

Proposals for Changes in the Structure of Collective Bargaining and Tripartism

At the turn of the twenty-first century there does not appear to be much interest in developing tripartite approaches to industrial relations in Australia. The coalition parties are principally concerned with finding means to contain or reduce the unions' influence. The Labor party tends to favor the establishment of tripartite bodies when in government (such as the Economic Policy Advisory Council, established by the Hawke Labor government), but neither the employers nor the unions have exhibited strong support for these initiatives in recent years. It is unlikely that a future Labor government would assign high priority to reviving such arrangements, unless they were strongly supported by the employers and the union movement.

In this environment, and given the considerable decline in unionization rates, there has been some resurgence of interest in alternative representative mechanisms for employees. McCallum (2001) has argued that a future Labor government should give priority to reforming labor law using a "rights based approach" that would enact positive employee rights and employer obligations into statute law. According to McCallum, "Only when enterprises are required to bargain with recognized trade unions will bargaining in good faith laws be truly operative." Rather that simply relying on collective bargaining, however, McCallum argues that the federal parliament should also legislate minimum terms and conditions of employment for all workers who are covered by federal labor law. The following issues would be included: hours of work; standards for full-time, part-time, and casual employment; major public holidays, annual leave, and family leave including enforceable parental, cultural, and bereavement leave; minimum period of notice on termination and redundancy payment entitlements. To date these have been matters included in awards and agreements and are therefore negotiable. Consequently, a weakness of the current bargaining system, argues McCallum, is that it has involved employees exchanging their entitlements for cash payments.

Recently, the ACTU issued a discussion paper that discussed the merits of works councils, similar to those in Europe, which could provide an additional means of influence for workers in decision-making at the enterprise level. While the ACTU secretary, Greg Combet (2001), argued that works councils could provide an avenue for unions to recruit new members, there was not widespread support for this view within the union movement. Nevertheless, there has been debate among academic industrial lawyers about how legislation could be introduced to provide a "voice" for nonunionized workers as a means of strengthening "industrial citizenship," and this proposal could gain momentum under a Labor government.

McCallum (2001) argues that in order for employees to collectively participate in workplace governance, the federal parliament should encourage the establishment of elected works councils in enterprises with one hundred or more employees. These bodies could consult with employers on a wide range of issues, including the introduction of technological change, rostering arrangements, and amenities. The government should establish programs to train employee and employer works council representations to ensure that they understand their rights and responsibilities.

Despite the debate about the need for innovation, it is unlikely that the current government will introduce such measures, as they are contrary to the underlying philosophy and approach of federal government policy. As noted above, the emphasis is on promoting direct employee-employer relations and restricting the influence and activities of third parties such as unions and the commission.

CONCLUSION

It has been almost a century since an "historic compromise" was forged between labor and capital in Australia, after the disastrous strikes of the 1890s, with the enactment of the Commonwealth Conciliation and Arbitration Act of 1904, which gave birth to the federal tribunal and industrial relations system. During the past two decades, significant changes have occurred in the nature and structure of collective bargaining in Australia, as the "social settlement," which characterized industrial relations for most of the twentieth century, has been gradually dismantled by successive Australian governments.

The spread of enterprise bargaining and the decline in the power and authority of the AIRC has undermined the long-established system of centralized wage determination. This has been accompanied by a reduction in tariff protection of manufacturing and services with the objective of making Australian industry more internationally competitive. The decline of unionization, resulting from structural change and other factors, has enabled employers to increase their bargaining power and expand the scope of individualized, nonunion agreements. The degree of tripartism, which underpinned the social settlement and consensus on industrial relations, has also declined as the conservative coalition government has reduced its support for tripartite bodies.

The research evidence to date about the effects of industrial relations reform is somewhat inconclusive, though the patterns emerging suggest that for Australian workers there are growing inequities in wage rates, increasing insecurity at work, and a greater spread of working hours.

8 United States

The Spread of Coordination and Decentralization without National-Level Tripartism

Harry C. Katz

The United States historically has lacked national-level tripartism in part as a consequence of the prevalence of decentralized collective bargaining, a relatively small union sector, and strong market-oriented traditions. Although collective bargaining structures have become even further decentralized within the United States in recent years, through a number of private actions labor and management are taking steps to create coordinated structures regulating how they interact with one another. These steps are spreading coordinated and decentralized collective bargaining in the United States in ways that are similar to developments in other countries. For example, globalization is leading unions and multinational corporations to seek more centrally coordinated cross-national labor practices, and the intensification of plant-level collective bargaining is leading to a new form of national-local coordinated collective bargaining. In parallel fashion, while tripartism at the national level remains absent, regional tripartite activities are spreading *within* the United States to help spur work reorganization and up-skilling strategies.

Thus, there was not a simple decentralization trend underway in U.S. labor-management interactions. Rather, there was movement toward varied forms of coordination and decentralization in the structure of labor-management interactions, although given U.S. peculiarities, these developments lacked a national tripartite component.

THE HISTORICAL LACK OF NATIONAL-LEVEL TRIPARTISM

Historically, national-level tripartite activities involving labor, management, and government actors have been infrequent in the United States. The factors contributing to the infrequency of tripartism include the strong voluntarist traditions within the U.S. industrial relations system, the fact that employer organizations are relatively unimportant in the United States, and management's preference for the outcomes produced by decentralized collective bargaining in an industrial relations system that included a relatively small union sector.

Exceptions to this pattern include the national labor-management committees that surfaced during war periods or reform eras. At the turn of the century, for example, various national investigative commissions examined labor conditions and problems. Industrial relations commissions issued reports in 1880, 1902, and 1915, and these reports were used as background material for New Deal labor legislation in the 1930s.

Presidents Woodrow Wilson and Franklin Roosevelt created national war labor boards to promote labor peace and wage stability during the First and Second World Wars, respectively. Although these boards were generally successful in fulfilling their mandate during the course of the wars both, however, failed to keep labor and management working together at the national level after the wars. In 1945, for example, following the end of World War II, President Truman called labor and management representatives together in a national conference to try to work out principles for continuing the cooperation achieved during the war. But efforts to reach an accord broke down over labor's demand for a commitment to union security and management's demand for an explicit limit on the scope of labor's influence over employment issues.

While every president from the 1930s through the 1960s established one or more top-level labor-management advisory committees to deal with various issues, this tradition was later abandoned, although some of the committees that functioned with government encouragement continued to meet privately after the public effort dissolved. For example, the top-level committee that functioned when John Dunlop was secretary of labor in 1974–75, continued to meet under private auspices with Dunlop as chairman for years after he left office. This group discussed various labor policy issues other than collective bargaining problems under the premise that collective bargaining issues are best discussed at more decentralized levels between the parties that are directly involved.

A number of factors have made it difficult to change labor-management relations through national-level dialogue in the United States. These difficulties are well illustrated in the ill-fated tripartite committee active during the Clinton administration, the Dunlop Commission.[1]

The Dunlop Commission was charged with recommending what, if any, new collective bargaining practices and related legal framework should be encouraged to enhance workplace productivity through labor-management cooperation, employee participation, and direct workplace problem resolution.[2] The commission issued two reports: (1) a Fact Finding Report in which it reviewed the current state of labor management relations and arrayed the evidence presented to it on these questions, and (2) a Final Report and Recommendations outlining its proposal for reform. The recommendations sought a compromise within the existing framework of the National Labor Relations Act by loosening the constraints on employee participation in nonunion settings, something of great concern to the business community, and strengthening the protection of workers seeking to organize a union.

Yet, neither labor nor the business community supported this compromise. The business community generally perceived few problems in the nature of industrial relations in recent years as relative bargaining power shifted to their advantage because of, among other things, globalization and union decline. Furthermore, the shift in control of the Congress from a Democratic to a Republican majority that occurred in November 1994, in the midst of the commission's work, ended any hope for a change in labor policy by further polarizing the positions of business and labor. Thus, the experiences of the Dunlop Commission reinforced the record of little direct effect of national forums on labor-management relations.

While national tripartism languished, another forum for tripartite interactions, regional training partnerships, have expanded markedly from the mid-1990s. These partnerships have become a vehicle for labor, management, and government officials to interact at the state and local level to promote "high-road" economic development (AFL-CIO 2002). The most noteworthy case is the Wisconsin Regional Training Partnership that provides assistance to firms and unions with the spread of new technologies and work processes and education and training programs (Parker and Rogers 2001, 256–72). The Wisconsin Partnership also forged an alliance with a state-level extension program providing assistance to small- and medium-sized firms.

Other related training initiatives have emerged as offshoots of multi-employer collective bargaining agreements. Examples include an initiative in the San Francisco hotel industry involving the Hotel Employees and Restaurant Employees Union and a number of major hotels and public agencies. Local 1199, now a part of the Service Employees International

Union (SEIU), negotiated a set of training and career development programs under the rubric of a multiemployer training fund. Tripartite learning consortiums have also emerged in the telecommunication industry; one such case involves Cisco, a nonunion company, and the Communications Workers of America (the CWA). Federal and state government grants and subsidies support this consortium and other regional partnerships.

Regional partnerships extended earlier skilled trades tripartite programs by covering a broader range of employee skills and promoting work restructuring and participatory labor relations. Their growth suggests that local tripartism that is closely tied to workplace issues and directly concerns employment generation or preservation can play a meaningful role in U.S. labor policy. Yet the decentralized nature of collective bargaining in the United States limits the scope of local (or regional) partnerships and impending linkages across various partnerships.

THE DECENTRALIZATION OF COLLECTIVE BARGAINING IN THE UNION SECTOR

Compared to other countries, the United States in the post–World War II period experienced a relatively decentralized collective bargaining structure in the union sector, with most bargaining occurring at the company or plant level and a few cases of multiemployer bargaining. From the early 1980s on, the structure of collective bargaining began to decentralize even further, as most of the formally centralized structures broke down, the locus of bargaining shifted to the plant level within structures that maintained both company and plant levels, and pattern bargaining weakened.[3]

The use of multiemployer bargaining became even more infrequent as in a number of cases multiemployer bargaining ended, as was the fate of the basic steel agreement in 1986. In other industries, the number of firms and unionized employees covered by a multifirm agreement declined as companies withdrew from master agreements. Examples of this decline include the trucking industry (eroding the influence of the master freight agreement negotiated by the Teamsters and an employers association that had set employment terms for intercity truck drivers) and the underground coal mining sector (eroding the influence of a master agreement negotiated between the United Mineworkers and the Bituminous Coal Operators Association) (Kochan, Katz, and McKersie 1994, 128–30; Katz and Kochan 2000, 169–70).

The depth and importance of plant-level collective bargaining agreements increased, and this provided a further push for decentralization. In many cases, such as the tire and airline industries, decentralized collective bargaining included the negotiation of local pay and/or work rule concessions. Often these negotiations involved whipsawing by management (that is, forcing plants to compete against each other through concessions), with local unions and workers being threatened with the prospect of a plant closing if adequate concessions were not granted (Cappelli 1985; Kochan, Katz, and McKersie 1994, 117–27). In some cases, concessions on work rules were accompanied by new arrangements that provided extensive participation by workers and local union officers in decisions that had formerly been made solely by management (Kochan, Katz, and McKersie 1994, 146–205). Work rule bargaining increasingly involved a decision about whether or not to implement a joint team-based approach or disputes concerning the specific form or operation of this approach.

Even where company-level collective bargaining continued, greater diversity in collective bargaining outcomes appeared across companies. This diversity replaced the strong pattern bargaining that had served to centralize bargaining structures to the multiemployer level through either formal collective bargaining agreements or informally through pattern bargaining. For example, in the aerospace and agricultural implements industries, over the post–World II period until the mid-1980s, company-level pattern bargaining had included the same cost-of-living adjustment (COLA) clause and 3 percent annual improvement factor (AIF) wage increases found in the Big Three auto agreements. Yet, Erickson (1992 and 1996) documents the weakening of pattern bargaining and the emergence of significant intercompany variation in the aerospace industry and agricultural implements industries from the 1980s.

Bargaining at the plant and work group level now typically involves team systems, pay-for-knowledge, and other contingent compensation mechanisms, and changes in work time arrangements (Kochan, Katz, and McKersie 1994, 146–205; Cutcher-Gershenfeld 1991; Arthur 1992). More direct communication between managers and workers appears in many parts of the union sector in the United States (Eaton and Voos, 1992; Kochan, Katz, and McKersie 1994, 132–34).

Developments in the auto and telecommunications industry are examined below because these industries are economically important and the changes underway in each of these industries are representative of changes occurring in other unionized settings. While the changes in employment relations that occurred in the auto and telecommunications industries bear many similarities to those occurring elsewhere in the U.S. economy, certain characteristics of these two industries are noteworthy and affect the degree to which these industries are representative of broader changes underway in the United States. For example, the auto and telecommunications industries have much high levels of unionization and are dominated by very large firms. As a consequence of the former, labor-management relations in these two industries traditionally have been relatively highly structured and formalized.

THE AUTO INDUSTRY

Prior to 1979, the bargaining structure among the auto assembly firms involved very strong pattern following within and across the auto companies. In the traditional bargaining structure that prevailed at the Big Three (General Motors, Ford, and Chrysler) compensation is set by national, company-specific, and multiyear (since 1955 they have been three-year) agreements. Some work rules, such as overtime administration, employee transfer rights, and seniority guidelines, are also set in the national contracts. Local unions, in turn, negotiate plant-level agreements, which supplement the national agreements.

The influence of the agreements reached in the auto assembly firms traditionally extended to the auto supplier industry and beyond. The United Autoworkers (UAW), for example, used the auto assembly agreements as a pattern setter in their negotiations in the agricultural implements industry. Other unions, especially those linked to auto production such as the rubber industry, also looked to the contracts in the auto assembly firms as pattern setters. From the early 1950s until the late 1970s, the extent of interindustry pattern following varied somewhat over time, but generally there was a high degree of pattern following.

A key feature of the auto bargaining process was that from 1948 until 1980, formulaic mechanisms were utilized to set wage levels in collective bargaining agreements in the Big Three.[4] The formulaic wage-setting mechanisms traditionally included in the contracts were an AIF that after the mid-1960s amounted to 3 percent per year, and a COLA escalator that often provided full or close to full cost-of-living protection.

As import share rose in the 1980s and economic recession took hold, the absolute power of labor and management at the Big Three declined and the contracts negotiated in the early 1980s reflected this power decline. In addition, the relative bargaining power of the UAW was weakened by factors such as the rise in imports, the ease by which the companies could move production offshore, and the erosion of strike leverage due to excessive production capacity.

As a result, in collective bargaining at the Big Three the wage rules traditionally used to set wage levels were modified significantly, first as part of efforts to avoid bankruptcy at Chrysler in 1979 and 1980. Significant intercompany variation followed across the Big Three as a result of extra concessions granted to Chrysler to stave off its bankruptcy and because of the emergence of profit sharing as a significant component of pay and the subsequent variation that appeared in the annual company profit-sharing payouts. The profit-sharing payouts between 1982 and 2000 at General Motors (GM), Ford, and Chrysler, respectively, totaled $6,916, $47,545 and $45,025 (Katz, MacDuffie, and Pil 2002, 74).

From the early 1980s, however, the degree of pattern following declined across the Big Three and cross-company variation increased with the entry of Japanese- and German-owned transplants. The pay concessions and the move to contingent compensation schemes that tied wages to company performance increased the variation in employment conditions across the auto assembly companies. In addition, sizeable variation was created through the addition of the unionized transplants and the Saturn subsidiary, each of which had a separate collective bargaining agreement with the UAW, and through wage and benefit policies at the nonunion transplants.[5] Furthermore, in the 1980s the interindustry pattern-leading role of the Big Three settlements declined (Budd 1992).

Because work rules and work organization have been modified in different ways and at a varied pace across auto assembly plants, even greater variation now appears in the work practices used in unionized auto assembly plants. The threat of increased employment loss because of increased foreign sourcing of vehicles, plant closings due to excess capacity, or the outsourcing of certain operations all created pressures to lower costs and improve product quality. Ultimately, the pressure for increased interplant work rule divergence came from the same source as the pressure for intercompany pay variation, the fear that even greater losses in employment would result if previous policies were maintained. Companies often used investment decisions as explicit leverage for these changes, a strategy unions viewed as "whipsawing."

Substantial variation also appears in how teams and the team-based approach are being implemented. In team plants, for example, there is wide variety in the procedures used to select team leaders and the role that hourly team members exert in that selection process. Some team plants use strict seniority rights to determine who serves as the hourly team coordinator, while other teams allow team members to directly elect their team coordinator.[6] The procedures used to select team leaders are not an incidental matter. This is revealed by the fact that this selection procedure has been a key issue in disputes (some of which have entailed work stoppages).

There is also wide variety across plants in the specific duties performed by team members and leaders. In some plants team members have the authority to directly contact and visit parts vendors to resolve production problems. A number of plants have put hourly workers on scrap and quality-control tasks forces and freed workers from assembly line responsibilities to give them the time to carry out new duties. Pay-for-knowledge has been adopted along with teams in some plants to encourage workers to learn more jobs in their work area and in the process become more capable of understanding the linkages between jobs in and across work teams. The presence and form of pay-for-knowledge varies across plants, which provides a source of earnings variation across plants in contrast to the traditional work system that served to dampen such variation.

Thus plants of the Big Three now differ in terms of whether they use the traditional or a team-based work system, and there is much variation across team plants in terms of the specific way that teams are being introduced. Team systems have led to increases in the variation in work organization and work practices across auto plants through their operation as well as a result of the varying structure of team administration. Along with the variation produced by team systems there is wide variation appearing across assembly plants in the role that workers play in business decisions.

The broader involvement of workers and union officers in plant affairs has been spurred by a decentralization occurring within the ranks of management. As the negotiation of work practice change has intensified at the plant level and in the face of the wide plant-level (and within-plant) variations that have appeared as a consequence of these negotiations, in unionized settings the influence of plant-level industrial relations or employee relations managers has increased relative to their corporate counterparts. In addition, the involvement of operating managers (such as production managers or production superintendents) in employee relations matters has increased in part through the reduced role that the formal grievance procedure is playing in conflict resolution and the increasing role of informal discussions held between operating managers and workers (and union officers). Some of these discussions arise out of the natural operation of teams, while others occur as result of the broader roles workers are playing in problem-solving forums or through the activities of the various joint committees operating on the shop floor.

In some plants a formal "area" management structure is spurring the decentralization of industrial relations down to the shop floor. In these plants typically three or four key operational areas are designated and reporting lines are adjusted to fit these areas rather than the traditional plant hierarchy. In the traditional management structure, labor relations staff report upward to the plant industrial relations (or personnel) director and not to an operating manager. In an area management structure, in contrast, the employee relations support staff report directly to an area-operating manager and report in a matrix manner to an employee relations (or industrial relations) director. Area management represents a business-unit style of operation at the plant level and is intended to bring awareness and responsiveness to cost and profit pressures down to the work area. This is leading to a reorganization of the employee relations function within management as well as a broader involvement of workers and union officers in plant operations.

By the mid-1990s the UAW had regained substantial bargaining power relative to the Big Three, and this gain was reflective in favorable contract terms and a return to strict pattern bargaining across the Big Three companies. The UAW gained 3 percent annual base pay increases on top of income security guarantees and plant closing moratoriums in their four-year agreements signed in near identical contracts at the Big Three in the fall of 1999 (Katz, MacDuffie, and Pil 2002, 72). While pattern bargaining returned to wage setting, diversity in work rules and labors' decision-making role continued to spread across (and within) plants.

The UAW was not the only U.S. union to take advantage of a tight labor market during the mid- and late 1990s to gain favorable contracts and reintroduce pattern bargaining. Pilot bargaining at Delta, United, and American Airlines and bargaining involving International Association of Machinists (IAM)-represented machinists at Boeing exhibited these characteristics. In these firms, unions retained significant membership and benefited from the effects of the strong macroeconomic growth experienced in the United States in the 1990s.

THE TELECOMMUNICATIONS SERVICES INDUSTRY

As in the auto industry, in the telecommunications industry labor-management interactions became more decentralized, though in the latter, the domestic pressures, particularly from the divestiture of AT&T in 1983, rather than heightened international competition drove this change. Decentralization and variation increased in telecommunications collective bargaining as the Regional Bell Operating Companies (RBOCs), such as Verizon and SBC, pursued a variety of business and industrial relations strategies and the focus of industrial relations shifted downward within both AT&T and the RBOCs.

This decentralization occurred within a bargaining system that had by the early 1970s become very centralized. Responding to strong pressures from the CWA and AT&T's own interests in coordinating a national telephone system, the traditional collective bargaining structure involved a heavy role for the corporate officers of AT&T and national union officers. Prior to divestiture, AT&T and its Bell operating companies bargained at two levels. At the first level, called "national bargaining," Bell systemwide agreements were reached on wages, benefits, and employment security. At the second level of bargaining, "local bargaining," the individual Bell operating companies bargained with local union leadership over work administration and work rules (Keefe and Batt 2002, 278).

A centralized bargaining structure had fit with high levels of union representation in the "Bell system" and the strong influence of national-level officials within the respective telecommunications unions. Prior to divestiture, in 1983, unions represented 55.5 percent of the entire work force in the telecommunications industry, with nearly total representation of operators and field service technicians (the latter install and repair equipment and the network phone lines) and heavy representation among customer service representatives (who handle billing, complaints, and service requests) (Keefe and Batt 2002).

The breakup of the Bell system led to variation in employment relations by fragmenting a formerly coordinated national administrative structure and by creating the preconditions for intense competition between AT&T and the RBOCs. Yet, even with divestiture, the CWA and the International Brotherhood of Electrical Workers (IBEW) might well have been able to more successfully limit the ensuing variation in industrial relations if those unions had not confronted pressures emanating from the growth occurring in nonunion employment in the telecommunications industry. Nonunion employment grew dramatically within AT&T and the RBOC's, and it grew even more sizably through the entry of new nonunion firms into the telecommunications industry. By 1998, unions represented only 27.7 percent of the work force in the industry (Keefe and Batt 2002). Nonunion employment growth was in part a consequence of divestiture, but also was driven by factors that were independent from the corporate reorganization of the Bell system.

GENERAL UNION DECLINE

More generally throughout the U.S. economy, declines in the share of the work force represented by unions led to the ultimate form of decentralization in labor-management relations, namely, deunionization. In 2000, only 13.5 percent of the total workforce was unionized (Bureau of Labor Statistics 2001). Procedures that relate pay and other employment terms to individual traits have become a common feature in nonunion employment systems. The resulting "individualization" of the employment relationship in nonunion settings produced much higher variation across individuals, companies, and industries as compared to union employment systems.

In those industries where unions were never dominant, the expansion of nonunion employment per se did not create an entirely new type of employment system as in these industries there always had been large differences in the employment conditions in union and nonunion firms. But union decline did lead to greater variation in employment conditions in those industries because nonunion firms put greater emphasis on personnel procedures that linked rewards to individual traits, and these procedures contrasted sharply with the standardized employment conditions found in unionized settings. Furthermore, there were a number of industries such as steel and rubber, and sizable sectors within other industries such as over-the-road trucking and underground coal mining, that, like the auto and telecommunications industries, were once completely, or nearly completely, unionized and then experienced substantial nonunion growth (Kochan, Katz, and McKersie 1994). In these once heavily unionized industries a critical way the expansion of nonunion employment increased employment system variation was through the creation of an alternative to the once dominant union norm.

UNION REVITALIZATION

Faced with declines in membership and bargaining power, U.S. trade unions have taken a number of steps in recent years in pursuit of revitalization. An innovative aspect of recent union revitalization is the extent to which union activities in one sphere of influence, such as organizing, interact with activities in other spheres, collective bargaining or political action, for instance. This activity integration involves the coordination of union actions and thus, has a number of similarities to the kind of coordination emerging in other domains of U.S. collective bargaining.

The ongoing revitalization efforts of the CWA provide a clear illustration of union activity integration (Katz, Batt, and Keefe 2003). While the CWA has longed engaged in *parallel* activities in these three spheres, the integration strategy involves the simultaneous and *interactive* use of activities in all three domains. The CWA is linking activities across all three arenas in a strategic and sophisticated manner. For example, through novel language won in collective bargaining agreements with the RBOCs, the CWA is gaining card check recognition and employer neutrality in representation elections, key parts of the union's organizing initiative. And similarly, the union's collective bargaining efforts are being strengthened by political actions toward regulatory bodies and public relations campaigns. Another example is provided in the way the CWA's traditional top-down approach to organizing has been supplemented through the involvement of grassroots campaigns staffed by mobilized members.

Over the post–World War II period, CWA president Beirne and other early leaders of the union saw the need for activities in three spheres— collective bargaining, politics, and organizing—and fitting with the relatively stable environment the union faced in that period (and following the organizational principle outlined by Lawrence and Lorsch [1969]), the CWA's activities in those areas were conducted in a segmented manner. Postdivestiture, as the CWA's environment became more complex and unstable and the union's traditional sources of bargaining power declined, the CWA shifted to an integration strategy that linked previously segmented units and tactics. The activity integration that emerged at the CWA is consistent with another organizational principle articulated by Lawrence and Lorsch (1969, 11), namely, that "integration" and "integrating mechanisms" emerge in organizations that face environmental complexity and uncertainty. Given its particular constraints and objectives, for the union a key reason for the shift to activity integration was the need to develop new sources of bargaining leverage.

The CWA efforts to use activity integration to increase its membership and bargaining power led to ever more complex interactions with a wide array of constituents. The CWA faced much greater uncertainty in the postdivestiture era because the new environment threatened its institutional security and undermined its bargaining power. In the face of ongoing corporate restructuring and ownership changes, the union could not depend on traditionally stable and predictable bargaining behaviors, norms, and outcomes. To regain power and revitalize, the CWA turned to activity integration, a type of coordination that has many similarities to other "private" coordination activities underway in recent years involving U.S. collective bargaining.

CROSS-NATIONAL UNIONISM

The activity integration underway in the CWA and other U.S. unions primarily involved domestic collective bargaining, organizing, and political actions. Yet, as economic globalization gained steam, the CWA and other unions increasingly came under pressure to find ways to add an international dimension to activity integration.

Globalization has spurred both unions and management to realign their cross-national labor practices. With regard to labor, globalization puts pressure on labor movements all over the world to extend bargaining and bargaining structures across national borders. The expansion of international trade and the accelerated expansion of multinational corporations extend the market internationally. In his classic analysis of early union formation among American shoemakers, John R. Commons explained that as the extent of the market expanded, unions at the beginning of the twentieth century shifted to a national structure to counteract "competitive menaces" and retain bargaining power (Commons 1909). This provided a structure of representation that was parallel to the emerging national structure of markets.

The problem now confronting labor movements is that they confront the need for cross-national unionism, but their efforts to create such unionism face substantial barriers. These barriers include divergent interests (i.e., each labor movement wants the employment) and national differences in language, culture, law, and union structure.

Yet, even in the face of these barriers, there are some recent signs of increased international activity among U.S. unions, particularly U.S.-Mexico and U.S.-Canada cross-border activities (Compa 2001a, 53–54). American unions have engaged in cross-national pressure campaigns by filing North America Free Trade Agreement (NAFTA) complaints.[7]

Some "international" unions do have members in both the United States and Canada. This has led to cross-border information sharing along with organizing and strike support. There are also nascent efforts underway in the railroad and constructions industries in the United States and Mexico to engage in coordinated collective bargaining.[8] At the same time, there are also cases where once stronger cross-border ties have weakened. The most famous example involved the end to UAW negotiation of company-level collective bargaining contracts covering Canadian workers when the Canadian Autoworkers Union (CAW) was formed and broke with the U.S.-based UAW in 1985 (Katz, MacDuffie, and Pil 2002, 57). The only sustained case of cross-border collective bargaining that actually occurs in North America involves professional sports in the United States and Canada.

While overall cross-border contacts and cooperation between North American labor movements are increasing, as Compa (2001a, 57) notes, "The scope of cross-border union activism on trade and labor rights should not be overstated. Among U.S. unions it involves only the most internationally active unions, still a minority of the overall labor movement. In Mexico, it involves mainly small, independent opposition labor groups." Where it exists, cross-national labor activity at this point largely involves transnational networks of labor rights partisans. Thus, while globalization is putting pressure on heretofore national labor movements to create cross-border ties, and potentially, cross-border collective bargaining structures, to date the impediments to cross-border linkages have proven daunting.

Globalization is likely to lead unions to extend efforts to coordinate actions across national borders. At the same time, the rise in the importance of plant-level issues is leading national unions to coordinate national-local union interactions. Unions thereby are under pressure to find coordinating structures and mechanisms *across and within* national boundaries. As discussed below, similar pressures appear within corporations.

THE GLOBALIZATION OF INDUSTRIAL RELATIONS WITHIN U.S.-BASED MULTINATIONAL CORPORATIONS

To fully understand the structure and nature of labor-management interactions it is essential to examine the internal structuring of industrial relations within corporations. The discussion above suggests that the pressures for decentralization have led many corporations to shift area management or business unit structures to gain flexibility in industrial relations administration and in some cases, bargaining power advantages. Yet globalization pressures are also leading to shifts in the internal operations and structure of multinational corporations (i.e., how and where various tasks are conducted within the corporation). A special dilemma for industrial relations managers in the multinational corporation arises from the fact that culture, law, and institutions retain much of their international diversity at the same time that globalization has increased the premium on coordination and central control. The internal restructuring pressures that exist within the industrial relations function of multinational corporations are analyzed below through a case study of the changes taking place in a U.S.-based multinational corporation that produces and sells consumer products.

Cross-national differences in culture, law, and institutions have long been the source of control and coordination problems for multinational firms. Traditionally, multinational firms responded to this problem by maintaining a high degree of local control (decentralization) in the internal direction of industrial relations (Kujawa 1980). Previous research shows that generally the administration of industrial relations was more decentralized than other management functions such as finance or marketing in multinational corporations. Multinationals found that there were substantial benefits to be gained from the decentralization of industrial relations. These benefits include the ability to respond flexibly to various kinds of diversity. By allowing local managers in each country to fashion industrial relations policies, these managers could create policies and procedures that fit with local conditions and events. Yet the case described below illustrates the shift underway in multinational corporate strategy and structure because of the pressures of globalization.

CASE STUDY OF THE SHIFT OCCURRING IN THE INTERNAL STRUCTURE OF THE INDUSTRIAL RELATIONS FUNCTION AT A U.S.-BASED MULTINATIONAL CORPORATION

The U.S.-based multinational consumer products firm that forms the basis for this case study has more than a hundred manufacturing facilities in thirty countries and eighty fully owned subsidiaries that are organized in a regional and core business matrix. Labor relations and human resource management traditionally were very decentralized in the company, with most decisions being made by facility managers or "focused-factory" managers within facilities. In the past, country- or corporate-level presidents and directors of manufacturing only became involved in facility issues in the midst of a clear crisis. A small corporate staff (a vice-president of human resources and a vice-president of industrial relations) located in the home country provided strategic guidance to country- and facility-level managers on industrial relations and human resource matters.

Pressure for change in the company's internal industrial relations and human resource function, however, began to build as the company became increasingly global in its operations. In the mid-1990s regional and global shifts occurred in the company's basic business structure and strategy, and these shifts spurred the changes in the industrial relations and human resource function. There was a movement toward regional "centers of excellence" through manufacturing consolidation as the company moved away from its past practice of having multiple plants within a region produce the same product. This reorganization was spurred by regional trade pacts that reduced tariffs and facilitated cross-border trade. Manufacturing consolidation was also being encouraged by technological improvements that made it possible to produce greater volumes within a single plant and organizational (and industrial relations) changes that allowed for three-shift-a-day, seven-day-a-week production operation.

Inside the multinational corporation, in recent years there has also been a move toward a more simplified global supply chain (i.e., more global sourcing and fewer preferred suppliers) and less product variety across countries ("less tinkering with the product"). The latter is associated with moves toward more globally similar (if not, coordinated) products to take advantage of production scale economies and marketing standardization. Furthermore, the ease by which consumer information now moves across countries is leading the corporation to seek greater central control of marketing and products. These pressures are all leading to greater centralization within the corporation. Furthermore, international (i.e., non-U.S.) sales now constitute most of the company's profits. Centralization and standardization of industrial relations and human resource management is facilitated by the fact that although the specific products differed in the various business units in the United States (and elsewhere in the company), there is a lot of similarity in the nature of the business and technologies in the company's different business units.

Most of the workers in the company's manufacturing facilities are represented by unions, yet very few of the company's new "greenfield" plants are unionized. From the early 1980s on, a number of the facilities at one time or another have launched work redesign or quality improvement initiatives. By the mid-1990s, corporate officers had come to the conclusion that most plants had little to show for these efforts, in part because they were launched without the involvement of unions, workers, or other employees in the design and planning process. The company perceived that in its facilities there has been a problem "integrating its high commitment efforts with labor relations changes." Corporate management believed that plants tend to think of labor relations in terms of firefighting over the latest crisis, and in the process, plant-level managers failed to gain the benefit of work rule changes and other contractual and operating improvements.

To address these problems the company launched a global industrial relations initiative (labeled its "global industrial relations strategy"). A new position, a regional director of human resources (and industrial relations), was created to help coordinate the change effort and provide continuing coordination of human resource and industrial relations initiatives. This coordination included semiannual review and planning meetings bringing together key plant- and country-level human resource and industrial relations and manufacturing managers.

Related changes in the company's human resource function involve greater centralization and regionalization. For example, there are efforts underway to adopt standardized and regionalized "shared services" administration of pay and benefits through the introduction of standardized computer software and regional information call centers. There also has been a gradual move inside the company toward regional compensation professionals who replace country-level human resource specialists in compensation, linked to the broader shift to shared human resource services in the company. Managerial succession planning for the United States, Europe, and Asia is also becoming more centrally coordinated.

Developments at the consumer products multinational corporation described above illustrate how globalization is leading U.S.-based multinational firms to increase the central control and administration of industrial relations even in the face of some difficulties and a heavy U.S. bias in the actors promoting this centralization. While other case studies are needed to tell if the experiences in the consumer products multinational analyzed in this case study are common to other companies and countries, there are reasons to expect that they are.

Centralization of a corporate function has always had the advantage of providing consistency and scale economies. Although diversity in local environments overwhelmed these advantages in the past, the integration of production across national boundaries spurs multinational firms to narrow variation in industrial relations policies. The opening of trade through mechanisms such as the European Union, the North American Free Trade Agreement, and the formation of other regional trading blocs are providing further impetus to corporate globalization and a rebalancing of the locus of the internal corporate industrial relations (and human resource) function.

As a result, corporations face pressures to reorganize their internal administration of industrial relations and human resource management both within and across countries. The increasing importance of plant and subplant (i.e., work-group) level labor-management interactions also is leading to the expansion of coordinating actions and structures within countries. Meanwhile, global pressures are promoting the enhancement of regional-level management global coordinating internal structures, in part to spur awareness of common problems and learning.

The emerging organizational structure in the U.S. consumer products multinational corporation involves a hybrid form involving "geocentric" and "polycentric" structures similar to structures found at ABB by Berggren (1999). The current push to regionalization, combined with efforts to enhance corporate guidance of human resource activities, is leading to a hybrid structure that involves a form of coordinated decentralization within the internal structure of the firm. In this structure, while a number of human resource and industrial relations decisions are still left in the control of local (plant- or country-level) managers, the expanding influence of regional and corporate managers simultaneously functions as a coordinating influence.

While insight is gained from analysis of the developments occurring within particular firms, the broader economic performance of the U.S.

economy also exerted a critical influence on developments in the structure of labor and management interactions.

U.S. ECONOMIC PERFORMANCE

The U.S. economy performed well in the 1990s with regard to gross domestic product (GDP), employment, and inflation, and this led to little political pressure for a shift away from the traditional strong role played by the market in the determination of employment conditions. GDP, for example, grew at rates above 2.5 percent per year from 1995 to 2000, with particularly strong growth (between 4.1 and 4.4 percent per year) from 1997 to 2001. Civilian employment grew 1.3 percent per year from 1989 to 1999 (it had grown by 1.7 percent per year from 1979 to 1989). Concerns that this growth in employment masked deterioration in the quality of jobs were lessened by the fact that from 1995 to 1999, the share of regular full-time employment rose from 73.6 percent to 75.1 percent (Mishel et al. 2001, 7) of the work force. Inflation was particularly low in the 1990s, with the consumer price index rising only 1.6 percent per year, for example, in 1998 and 2001. Meanwhile, unemployment fell to levels that had not been seen since the Vietnam War buildup, falling as low as 4 percent in 2000.[9]

The tightening of the labor market that occurred in the late 1990s led to real growth in average wages, reversing the stagnation that had occurred in mean earnings in the preceding twenty-year period. The median wage for all workers, after adjusting for inflation, grew by 7.3 percent (2.7 percent per year) from 1995 to 1999 (Mishel et al. 2001, 5). Although U.S. economic growth was clearly impressive, as the per capita income growth experienced in the United States between 1989 and 1999 (1.6 percent per year) exceeded the rates of income growth in Germany, Japan, and Italy, it is also noteworthy that U.S. income growth was below the rates of growth experienced in the Netherlands, Australia, and Ireland over the same period (Mishel et al 2001, 373).

The increase in average earnings occurring in the United States in the late 1990s also did not alter the fact that the United States has the most unequal income distribution and one of the highest poverty rates among all the advanced economies in the world. Much economic research has documented the extent and causes of the increase in income inequality that occurred in the United States from the early 1980s (Levy 1998; Blau and Kahn 1996). The general pattern is well described by Mishel et al. (2001, 13–14) who note that in the United States, "in the 1980s, inequality "fanned out"—the top pulled away from the middle, and the middle pulled away from the bottom. In the 1990s, however, wages at the bottom and middle grew closer, while the top pulled further away from the middle."

Katz and Darbishire (2000) argue that the low level of unionization found in the United States contributed to that country's wide variation in employment practices and income inequality as compared to outcomes in other advanced economies. The absence of tripartism and other mechanisms that could coordinate wage setting across economic sectors or occupations also contributed to the institutional context that allowed market forces to produce the relatively wide income inequality and sluggish average real wage growth that characterized the United States.

The economic performance picture clouded even further with the collapse of the dot.com bubble in spring 2000 in the United States. An economic recession deepened after the September 11, 2001, terrorist attacks, and this led to an increase in the U.S. unemployment rate (the rate was 6.1 percent in May 2003) and the return of stagnant wages (real GDP grew only .3 percent in 2001).

Osterman et al (2001) pointed to the persistent problems that plagued the U.S. labor market and suggested the need for enhanced labor market intermediaries that could help workers develop their skills and labor market opportunities. Embedded in the recommendations provided by Osterman et al., Freeman and Rogers (1999), and other industrial relations researchers was support for steps that would make it easier for unions to organize and make use of a broader array of representation tools.

In 2002, the Enron, WorldCom, and other corporate financial scandals further spurred debates about potential alterations in employee and stockholder governance. Yet, there was no serious policy discussion of the potential contribution that tripartism might play in the United States. The historical prominence of market forces and the strong performance of the U.S. economy in the 1990s make it difficult for national-level tripartism to become a part of policy discussions.

SUMMARY

There is a strong tendency toward further decentralization and individualization in labor-management interactions in the United States. In the union sector collective bargaining is shifting toward the plant or subplant (workgroup) level and pattern bargaining generally has eroded. Labor and management are ever more likely to interact informally, outside of formal collective bargaining structures, to discuss a reorganization of work or productivity initiative or some other workplace issue. Meanwhile, individualization of employment condition determination is spreading even more dramatically because of the prevalence of nonunion employment.

At the same time that these decentralizing tendencies are spreading, in other dimensions there are centralizing tendencies underway in the structure of labor-management interactions. These include a growth in regional tripartite training forums and efforts by unions and management to create more globally coordinated industrial relations strategies. Globalization is challenging labor to overcome the formidable barriers that limit cross-national labor structures and actions. In response to these challenges, meaningful cross-national efforts are underway within the U.S. labor movement, particularly focused on enhancing linkages to the Mexican labor movement. Nevertheless, cross-national collective bargaining in North America remains a distant hope. Meanwhile, as suggested by our case study of a multinational corporation, globalization is spurring corporations to globally coordinate labor policies and practices both to take advantage of more globally coordinated production strategies and to spread corporate-sanctioned bargaining and workplace practices.

Behind many of these trends, corporate global work practice coordination, the further decentralization of the structure of collective bargaining, and the increasing importance of regional training consortiums, are pressures linked to work reorganization and workplace productivity initiatives. The common result is various forms of coordinated decentralization as the parties seek to combine the advantages of local variation and flexibility with the stability and coherence provided through central coordination. Given its particular institutional and historical legacies, coordinated decentralization in the United States does not involve national-level tripartism, and the local variants of coordination emerging in a variety of industrial relations settings largely occur through private initiative.

Although the U.S. economy exhibited great strength in the 1990s, a difficult recession started with the bursting of the dot.com bubble in spring 2000 and this recession accelerated after the September 11, 2001, terrorist attacks. The recession put stagnant earnings growth and unemployment back on the policy agenda along with new concerns about corporate governance brought to the fore by the Enron, WorldCom, and other corporate financial scandals. While these recent economic travails provided support to calls for stronger labor market intermediaries and unions, significant support for national-level tripartism was not surfacing, even in the face of the success social pacts and related forms of national-level tripartism were having in a number of European countries (as documented elsewhere in this book).

Yet even though national-level tripartism was lacking historically and not on the policy agenda, various forms of coordination were expanding in the United States in a manner that was similar to developments in other countries. Coordination of labor market activities came, for example, through the expansion of regional training partnerships, efforts at cross-national unionism, and attempts by multinational corporations to develop more regional and global human resource and industrial relations strategies and structures. The United States also experienced increasingly decentralized collective bargaining in firms where unionism continued, and extensive growth occurred through the spread of the ultimate form of decentralized employment relations, namely, nonunionism.

Thus, while exceptional in the extent to which national-level tripartism conflicted with labor market traditions and prevailing political ideology, as compared to the other countries analyzed in this book, through the expansion of various forms of labor market coordination and the general downward shift occurring in the locus of labor-management interactions, the United States was not exceptional.

Summary

Reconstructing Decentralized Collective Bargaining and Other Trends in Labor-Management-Government Interactions

Wonduck Lee, Joohee Lee, and Harry C. Katz

Previous research has shown that a widespread downward shift occurred in the 1980s in the locus of collective bargaining, often from a national level or multicompany level to the firm or plant level. Yet, somewhat surprisingly, in the 1990s even though in some ways the structure of collective bargaining continued to decentralize, in many countries this decentralization was accompanied by mechanisms that provided greater coordination and cooperation between labor, management, and government. National-level tripartism, seemingly discredited by the failure of incomes policies to stem inflation in the 1970s, resurfaced in a number of countries as an effective social policy. But how was it possible for bargaining structures to simultaneously trend in both upward and downward directions? And what, in particular, are the long-term implications of the reemergence of national-level tripartism? These issues are addressed in this summary chapter.

DECENTRALIZATION AND INDIVIDUALIZATION

In the countries analyzed in this volume there are common trends toward increased decentralization in the locus of labor-management interactions and greater individualization in the determination of employment conditions. At the same time, the specific form and roles played by decentralized collective bargaining and the more individualized determination of employment conditions varies much within countries. Furthermore, countries vary enormously in whether, and if so how, these trends interact with national-level tripartite activities.

The increase in the amount and intensity of subnational collective bargaining in most countries took the form of greater company or plant-level collective bargaining. In Italy, for example, Regini and Regalia report on the increasing use of company-level collective bargaining. Simultaneously in Italy, more localized collective bargaining also was appearing through an expansion in the amount of territorial collective bargaining. In the United States, in unionized settings plant–level collective bargaining intensified as company or multicompany agreements either fragmented or saw their influence weaken as they took on the role of framework agreements that allowed for more differentiation within local agreements.[1] Australia's previously highly centralized industrial relations system with a heavy role for a wage tribunal system and the Australian Industrial Relations Commission experienced a rapid spread of enterprise-based collective bargaining and, according to Baird and Lansbury, entered a phase of "fragmented flexibility."

In Germany, the formal structure of collective bargaining did not change as the dual interest representation system and sectoral agreements continued, yet the influence of works councils increased. As Bosch comments, "Works councils have become, de facto, grassroots union organizations through their negotiation of shop floor issues, particularly, work organization." In addition, the influence of sectoral bargaining lessened as hardship clauses that allowed for the negotiation of local exceptions to sectoral contractual standards spread, and especially in eastern Germany, some companies withdrew from sectoral bargaining.

In a variety of countries local collective bargaining became a vehicle by which shop floor productivity and workplace flexibility were used to develop particular solutions that met the needs of individual firms. Yet, although local collective bargaining came to play an increasingly important role, there was variation in the degree to which countries retained mechanisms that coordinated employment-related outcomes. In Germany, works councils continued to exercise a strong coordinating role. In the Netherlands, central pay targets and other policies agreed to in national *overlag* played a coordinating role across industry-level collective bargaining. In Italy, national-level social pacts provided framework agreements and set minimum conditions for local collective bargaining.

Nevertheless, increased coordination across the various bargaining levels within country systems did not occur everywhere. In the United States, the traditional coordinating role of pattern bargaining (historically limited by the low level of unionization) weakened further and nothing replaced it. In Australia, as the role of the wage tribunal system weakened and local (and in some cases individualized) bargaining increased, the traditional coordinating role played by the wage tribunal system and the Australian Industrial Relations Commission weakened (although the influence of these institutions did not go to zero).

As collective bargaining increasingly came to focus on work practice issues, all the countries analyzed in this volume experienced greater individualization in the determination of employment conditions. In European countries (Italy, Germany, and the Netherlands) and in Ireland, individualization was heavily focused around efforts to introduce greater flexibility and variation in working times. Slomp describes how in the Netherlands the resulting variety in working time arrangements led to a blurring in the distinction between full- and part-time work.

At the same time that the locus of collective bargaining was shifting downward due to the fact that local bargaining emerged as the central forum to address workplace issues, economic pressures were leading to a broadening in the scope of the collective bargaining that was still occurring at higher levels. Again events in the Netherlands provide a clear illustration of wider trends. Slomp reports how in the Netherlands the scope of industry-level collective bargaining broadened to include social security benefits, employee participation, childcare, and environmental issues. The country studies consistently also demonstrate that it was the need to address broad economic and social issues that was behind the reemergence of national-level social pacts.

THE REVIVAL OF NATIONAL-LEVEL SOCIAL PACTS

In the 1980s, many analysts argued that corporatism, high-level negotiations involving aggregate representatives of labor and management representatives that often directly or indirectly involved national governments, had failed and consequently, were unlikely to recur. Corporatism had become associated with wage inflexibility and thus considered too dysfunctional for the new competitive environment.

Events in the 1990s proved this analysis wrong. National-level social dialogue reemerged not only in countries with a strong tradition of corporatist policy-making coordination (e.g., the Netherlands), but it also appeared in those countries where the traditional prerequisites had been weak, as the cases of Italy, Ireland, and Korea described in this book demonstrate.

National emergencies played a key role in promoting social pacts. For some members of the European Union (Italy, the Netherlands, and Ireland) a primary motivation for the social pacts reached in the 1990s was the need to bring inflation rates and public debts into conformance with "parameters" set for membership in the European Monetary Union (EMU).[2] The Asian financial crisis played a parallel role in Korea, leading the parties there to turn to a tripartite commission to formulate recommendations concerning labor market and labor law policy reforms. The goal in Korea was to revive the economy and maintain social peace through a difficult period of economic adjustment.

While national emergencies emerged as a distinctive new factor encouraging social pacts, this did not imply that social pacts bore no similarities to earlier corporatism. According to Teague and Donaghey, the central goal of the social partnership initiatives adopted in Ireland since 1987, like earlier corporatism, was wage moderation.

Yet, in a number of important ways the social pacts negotiated in the 1990s differed from previous corporatism, including differences in the methods used to determine pay. For example, in Ireland's social pacts pay increases were tied to projected economic growth rates and not to expected rates of inflation, as had been the case as part of past incomes policies. The social pacts of the 1990s also were distinguished from early income policies in the way the pacts allowed for the sharing productivity gains through company-level collective bargaining, as in Italy and Ireland.

The scope of tripartite agreement also broadened beyond the focus of previous incomes policies or corporatism. In Ireland, for example, the Partnership 2000 program promoted participatory workplace restructuring. Employee and union participation became attractive to Irish unionists who worried about the effects that macroeconomic targets would exert on workplace outcomes and conditions. Meanwhile, employers viewed partnership at the enterprise level as a mechanism for sustaining economic competitiveness.

Regalia and Regini describe how unstable political exchanges of the 1980s in Italy were transformed into effective tripartism in the 1990s. The making of social pacts during the 1990s was facilitated by the strengthening of the Italian union movement that was greatly assisted by the reforms that took place in 1993 involving the introduction of a new workplace representation system (RSU's). The new workplace representative bodies helped revitalize unions by reconnecting them with workers and by clarifying the relationship between shop floor labor-management interactions and interactions taking place at other bargaining levels in the Italian industrial relations system. In the process, cooperation among the three major union confederations was restored. In particular, the consolidation of efficient channels for employee voice and the coordination of union activities proved to be crucial ingredients in the success of the 1995 pension reforms.

In a number of countries the processes that produced the social pacts that emerged in the 1990s included participation of a broader range of interest groups than was characteristic of earlier corporatism. In Ireland, for example, in addition to the traditional labor and management representatives, representatives of the not-for-profit sector and organizations representing the unemployed, women, and the socially excluded were included in the negotiating process from the mid-1990s. The participation of civic associations (i.e., civil society) improved the problem-solving capacity of social dialogue and helped facilitate the inclusion of new topics in tripartite discussions concerning matters such as the rationalization of public services, education, poverty, and equal opportunities.[3]

THE EFFECTS OF TRIPARTISM ON ECONOMIC PERFORMANCE AND SOCIAL POLICY REFORM

Much has been accomplished through the new wave of national-level tripartite dialogue and pacts. In the Netherlands, Ireland, and Italy social pacts successfully promoted wage moderation, which in turn helped stimulate declines in unemployment and positive economic growth. In effect, the social pacts triggered particularly virtuous economic cycles that continue to this day in the Netherlands and Ireland. Ireland, a country that once faced the dual economic problems of high public debt and high unemployment, now enjoys virtually full employment and impressive economic growth (and stable industrial relations). The Netherlands also experienced a dramatic reduction in the unemployment rate after instituting the "Polder model," becoming one of the best-performing economies in Europe (with the lowest unemployment rate in the European Union in 2002).

Social pacts also led to pension system reforms and promoted labor market flexibility by stimulating legal and other institutional changes that facilitated expansions in part-time and temporary employment. And the improvements in national economic performance and government budgetary position brought by social pacts, by helping the respective countries conform to the requirements of the European Monetary Union, also helped stabilize the European Union.

In Korea and Italy, the structure of labor relations was reformed through national-level social dialogue. As discussed above (and more fully in Regalia and Regini's chapter) in Italy, the role of workplace representation structures was clarified, as was the relationship between industry and company (and other forms of local) collective bargaining. In Korea, the Tripartite Commission legalized the right of unions to engage in political activity, made it legal for public school teachers to unionize, and established works councils for government officials.

While this is an extensive set of accomplishments, the items in this set provide few direct and immediate benefits to unions and the workers they represent. The labor movement clearly benefits in the long run from the virtuous economic cycle stimulated by social pacts in the Netherlands and elsewhere, and labor gains long-term benefits from the stabilization of European Union and the long-term advantages of pension reforms and government account balancing. Yet, for labor, these were all long-term and indirect benefits, if benefits at all. One can then understand why labor was both a reluctant partner in the formation of many of the tripartite arrangements and continues to debate whether to support those endeavors. The limited direct benefits gained by labor movements from social pacts also helps explain why unions often put their focus not on the promotion of social pacts, but rather on the maintenance or introduction of national-level collective bargaining.

The potential of national-level collective bargaining as a mechanism to first define and then raise employment standards is clear to the labor movement. As Lee and Lee report, the Korean labor movement (and especially a key labor confederation, the KCTU) views the creation of industry-level collective bargaining and industrial unions as prime objectives. While some industry-level collective bargaining has emerged in recent years in Korea from this push from the labor movement (the banking industry is an interesting case), employer opposition has stifled the spread of industry-level collective bargaining.

The lack of labor movement excitement over the contributions of national-level social pacts contributes to the "exhaustion" that now seems to surround social pacts in Italy, and to some extent in Ireland. For business and government, in contrast, the benefits from social pacts are both more direct and short run. The wage moderation and government budget balancing accomplished through the pacts were sufficient to convince business and government in a number of countries to support them.

Yet, the business community and governments have not solidly endorsed social pacts. Even in the face of the clear advantages to the pubic interest provided by the social pacts of the 1990s, the Berlusconi government in Italy and the Howard government in Australia, in particular, saw no value in national-level pacts. Both of these governments instead preferred to rely on the "unimpeded" market as a method to determine labor market outcomes. This pattern also clarifies one of the key determinants of temporal and cross-country variation in the use of tripartite pacts: the political choice of governmental actors rather than the performance of social dialogue.

A factor that made it difficult for political actors to assess the economic performance implications of national-level tripartism was the strong economic growth that took place in United States (up until spring 2000), which occurred without the benefit (and some argued because of the very absence) of national-level tripartism. Our reading of the economic evidence, supporting the claims of the "varieties of capitalism" research literature (discussed more fully below), is that there is no one best way to organize national industrial relations systems and national economies. The successful economic performance of the Netherlands and Ireland in the 1990s suggests that social pacts can make a very positive contribution.[4] Yet the U.S. economic growth experience of the 1990s indicates that there is an alternative market-based path to economic growth.

The country chapters do suggest that with regard to social welfare concerns, the use of national–level tripartism appears to make a clear positive contribution. For, although the U.S. (market) model provides one road to strong economic growth, it appears to be a road that includes very large increases in income inequality and the absence of forums for addressing social welfare problems. In contrast, as discussed above, social pacts helped facilitate social policy reforms in a number of countries.

At the same time, evidence from the countries analyzed in this book suggests that while accomplishing much, national-level tripartism does not have the capacity to completely stop (or reverse) the trend toward increasing income inequality. Income inequality rose in the 1990s even in the Netherlands and Ireland where social pacts were strong as well as in countries where tripartism was lacking (the United States and Australia). What is less obvious is whether the presence of social pacts served to moderate market forces that otherwise would have produced even more economic inequality in those countries that had social pacts if those social pacts had not been in place.

EVER MORE DIVERSE "VARIETIES OF CAPITALISM"

A core principle in the modern field of comparative political economy is conceptual differentiation between "coordinated market economies" and "liberal market economies" (Soskice 1990; Hall and Soskice 2001). The former, including much of Western Europe, exhibit deep institutional linkages between firms and banks. Coordinated market economies also possess industrial relations systems with "coordinated" and often centralized wage setting. In contrast, liberal market economies are characterized by market-driven financial sectors and arms length separation in the interests and roles of firms and banks. Industrial relations systems in liberal market economies, as in the United States and the United Kingdom, involve weak unions and decentralized (mostly market-based) pay determination. A related classification scheme has been proposed by Traxler (1995a) who, when analyzing industrial relations changes in the 1990s, differentiates between those countries that experienced "coordinated" and "uncoordinated" decentralization in the structure of collective bargaining.

This book demonstrates the inadequacy of these dichotomous categories by revealing the high degree of variation that exists in the role and nature of the tripartite social dialogue that appeared in a number of countries in the 1990s. The range of variation includes the absence of national level tripartism in the United States, and the elimination of a previously important national-level government-labor "accord" in Australia. But instead of a contrasting common form of coordinated market economy or coordinated decentralization, what this book reveals is wide diversity in the nature, function, and operation of national-level social pacts. The Netherlands, Ireland, and Italy all made successful use of national-level tripartism in the 1990s. And in Germany, even though wage setting did not occur at the national level, tripartite social dialogue has been used successfully, as Bosch notes, to address training and a number of other issues, including employment security and job creation (through "employment pacts"). Yet even within these countries there was much variation in the specific employment issues and social policies addressed through tripartite pacts. Meanwhile, in Korea and Japan, the use of tripartite pacts has appeared only in particular episodes over the last twenty years with little effective national-level wage setting in recent years.[5]

Furthermore, in contrast to previous research, the country chapters reveal common trends in the structure of collective bargaining in countries that have been labeled "coordinated" or "uncoordinated," including expansion in various types of decentralized and individualized determination of pay and other employment conditions. As a result, greater refinement is needed in analysis of the shifts underway in labor, management, and government interactions than that provided by the dichotomous categories used in previous research.

Another key finding of this book is that the presence of some common trends within countries in the changes occurring in labor, management, and government interactions is not inconsistent with the fact that there is an expanding variation in capitalist economies. In this way, this volume follows many of the core concepts within the varieties of capitalism literature. For example, the country studies in this volume similarly find that various economic institutions and structures, including industrial relations practices, reinforce one another and fit together into discreet patterns. And consistent with the varieties of capitalism literature this book lends support to the view that there is no one best way to organize industrial economies, as effectively integrated systems may differ in the terms of their integration, yet produce equally efficient outcomes. The key challenge for policymakers continues to be to insure that the various parts of economic systems fit together and reinforce one another in a positive direction.

This book also contributes to comparative political economy by showing the advantages to be found in research that includes within comparative studies Asian economies rather than the traditional exclusive focus on English-speaking and European countries. Japan is particularly interesting because it entered the 1980s with an industrial relations system that relied heavily on enterprise-level collective bargaining with a strong informal role played by the Spring Wage Offensive, which served to coordinate wage setting across firms. In Korea, on the other hand, determined efforts at national-level labor policy dialogue emerged only in the aftermath of periodic economic crises.[6]

THE FUTURE?

It is difficult to forecast future developments in the structure of labor, management, and government interactions. Despite the revival of social pacts in the 1990s in a number of countries, there is widespread evidence of a declining influence of collective bargaining and declining union membership and representation. Even in Germany, the coverage of sectoral bargaining is decreasing and sectoral agreements increasingly are not respected at the enterprise level.

Serious problems are being created by the falling union membership rates and associated union weakening occurring in nearly all the countries analyzed in this volume. Japanese trade unions, for example, lost much political influence and membership after the Heisei recession during the 1990s. In Australia, union membership fell from 49 percent of the work force in 1990 to 25 percent in 2000. While Regini and Regalia take note of the positive role that union democracy played in generating grass-roots support for social pacts in Italy, it should be noted that union democracy is of little value if the labor movement's power and influence becomes marginalized.[7] Here again there was much variation across countries with unions faring somewhat better in those countries that had a more coordinated bargaining structure as compared to unions in countries that lacked such coordination.

Growing individualization in the determination of employment conditions also posed a serious threat to the institution of collective bargaining and was detrimental to the maintenance of equity among workers. In Korea, for example, severe social problems were created by the increasing use of atypical employment and the replacement of regular and long-term employment by "irregular" employees who lacked employment security and received significantly lower pay and benefits. The temporary and day workers who are not allowed to join enterprise unions in Korea are bound to be subject to individualized employment contracts and do not possess the bargaining power necessary for the promotion of decent work conditions.

Atypical work, commonly outside the influence of collective bargaining and regulated on an individualized basis, was on the rise in a number of countries. The pressure for individualization of the employment relationship also reached into the upper tier of the labor market, as highly skilled employees in countries such as the Netherlands and Australia were shifted from collective to individual contracts. Meanwhile deunionization, which Katz labels, "the ultimate form of decentralization," spread rapidly in a number of countries, with individualized employment relationships appearing as the alternative to collective bargaining in most nonunion settings. In Australia, a clear challenge to collective representation emerged through the Howard government's promotion of the Australian Workplace Agreements (i.e., individual contracts).

All these changes make it especially difficult to construct and sustain tripartite dialogue as the power of one of the key participants in dialogue, namely unions, declined.[8] It was only natural that employers increasingly pushed for market-based outcomes and governments increasingly went along with this push in countries where unions became marginal members of the economic and political system. With a strong trend toward lower union density and collective bargaining coverage, it is difficult to sustain either highly coordinated collective bargaining or effective social pacts.

Labor, management, and government interact increasingly at a number of different levels. While certain aspects of collective bargaining have become more decentralized and individualized in recent years, in some countries at least, this was not inconsistent with the successful use of national-level tripartism to address a variety of economic and social problems. The research presented in this volume suggests that the use of social dialogue in the future will be determined by whether governments have the political will, employers the inclination, and unions the strength to support this variety of capitalism.

Notes

CHAPTER 1

1. The term "Republic of Ireland" is used in this instance. However, throughout the paper the terms "Ireland" and "Irish" refer to the Republic of Ireland and not to Northern Ireland, which has a very different system of employment relations.

2. (1) Competitiveness, adaptability, flexibility, and innovation in the enterprise; (2) Better systems of work organization; (3) Training and development that is linked to lifelong learning; (4) Measures to promote equality of opportunity and family friendly working arrangements; (5) Problem solving and conflict avoidance; (6) Occupational safety, health and safety issues including physical environment of partnership and improvement; (7) Information and consultation; (8) Time off, facilities and training for staff representatives; and (9) Financial forms of involvement.

3. Established initially as the National Centre for Partnership under Partnership 2000.

CHAPTER 3

1. For discussion of these features and more details, see Cella (1989), Ferner and Hyman (1992), and Regalia and Regini (1995; 1998).

2. The categories of workers covered by agreements at this level vary greatly and have been repeatedly redefined. The metalworkers agreement, for example, is an extremely broad (multi-industry) sectoral collective bargaining agreement, while the coverage of agreements in the chemical and textile industries is much more limited.

3. In the late 1940s the initially unified CGIL split along ideological lines and two other major confederations, CISL and UIL were created. Originally the three confederations were linked respectively to the Communists and Socialists (CGIL), the Christian Democrats (CISL) and the small lay parties, including the Republicans, the Social Democrats, and the reformist wing of the Socialists (UIL).

4. Besides the industrial unions affiliated to the three main confederations, the Italian trade union system also includes other minor organizations termed "autonomous" unions in that they are not affiliated to any of the three main union confederations and may have their own confederations.

5. The agreement on the *scala mobile* was rapidly converted into law. However, in a period of growing inflation, it had the undesired effects of flattening pay levels, reducing the space for collective bargaining, and fueling inflation. Consequently, as we shall see in the next section, it became one of the most contentious issues involving the social partners during the 1980s until its abolition in 1992.

6. Tax deductions were offered to offset the increase in taxation due to the growth of nominal wages in this period of high inflation. Without this compensatory mechanism, in a progressive fiscal system like Italy's, workers' real wages would actually have decreased.

7. "Clean Hands" was the campaign conducted by the Milanese judiciary against political corruption.

8. Under the tripartite agreement of July 1993, all the actors agreed that a single pattern of workplace representation would be introduced throughout the economy and be named Rappresentanza sindacale unitaria (RSU, unitary union structure) (Carrieri 1995). Like the previous works councils, this was a representative body elected by all workers and provided representation to the trade unions, as they had priority in nominating candidates. For the first time the same representative system was to cover all economic sectors, including public employment. The novel features of the new system were produced by the fact that the employers realized that it was also in their interest to place in-company representative bodies on a sounder footing, so that they might have a reliable partner for decentralized bargaining. Accordingly, in December 1993, the employers' associations and the union confederations signed a national-level interconfederal agreement on the RSU, the first to regulate such matters after thirty years of informal arrangements. Not approved, however, was the proposal put forward by the minister of labor to give statutory definition to the RSU (this came later, in 1998, but only for the public sector). This failure is responsible for the marked instability and weakness of the system, as demonstrated by recent figures that show the limited spread of RSU in the private sector of the economy (Cnel 2000, 335–48).

9. According to figures issued by the OECD and the European Commission, quoted in *La Repubblica Affari & Finanza* 11, no. 15 (22 April 1996): 1–3, in 1993, overall social spending excluding education was 25.8 percent of GDP in Italy as compared to the European average of 28.5 percent. However, spending on pensions in Italy was 15.4 percent of GDP compared to an average of 11.9 percent in the twelve countries of the European Union.

10. The CGIL especially has been concerned with the possibility that acceptance of substandard wages and employment conditions, even though targeted on less developed areas and conceived as experiments of limited duration subject to monitoring and possible revocation, may end up becoming a "Trojan horse" by fostering wider deregulation.

11. See the Ires Lombardia periodic survey on company-level industrial relations (Regalia and Ronchi 1988–92; Lizzeri 2002).

12. Or at least it did so until 2000, when the resumption of inflation widened the gap between the real and planned inflation rates on the basis of which wage increases had been fixed by industry-level collective bargaining since the 1993 agreement.

13. In the late 1990s, new unions affiliated to CGIL, CISL and UIL were set up to represent contingent workers (temporary or self-employed workers) (Regalia 2003; Ballarino 2002). Although membership is still very low in these unions, this may signal the beginning of a significant extension of collective bargaining.

14. For similar estimates from other regional surveys see Fabbri and Pini's (1999) analysis of Emilia Romagna; Lizzeri's (2002) analysis of Lombardy; and Giaccone's analysis (2001) of Veneto.

15. For another example of an area (Gioia Tauro) contract, see Cnel (2000, 579–609).

CHAPTER 4

1. The Federal Labor Court (*Bundesarbeitsgericht*) decided in 1968 that the wage drift negotiated by work councils did not have the protections afforded to collective agreements (Keller 1993, 3d ed., 117).

2. The terms *East* and *West German* refer to the eastern and western regions of unified Germany.

3. Collectively agreed annual wages are somewhat below this level, however, since supplementary payments such as holiday pay and the thirteenth month's salary benefit are lower. Moreover, the agreed weekly working time is on average 1.7 hours longer than in West Germany (BMA 2001, 21–24).

4. German companies outsource less than their U.S. counterparts. In the United States only 37 percent of employees in the manufacturing industry are

involved in service activities, compared with 48 percent in Germany (Wagner 1998).

5. The percentages cited here add up to 103 percent because a few works councilors gave more than one answer.

6. The situation was very different in other countries. France, for example, did not use municipal companies to provide water, public transport, and energy as in Germany. Such services were provided in France by large private companies, such as the former Générale des Eaux, and Lyonnaise des Eaux and Electricité de France (EDF).

7. After I finished this article the German government abolished the Alliance of Work in the beginning of 2003. The government argued that the social partners were not able to find agreements on necessary reforms of the welfare state. It was, however, obvious that the government did not want to find a compromise with the unions any more. After the abolishment of the Alliance of Work it announced its Agenda 2010 with substantial cuts in unemployment benefits and deregulation of job protection legislation.

8. Sengenberger and Campbell (1994) differentiate between substantial, promotion, and procedural standards.

CHAPTER 5

1. In 1964, for example, enterprise unions accounted for 93.6 percent of all unions, while craft and industrial unions, respectively, accounted for only 1.6 percent and 3.1 percent of all unions (Rōdōshō 1964).

2. Enterprise unions (*Kigyōbetsu Kumiai*) refer either to plant unions or to enterprise-level federations of plant unions (if there is more than one plant in an enterprise). The relationship between plant unions and their federation varies with enterprises. Some enterprise unions concentrate their decision-making authority at the federation level, while other enterprise unions delegate decision-making authority to plant unions (Shinoda 1989, 16–17).

3. There have been some exceptions to this rule. Some industry-level federations, such as the All Japan Seamen's Union (the AJSU) and the General Federation of Private Railway Workers' Unions (the GFPRWU), engaged in industry-level collective bargaining with industry-level employers' associations (the industry-level bargaining in the private railway industry collapsed in the mid-1990s and bargaining was then decentralized to the enterprise-level). Collective bargaining was also conducted above the enterprise level in some branches of the textile industry, such as the cotton and synthetic fiber sectors, between the branch organizations of the federation of textile workers' unions and the labor relations committees of business associations (organized along product lines).

4. In subsequent JEIU surveys, the proportion of those who express either negative or indifferent views decreased to 40 percent in 1984 and then increased to 48 percent in both the 1989 and 1994 surveys (Chōsa Jihō 1990, 129; Chōsa Jihō 1995, 144).

5. The variance in wage increases among large steel firms decreased from 17.43 in 1960 to 14.66 in 1964 to 3.60 in 1970. The variance in wage increases among large firms in other major industries showed similar declines. Interindustry wage increase variance among large firms also decreased from 38.39 in 1961 to 17.75 in 1970 (see Lee 2000, 36–37; Rōdōshō 1972, 498–99).

6. IMF-JC is a loose confederation of industry-level federations in the metal industries. Members of the IMF-JC belonged to various national confederations. The Japan Federation of Steelworkers' Unions (the JFSWU) belonged to Sōhyō. The Confederation of Japan Automobile Workers' Unions (the JAW) and the Japan Confederation of Shipbuilding and Engineering Workers' Unions (the JCSEWU) belonged to Dōmei. The Japanese Electrical, Electronic, and Information Union (the JEIU) belonged to Chūritsu Rōren.

7. An increase in the influence of opposition parties in the Diet was largely due to the negative reaction of the public to political scandals and corruption in the ruling party, rather than to the increased power of organized labor.

8. This reflects the government's nonrecognition policy toward the two smaller leftist confederations.

9. Dispatched workers are employed (full or part-time) by manpower dispatching companies. Client companies pay fees to these companies and receive dispatched workers when they are short of manpower. Client companies can send these workers back to the manpower dispatching companies when they are no longer needed.

10. Interindustry wage coordination among employers during *Shuntō* declined in this period. The Eight Company Round Table Meeting (*Hasshakon*), established in 1976 as an "informal gathering of eight companies, two from each of the four key metal sectors" (including steel, autos, and electronics) to exchange information on an amount of wage increases, was discontinued in the 1999 *Shuntō*. Although the wage pattern had been set at the meeting in the past, it outlived its usefulness as a body for interindustry coordination because of the growing differences in economic conditions and performances across these industries (Sako 1997, 255; Weathers 1999, 964–65; Asahi Shimbun 1998).

11. It is too early to tell conclusively whether or not the decentralization trend within *Shuntō* wage bargaining is influencing wage settlements. However, the variation in wage increases among major corporations did increase slightly after 1996 (see table 5.2).

12. The discretionary work scheme gives workers "discretion" in carrying out their jobs as well as in how they spend working hours as long as they produce results. Under this work arrangement, employers do not have to pay overtime pay to workers.

13. There were other regional unions not affiliated with this federation. If the members of these unaffiliated unions are included, the total membership of regional unions is estimated to be just below thirty thousand (Takagi 1999a).

14. While most of the workers who receive counseling services are unorganized workers, some of them are members of enterprise unions. These workers are seeking help from regional unions because their enterprise unions do not offer much help in solving the disputes these workers have with their employers (interview with a Rengō official, December 8, 2001).

15. Rengō started a new organizing program in 1996 that emphasizes organizing part-time workers and forming regional unions (OISR 1999, 194).

16. The Nissan Workers' Union had exerted a strong influence on the pace of rationalization efforts of management based on the union's shop floor organization until the mid-1980s (Totsuka 1995).

17. The changed attitude of employers was indicated by Nikkeiren's policies. The employers' association proposed the division of regular employees between "flow" and "stock" types in 1992, and further elaborated this idea in 1995 in a document titled "Japanese-Style Management in a New Era." In this document, Nikkeiren proposed, among other things, the division of regular employees (whose employment status had been secure) into three groups with a different duration of employment as well as a shift from seniority-based wages to wages strictly based on workers' ability and performance (SRN 1995).

18. Katz (1993) points out three main hypotheses for the decentralization of bargaining structure; "shifts in bargaining power," "productivity coalitions focused around changes in work organization," and "diversification of corporate structure and worker interests." Due to a limit of space, I cannot examine each of these hypotheses in relation to the Japanese case. As the following passage indicates, however, the first hypothesis seems to offer the most plausible explanation for the decentralization trend that emerged in Japan in the 1990s.

19. Although no statistical data showing how part-time workers perceive discriminatory treatment are available to the author's knowledge, one of organizers of Zensen Dōmei (The Japanese Federation of Textile, Garment, Chemical, Mercantile, Food and Allied Industries Workers' Unions, one of the few industry-level federations that actively organize part-time workers) told the author that the sense of moral indignation was widespread among part-time workers (interview, September 14, 2002).

CHAPTER 6

1. A strong leftist labor movement emerged after the liberation from Japanese colonial rule in 1945, but the American Occupation Government effectively destroyed these unions, replacing them with state-controlled unions. Since then, the independent union movement in South Korea has always been regarded as some sort of a "communist" movement, which made unionism very vulnerable to both ideological and physical attacks from the state.

2. The average number of strikes from 1977 to 1986 was 173.6 per a year. For a comprehensive evaluation of industrial relations in Korea from the 1987–97 period, see Lee (1998).

3. The Asian financial crisis, which originated in Bangkok and spread to Korea in the winter of 1997, forced the Korean government to turn to the IMF for emergency credit. In return for the rescue package that prevented a lending-moratorium, the IMF imposed far-reaching structuring reforms along with its usual austerity policies. Since then, the government has faithfully followed suggestions attached to the IMF lending program, which required comprehensive restructuring of the financial sector, increasing transparency in corporate governance and flexibility in the labor market. After a few years of intensive structural adjustments, Korea appears to be on track for recovery.

4. In May 1996, the Presidential Commission on Industrial Relations Reform was organized to revise the labor law. Lee (1997) provides an overview of the activities of the commission and the contents of the labor law revision.

5. The most common change in developing countries that have recently experienced democratization and economic reform is a move toward a greater degree of flexibility in both individual labor law and collective labor relations, and toward a greater degree of liberalization in systems with a previously high degree of state intervention (Cook 1998). Korea was not an exception.

6. The rapid increase in nonstandard employment has not been a gender-neutral process. Despite the impact of the financial crisis, the proportion of male *regular* workers among the total male employed increased to 65.1 percent in 1998 from 64.7 percent a year earlier. But during the same period, the proportion of female *regular* workers among the total female employed sharply decreased to 34.2 percent from 38.2 percent.

7. Despite the depth of the problem, the initial response of the Korean government was fairly simple: "The capacity of the new Employment Insurance system will be strengthened to facilitate the redeployment of labor, in parallel with further steps to improve labor market flexibility" (IMF Stand-by Arrangement, Dec. 5, 1997).

8. Hyundai Motor Company, because of its privileged position in the economy, more or less has played the role of "pattern setter" in the manufacturing sector.

9. Most enterprise unions do not accept workers with temporary status as members.

10. This practice was justified during the authoritarian regimes, as the military government regulated the amount of union dues by law (it was abolished in 1996) (Kim 2000). The revised labor law in 1996 declared that any employer's payment of wages to full-time union officers constitutes an unfair labor practice, but the implementation of this revised law was delayed until the year 2007.

11. The bank mergers were conducted through a purchase and assumption arrangement, under which healthy banks were able to select the assets and liabilities of the weak banks (*Financial Times*, June 29, 1998).

12. This was the predecessor of the Ministry of Finance and Economy.

13. Urgent managerial reasons include takeovers, mergers, and acquisitions of businesses to avoid managerial difficulties.

14. Bonus and overtime have been more sensitive than regular wages to fluctuations in economic conditions. In 1998, these payments decreased more than 15 percent, while regular earnings recorded a 3 percent increase during the same period.

15. The FKI was established in 1961 as "a self-defense interest and lobbying organization," by a group of businessmen threatened by the new military regime's attempt to assure the *chaebols*' subservience to the state (Fields 1992). Since then, the FKI has gradually expanded its own research and supplemental facilities to improve its lobbying abilities.

16. The concept of the welfare state is a rather elusive one, but it is generally agreed that the definition is based on the extent to which equality in basic living conditions has been achieved among the citizens (Korpi 1980 and 1989). Hence, the levels of general public expenditures and public expenditures on social security, in particular, have been most extensively utilized as measures of welfare state development. When Korea joined the OECD in 1995, welfare expenditures constituted only 1.8 percent of GPD and 8.3 percent of government expenditure (Kim 1999).

17. Campbell (2000, 75) from the ILO assessed that "it is not unreasonable to assume in the Korean case that the Tripartite Commission played an important role in the promotion of economic reform amidst relative social stability."

CHAPTER 8

1. This discussion relies heavily on Katz and Kochan (2000, 392–94).
2. *Fact Finding Report* 1994: xi.

3. Decentralization of collective bargaining in the United States began to occur earlier in some industries as noted in Kochan, Katz, and McKersie (1994). United States developments are compared to those in other countries in Katz and Darbishire 2000.

4. The history of wage setting in the U.S. auto industry is discussed in more detail in Katz (1985).

5. The transplants, both union and nonunion, typically pay wages that are close to Big Three levels. However, the transplants have pension, medical care, and other fringe benefits that differ substantially from the benefits provided at the Big Three (the transplants often provide lower benefits) and from one another, often based on local labor market conditions.

6. In some other assembly plants there is a joint labor-management selection committee that screens and interviews candidates for the team coordinator position in a jointly designed assessment procedure. Meanwhile, other plants (such as GM's Shreveport truck assembly plant) allow the teams to chose the team leader selection procedure and as a result the selection procedure varies by work group across the plant.

7. The labor side-agreements create National Administrative Offices authorized to investigate public charges that one of the NAFTA countries is not enforcing its own labor laws. See Compa, 2001b, 454–57, for a description of a number of the NAALC complaints.

8. This overview of the state of cross-border union activities relies heavily on Compa 2001b. For an informative account of cross-national activities involving the U.S.-based CWA, see Cohen and Early 2000.

9. Annual GDP, unemployment, and inflation statistics cited above are from Council of Economic Advisors 2001.

SUMMARY

1. Other countries not analyzed in this volume, such as Sweden, also experienced more decentralized collective bargaining (Katz and Darbishire 2000).

2. Numerous East European countries also experimented formally with macrolevel corporatism during their transition period. Although they were mostly modeled on West European experiences, the creation and survival of corporatism in these countries has been much more dependent on governmental initiatives (Schmitter and Grote 1997).

3. Jørgensen (2000, 21) suggests that tripartism should now be described not so much by structural requirements, such as centralized unions and employers' organizations, but by the functional roles developed through the participation of labor and capital in agenda setting and policy development.

4. Kenworthy (2001), using a quantitative analysis of sixteen OECD countries, finds that the effects of corporatist institutions on low unemployment

disappeared in the 1990s, largely because employment outcomes in low-coordination countries improved rather than because outcomes in high-coordination countries deteriorated.

5. Interesting comparative studies of industrial relations that analyze European experiences include Crouch and Traxler (1995); Ferner and Hyman (1992a); and Iversen et al. (2000). Insightful comparisons between European and North American industrial relations systems are provided in Golden and Pontusson (1992).

6. Note, while the industrial relations systems in these two East Asian countries have been frequently described as similar, with enterprise unions being the most prevalent form of union organization in both, industrial relations in these countries significantly differ in several other respects. Perhaps most critical is the fact that while Korean enterprise unions are mostly composed of blue-collar production workers, Japanese enterprise unions recruit both blue-collar and white-collar workers. The latter nonproduction workers usually consider their work experience in trade unions as a step leading to higher managerial positions. As a result, the overall orientation of the Japanese labor movement has been quite cooperative towards management, whereas militant Korean union leaders promoted adversarial relations with employers.

7. Also see Baccaro (2002) for an interesting and consistent account of the positive role played by internal union democracy in the Italian pension reform process.

8. Visser (2002) also worries that declining union strength will result in a decline in coordinated collective bargaining.

References

ABS (Australian Bureau of Statistics). 2001. Cat. no. 6248, Sept Quarter, Table 6.
———. 2000. *Employee Earnings and Hours Australia*. Cat. no. 6306.0 May.
ACTU (Australian Council of Trade Unions). 2001. *Our Future at Work*. Melbourne: ACTU.
———. 2000. *Unions at Work*. Melbourne: ACTU.
ACTU/CAI (Australian Council of Trade Unions/Confederation of Australian Industry). 1988. *Joint Statement on Participative Practices*. Canberra: Australian Government Publishing Service.
AFL-CIO. 2002. "Helping Low Wage Workers Succeed through Innovative Union Partnerships." Washington, D.C.: AFL–CIO Working for America Institute.
Allen, Kieran. 2000. *The Celtic Tiger: The Myth of Social Partnership in Ireland*. Manchester: Manchester University Press.
ALP/ACTU (Australian Labor Party/Australian Council of Trade Unions). 1983. *Statement of Accord between the ALP and ACTU Regarding Economic Policy*. Melbourne: ALP/ACTU.
Arbeidsinspectie. 1996–2001. *Najaarsrapportage CAO-Safspraken*. The Hague: Arbeidsinspectie (annual surveys).
———. 1996–2001. *Voorjaarsrapportage CAO-Safspraken*. The Hague: Arbeidsinspectie (annual surveys).
Arthur, Jeffrey B. 1992. "The Link between Business Strategy and Industrial Relations Systems in American Steel Mini-Mills." *Industrial and Labor Relations Review* 45 (April): 488–506.
Asahi Shimbun (Asahi Newspaper). 1998. "'Yokonarabi' Hōkai, Fukyōkan ga Kasoku, ōzume Shuntō." (The Collapse of the Side-by-Side Style,

the Deepening Sense of Recession, the Final Stage of Shuntō). March 14.
Australian Productivity Commission. 1999. *Microeconomic Reforms and Australian Productivity: Exploring the Links.* Melbourne: APC.
AWVN. 1998–2000 *Cao-overleg.* Haarlem: AWVN (annual surveys).
Baccaro, Lucio. 2002. "Negotiating the Italian Pension Reform with the Unions: Lessons for Corporatist Theory." *Industrial and Labor Relations Review* 55 (April): 413–31.
———. 2000. "Centralized Collective Bargaining and the Problem of 'Compliance': Lessons from the Italian Experience." *Industrial and Labor Relations Review* 53 (4) July: 579–601.
Bahnmüller, R., R. Bispinck, and A. Weiler. 1999. "Tarifpolitik und Lohnbildung in Deutschland am Beispiel Ausgewählter Wirtschaftszweige." WSI-Diskussionspapier No. 9: Düsseldorf, Göttingen, Tübingen.
Ballarino, Gabriele. 2002. "Contrattare L'eterogeneità: Il Sindacato Lo bardo e la Rappresentanza del Lavoro Atipico." In *Lavoro e Sindacato in Lombardia*, edited by Daniele Checchi et al., 229–56. Milan: Franco Angeli.
Ballarino, Gabriele, Matteo Bolocan Goldstein, Cinzia Fontana, Barbara Lizzeri, Emanuele Mascelli, and Gabriele Pasqui 2001. "The Regulation of New Forms of Employment and Work in Lombardy between Institutionalized Concertation and Experimentation." LocLevConc Working Paper, WP/01/17/EN. Milan: Ires Lombardia (also on www.ireslombardia.it).
Bamber, Greg J., and Russell D. Lansbury. 1997. "The Auto Industry." In *Changing Employment Relations in Australia*, edited by Jim Kitay and Russell D. Lansbury, 81–101. Melbourne: Oxford University Press.
Barbera, Filippo. 2001. "Le Politiche della Fiducia. Limiti e Possibilità dei Patti Territoriali." Ph.D. dissertation, University of Milan.
Barbieri, Marco. 1995. "Le Politiche Contrattuali dopo il Protocollo di Luglio: Continuità e Discontinuità Degli Assetti Contrattuali nel Pubblico Impiego." In *Le Relazioni Sindacali in Italia. Rapporto 1993/94*, edited by CESOS, 295–307. Rome: Edizioni Lavoro.
Barrett, A., T. Callan, and B. Nolan. 1999. "Rising Wage Inequality, Returns to Education and Labor Market Institutions: Evidence from Ireland." *British Journal of Industrial Relations* 37 (1): 77–100.
BCA (Business Council of Australia). 1999. *Managerial Leadership in the Workplace.* Melbourne: BCA.
Berggren, Christian. 1999. "Introduction: Between Globalization and Multidomestic Variation." In *Being Local Worldwide: ABB and the Challenge of Global Management*, edited by Jacques Belanger et al., 1–15 Ithaca, N.Y.: ILR/Cornell University Press.
Biagi, Marco. 2001. "Dopo la Riforma Costituzionale. Relazioni di Lavoro." *Il Diario del Lavoro*, 15 March.

Birindelli, Lorenzo, and Giuseppe D'Aloia. 2001. "Retribuzioni, Produttività e Distribuzione del Reddito Prima e dopo il 1993." Rome, Ires nazionale, Working paper.
Bispinck, R. 2001. "Betriebliche Interessenvertretung, Entgelt und Tarifpolitik." *WSI-Mitteilungen* 52 (2): 124–32.
Bispinck, R. and Tarifarchiv. 1999. "Das Märchen vom Starren Flächentarifvertrag, Elemente Qualitativer Tarifpolitik." 37. Dusseldorf: Hans-Böckler-Stiftung.
———. 1998. "Wage Setting System—An Analysis of Differentiation, Decentralization, and Deregulation of Sectoral Collective Agreements." In *The German Model of Industrial Relations between Adaptation and Erosion*, edited by Reiner Hoffmann, et al., 9–26. Dusseldorf: Hans-Böckler-Stiftung.
Bispinck, R., and T. Schulten. 2000. "Tarifpolitik und Bündnis für Arbeit." *WSI-Mitteilungen* 53 (6): 406–7.
Bispinck, R. and Tarifarchiv 2001. Tarifjahr 2000: Moderate Lohnabschlüsse plus "Beschäftigungsbrücke," *WSI-Mitteilungen* 54 (2): 133–43.
Blank, Rebecca. 1994. "Does a Larger Social Safety Net Mean Less Economic Flexibility?" In *Working Under Different Rules*, edited by Richard Freeman, 157–87. A National Bureau of Economic Research Project Report. New York: Russell Sage Foundation.
Blau, Fran and Lawrence Kahn. 1996. "International Differences in Male Wage Inequality: Institutions Versus Market Forces." *Journal of Political Economy* 106 (August): 791–837.
BMA. 2001. "Bundesministerium für Arbeit und Sozialordnung, Tarifvertragliche Arbeitsbedingungen im Jahr 2001." Bonn.
Bolocan Goldstein, Matteo. 2002. "Il Patto per il Lavoro di Milano." In *Lavoro e Sindacato in Lombardia*, edited by Daniele Checchi et al., 287–96. Milan: Franco Angeli.
Bolocan Goldstein, Matteo, Gabriele Pasqui, and Paolo Perulli. 2000. "La Programmazione Negoziata e la Concertazione Territoriale dello Sviluppo in Lombardia: L'indagine Empirica." Ires Working Paper. Milan: Ires Lombardia (also on www.ireslombardia.it).
Bordogna, Lorenzo. 1994. *Pluralismo Senza Mercato. Rappresentanze e Conflitto nel Settore Pubblico*. Milan: Franco Angeli.
Bosch, Gerhard. 2000. "The Dual System of Vocational Training in Germany: Is it Still a Model?" In *Vers de Nouveaux Modes de Formation Professionnelle? Rôle des Acteurs et des Collaborations*, edited by D. G. Tremblay and P. Doray, 91–114. Quebec: University of Québec.
———. 1997. "Annual Working Hours: An International Comparison." In *Le Temps du Travail: Nouveaux Enjeux, Nouvelles Norme, Nouvelles*

Mesures, edited by G. Bosch, D. Meulders, and F. Michon, 13–36. Paris: Editions du Dulbea.

Bosch, Gerhard, and M. Lallement. 1991. "La Négociation Collective sur le Temps de Travail en France et en Allemagne." *Travail et Emploi* 49: 31–45.

Bosch, Gerhard, and K. Zühlke-Robinet. 2002. "The Labour Market in the German Construction Industry." In: *Building Chaos: An International Comparison of Deregulation in the Construction Industry*, edited by Gerhard Bosch and P. Philipps, 48–72. London: Routledge Press.

———. 2000. "Der Bauarbeitsmarkt: Soziologie und Ökonomie einer Branche." Frankfurt: Campus–Verlag.

Bray, Mark. 1991. "Australian Unions and Economic Restructuring." Unpublished paper, Department of Industrial Relations, University of Sydney.

Brett, J. 1997. "Politics and Business Parted." *The Age Newspaper* July 17: 15.

Briggs, C. 2001. "Australian Exceptionalism: The Role of Trade Unions in the Emergence of Enterprise Bargaining." *Journal of Industrial Relations* 43 (1): 27–43.

Buchanan, J. 2002. "Certified Enterprise Agreements Outlook." Presentation to Wages Outlook Conference, ACIRRT, Sydney, March.

Budd, John W. 1992. "The Determinants and Extent of UAW Pattern Bargaining." *Industrial and Labor Relations Review* 45 (April): 523–39.

Bureau of Labor Statistics. 2001. "Union Members in 2000." Press release, January 18, www.stats.bls.gov/newsrels.htm

Calmfors, Lars, and John Driffill. 1988. "Bargaining Structure, Corporatism, and Macroeconomic Performance." *Economic Policy* 3: 13–61.

Campbell, Duncan. 2000. "Recovery from the Crisis: The Prospects for Social Dialogue in East Asia." Paper presented at the 12th International Industrial Relations World Congress, Tokyo, May 29–June 2.

Cantillon, S., C. Corrigan, P. Kirby, and J. O'Flynn, eds. 2001. *Rich and Poor: Perspectives on Tackling Inequality in Ireland* Dublin: Oak Tree Press/Combat Poverty Agency.

Cappelli, Peter. 1985. "Competitive Pressures and Labor Relations in the Airline Industry." *Industrial Relations* 24 (fall): 316–38.

Carrieri, Mimmo. 1995. *L'incerta Rappresentanza. Sindacati e Consenso Negli Anni '90: Dal Monopolio Confederale alle Rappresentanze Sindacali Unitarie*. Bologna: Il Mulino.

Casadio, Piero. 1999. "Diffusione dei premi di risultato e differenziali retributivi territoriali nell'industria." *Lavoro e Relazioni Industriali* (January–June): 57–81.

CBS. 1985–2002. *Sociaal–economische maandstatistiek*. The Hague: CBS.

Cella, GianPrimo. 1989. "Criteria of Regulation in Italian Industrial Relations: A Case of Weak Institutions." In *State, Market, and Social Regula-*

tion. New Perspectives on Italy, edited by Peter Lange and Marino Regini, 167–85. Cambridge: Cambridge University Press.
Cella, Gianprimo, and Tiziano Treu. 1998. "La Contrattazione Collettiva." In *Le Nuove Relazioni Industriali*, edited by Gianprimo Cella and Tiziano Treu, 183–255. Bologna: Il Mulino.
Chōsa Jih (Survey Report of the JEIU). 1995. No. 276.
———. 1990. No. 242.
———. 1983. No. 181.
Chōsa Jih (Survey Report of the JFSWU). 1989. No. 149.
CNEL, ed. 2000. "Le Relazioni Sindacali in Italia 1997–1998." Report prepared for CNEL by CESOS, *Documenti CNEL* 32: Rome.
Cohen, Larry, and Steve Early. 2000. "Globalization and De-unionization in Telecommunications: Three Case Studies in Resistance." In *Transnational Cooperation among Labor Unions*, edited by Michael Gordon and Lowell Turner, 202–22. Ithaca, N.Y.: Cornell University Press.
Combet, G. 2001. "Employee Participation in an Australian Context." *Conference on Works Councils in Australia*, Royal Melbourne Institute of Technology, Melbourne.
Committee of Review into Australian Industrial Relations Law and Systems, chaired by K. Hancock. 1985. *Report*. Canberra: Australian Government Publishing Service.
Commons, John R. 1909. "American Shoemakers." *Quarterly Journal of Economics* 24 (November): 39–81.
Compa, Lance. 2001a. *The North American Agreement on Labour Cooperation*. Monograph in the series, "International Encyclopedia of Laws, Labour Law, and Industrial Relations," R. Blanpain, ed. The Hague: Kluwer Law Publications.
———. 2001b. "NAFTA's Labor Side Agreement and International Labour Solidarity." *Antipode* 33(July): 451–67.
Cook, Maria Lorena. 1998. "Toward Flexible Industrial Relations? Neo-Liberalism, Democracy, and Labor Reform in Latin America." *Industrial Relations* 37 (3): 311–36.
Cooper, R. 2000. "Organise, Organise, Organise! ACTU Congress 2000." *Journal of Industrial Relations* 42 (4): 582–94.
Council of Economic Advisors. 2001. *Economic Report of the President*. Washington, D.C.:
http://www.access.gpo.gov/usbudget/fg2003/erp.html#erp/
Crouch, Colin. 1985. "Conditions for Trade Union Wage Restraint." In *The Politics of Inflation and Economic Stagflation*, edited by Leon N. Lindberg and Charles S. Maier, 105–39. Washington, D.C.: Brookings Institution.
Crouch, Colin, and Franz Traxler. 1995. *Organized Industrial Relations in Europe: What Future?* Avebury: Ashgate.

Cutcher-Gershenfeld, Joel. 1991. "The Impact on Economic Performance of a Transformation in Workplace Relations." *Industrial and Labor Relations Review* 44 (January): 241–60.
Dabscheck, B. 2000. "The Australian Waterfront Dispute and Theories of the State." *Journal of Industrial Relations* 42 (4): 497–518.
———. 1995. *The Struggle for Australian Industrial Relations*. Melbourne: Oxford University Press.
Damiano, Cesare, and Mario Giaccone. 2001. "Le Prospettive del Modello Contrattuale Italiano." *Economia e Società Regionale* 3: 49–72.
D'Antona, Massimo. 2000. *Il Lavoro delle Riforme—Scritti 1996–1999*. Rome: Editori Riuniti.
Davis, E. M., and R. D. Lansbury. 1998. "Employment Relations in Australia." In *International and Comparative Employment Relations*, edited by Greg J. Bamber and Russell D. Lansbury, 144–69. Sydney: Allen & Unwin.
de Beer, P. T. 2000. "De Deeltijdbaan als Smeerolie." *Economisch-Statistische Berichten*: 904–6.
de Jong, Brenda, and Hans van den Hurk. 2000. *OR & cao's*. The Hague: Elsevier.
Delsen, Lei. 2002. *Exit Poldermodel? Socioeconomic Developments in the Netherlands*. Westport, Conn.: Praeger.
Department of Employment and Industrial Relations. 1986. *Industrial Democracy and Employee Participation*, Canberra: The Australian Government Publishing Service.
Dore, Ronald. 1990. "Japan: A Nation Made for Corporatism?" In *Corporatism and Accountability*, edited by Colin Crouch and Ronald Dore, 45–62. Oxford: Oxford University Press.
Eaton, Adrienne E., and Paula B. Voos. 1992. "Unions and Contemporary Innovations in Work Organizations, Compensation, and Employee Participation." In *Unions and Economic Competitiveness*, edited by Lawrence Mishel and Paula Voos, 173–216. Washington, D.C.: Economic Policy Institute.
Ebbinghaus, B., and Hassel, A. 2000. "Striking Deals: Concertation in the Reform of Continental European Welfare States." *Journal of European Public Policy* 7 (1): 44–62.
Ellem, B. 2001. "Trade Unionism in 2000." *Journal of Industrial Relations* 43 (2): 196–218.
Erickson, Christopher L. 1996. "A Re–interpretation of Pattern Bargaining." *Industrial and Labor Relations Review* 49 (July): 615–34.
———. 1992. "Wage Rule Formation in the Aerospace Industry." *Industrial and Labor Relations Review* 45 (April): 507–22.

Ettl, W., and A. Heinkenroth. 1996. "Strukturwandel, Verbandsabstinenz, Tariffucht: Zur Lage der Unternehmen und Arbeitgeberverbände im Ostdeutschen Verarbeitenden Gewerbe." *Industrielle Beziehungen* 3: 321–53.

European Commission. 2000. "Report on Industrial Relations in Europe." Brussels.

European Economy. 2001. "Supplement A: Economic trends." Luxembourg: Office for Official Publications of the European Communities.

Eurostat Yearbook 2001. 2001. Luxemburg: Eurostat.

Fabbri, R., and Paolo Pini. 1999. "La Contrattazione Decentrata in Emilia Romagna: Banca Dati e Caratteristiche della Contrattazione." Working paper, Ferrara University.

"Fact Finding Report." 1994. *Commission on the Future of Worker Management Relations*, Washington, D.C.: U.S. Departments of Commerce and Labor, May: xi.

Fajertag, Giuseppe, and Philippe Pochet, eds. 2000. *Social Pacts in Europe—New Dynamics*. Brussels: ETUI.

———. 1997. *Social Pacts in Europe*. Brussels: ETUI.

Federmeccanica. 1997. *Ventiduesima Indagine Annuale Sull'industria Meccanica*. Rome: Federmeccanica Publ.

Ferner, Anthony, and Richard Hyman. 1998. "Introduction: Towards European Industrial Relations?" In *Changing Industrial Relations in Europe*, edited by Anthony Ferner and Richard Hyman, x–xxvi. Oxford: Basil Blackwell.

———. 1992a. *Industrial Relations in the New Europe*. Oxford: Basil Blackwell.

———. 1992b. "Italy: Between Political Exchange and Micro-Corporatism." *In Industrial Relations in the New Europe*, edited by Anthony Ferner and Richard Hyman, 524–600. Oxford: Basil Blackwell.

Fianna Fail. 1987. *Program for National Recovery* (Election Manifesto).

Fields, Karl J. 1992. "Developmental Capitalism and Industrial Organization: *Chaebol* and the State in Korea." In *Political Authority and Economic Exchange in Korea*, edited by Hong Yung Lee and Dal Joong Chang, 207–50. Seoul: Oruem.

FNV. 2001. *Ruimte voor de CAO: Jaarboek 2000/2001*. Amsterdam: FNV.

———. 2000. *CAO Jaarboek 1999/2000*. Amsterdam: FNV.

Förster, G., and P. Hausmann. 2001. "Dezentralisierung der Tarifpolitik—Eine Kritische Analyse am Beispiel der IG BCE." *WSI-Mitteilungen* 54 (7): 458–63.

Freeman, Richard B. 1994. "How Labor Fares in Advanced Economies." In *Working Under Different Rules*, edited by Richard Freeman, 1–28. A

National Bureau of Economic Research Project Report. New York: Russell Sage Foundation.

Freeman, Richard B., and E. P. Lazear. 1995. "An Economic Analysis of Works' Councils." In *Works Councils: Consultation, Representation, and Cooperation in Industrial Relations*, edited by Joel Rogers and Wolfgang Streeck, 27–50. Chicago: University of Chicago Press.

Freeman, Richard B., and Joel Rogers. 1999. *What Workers Want?* Ithaca, N.Y.: ILR/Cornell University Press.

Frenkel, Stephen, and Jeffrey Harrod. 1995. *Industrialization and Labor Relations: Contemporary Research in Seven Countries*. Ithaca, N.Y.: Cornell University Press.

Fujita, Minoru. 1996. "Shuntō Kaikakuron no Kōzu to Ronri." (The Structure and Logic of the Shuntō Reform Debate). *Chingin to Shakai Hoshō* 1180: 16–35.

Garofalo, Mario Giovanni. 1994. "Legislazione e Contrattazione Collettiva nel 1992." *Giornale di Diritto del Lavoro e di Relazioni Industriali* 17 (61): 163–95.

Giaccone, Mario. 2001. "Le Relazioni Industriali in Veneto: Tra Federalismo Accentratore e Concertazione per lo Sviluppo." *Economia e Società Regionale* 3: 107–49.

Ginsburg, Helen Lachs, June Zaccone, Gertrude Schaffner Goldberg, Sheila D. Collins, and Summer M. Rosen. 1997. "Special Issues On: The Challenge of Full Employment in the Global Economy, Editorial Introduction." *Economic and Industrial Democracy* 18: 5–34.

Golden, Miriam, and Jonas Pontusson. 1992. *Bargaining for Change: Union Politics in North America and Europe*. Ithaca, N.Y.: Cornell University Press.

Gordon, Andrew. 1998. *The Wages of Affluence*. Cambridge, Mass.: Harvard University Press.

Government of Ireland. 2000. Program for Prosperity and Fairness. Dublin: Government Publications Office.

———. 1996. *Partnership 2000*. Dublin: Government Publications Office.

———. 1993. *Program for Competitiveness and Work*. Dublin: Government Publications Office.

———. 1990. *Program for Economic and Social Progress*. Dublin: Government Publications Office.

———. 1987. *Program for National Recovery*. Dublin: Government Publications Office.

Gunnigle, P. 2000. "Paradox in Policy and Practice: Trade Unions and Public Policy in the Republic of Ireland." *IBAR* 21 (2): 39–54.

Gunnigle, P., M. O'Sullivan, and M. Kinsella. 2001. "Organized Labor in the New Economy: Trade Unions and Public Policy in the Republic of

Ireland." Paper presented at the Irish Academy of Management Conference, Derry.
Hall, Peter A., and David Soskice, eds. 2001. *Varieties of Capitalism: The Institutional Foundations of Comparative Advantage.* New York: Oxford University Press.
Hancock, K. 2003. "Work in an Ungolden Age." In *Working Futures*, edited by R. Callus and R. D. Lansbury, 6–26. Sydney: The Federation Press.
Hardiman, Niamh. 1988. *Pay Politics and Economic Performance in Ireland, 1970–1987.* Oxford: Clarendon Press.
Hassel, A. 2002. "Der Mühsame Sprung über den Eigenen Schatten. Das Bündnis für Arbeit hat Keine Greifbaren Resultate Erzielt. Verkrampfte Gewerkschaften haben Chancen Verpasst." *Frankfurter Rundschau* 25 (1): 7. (It is a daily newspaper).
Hassel, A., and B. Rehder. 2001. "Institutional Change in the German Wage Bargaining System—The Role of Big Companies." MPIFG Working Paper 01/9 December, Cologne.
Hayakawa, Seiichirō. 1992. "Shuntō no Tenkai to Henbō." (The development and transformation of Shuntō). In *"Rengō Jidai" no Rōdō Undō*, edited by Ohara Shakai Mondai Kenkyō Jo, 243–63. Tokyo: Sōgō Rōdō Kenkyō Jo.
Hendricks, Wallace E., and Lawrence M. Kahn. 1982. "The Determinants of Bargaining Structure in U.S. Manufacturing Industries." *Industrial and Labor Relations Review* 35 (2) January: 181–95.
Higgins, H. B. 1915. "A New Province for Law and Order." *Harvard Law Review* 29 (1).
Howard, W. A. 1977. "Australian Trade Unions in the Context of Union Theory." *Journal of Industrial Relations* 19 (3): 255–73.
Hundt, D. 1998. "Ein reformierter Flächentarifvertrag hat Zukunft." *Arbeitgeber* 50 (3): 49–51.
Hyōdō, Tsutomu. 1997. *Rōdō no Sengoshi* (Postwar History of Labor). Tokyo: University of Tokyo Press.
Igarashi, Hitoshi. 1998. *Seito Seiji to Rōdō Kumiai Undō* (Party Politics and Labor Union Movements). Tokyo: Ochanomizu Shobō.
ILO (International Labour Organisation). 2000. *Year Book of Labour Statistics.* Geneva: ILO.
IMF. 1998. "Republic of Korea: Selected Issues." Washington D.C., IMF Staff Country Report No. 98/74: International Monetary Fund.
Inagami, Takeshi. 1996. "The Death of the 'Labour Movement' and the 'Japanization' of Industrial Relations." *Industrielle Beziehungen* 3. Jg., Heft 2: 173–86.
———. 1995. *Seijuku Shakai no Nakano Kigyō betsu Kumiai* (Enterprise Unions in a Mature Society). Tokyo: Japan Institute of Labor.

ISTAT. 1998. *I Principali Risultati della Rilevazione sulla Flessibilità del Mercato del Lavoro*. Rome.

Iversen, Torben. 2000. "Decentralization, Monetarism, and the Social Democratic Welfare State." In *Unions, Employers, and Central Banks: Macroeconomic Coordination and Institutional Change in Social Market Economies*, edited by Torben Iversen et al., 205–31. Cambridge: Cambridge University Press.

Iversen, Torben, and Jonas Pontusson. 2000. "Comparative Political Economy: A Northern European Perspective." In *Unions, Employers, and Central Banks: Macroeconomic Coordination and Institutional Change in Social Market Economies*, edited by Torben Iversen et al., 1–37. Cambridge: Cambridge University Press.

Iversen, Torben, Jonas Pontusson, and David Soskice. 2000. *Unions, Employers, and Central Banks: Macroeconomic Coordination and Institutional Change in Social Market Economies*. Cambridge: Cambridge University Press.

Japan Labor Bulletin. 2000. "Pension Reform Legislation Passed by Diet." June 1.

———. 1999. "Revised Worker Dispatching Law: Worker Dispatching Has Generally Been Liberated." September 1.

Jeong, Jooyeon. 1995. "Enterprise Unionism from a Korean Perspective." *Economic and Industrial Democracy* 16: 253–73.

Jørgensen, Henning. 2000. "From Deregulation to Co-regulation: Neo-Corporatism and its Contribution to a Theory of Coordinated Labor Market Regulation." Unpublished manuscript.

JTUC-RIALS (Japanese Trade Union Confederation Research Institute for Advancement of Living Standards). 2001. *Rōdō Kumiai no Mirai o Saguru* (Exploring the Future of Labor Unions). Tokyo: JTUC–RIALS.

Katz, Harry C. 1993. "The Decentralization of Collective Bargaining: A Literature Review and Comparative Analysis." *Industrial and Labor Relations Review* 47 (1): 3–22.

———. 1985. *Shifting Gears*. Cambridge, Mass.: MIT Press.

Katz, Harry C., Rosemary Batt, and Jeffrey H. Keefe. 2003. "The Revitalization of the CWA: Integrating Collective Bargaining, Political Action, and Organizing." *Industrial and Labor Relations Review* 56 (4): 573–89.

Katz, Harry C., and Owen Darbishire. 2000. *Converging Divergences: Worldwide Changes in Employment Systems*. Ithaca, N.Y.: ILR/Cornell University Press.

Katz, Harry C., and Thomas A. Kochan. 2000. *An Introduction to Collective Bargaining and Industrial Relations*, 2nd ed. New York: Irwin-McGraw Hill Inc.

Katz, Harry C., John Paul MacDuffie, and Frits Pil. 2002. "Autos: Continuity and Change in Collective Bargaining." In *Collective Bargaining in the Private Sector*, edited by P. Clark et al., 55–90. Champaign, Ill.: Industrial Relations Research Association.

Katzenstein, Peter. 1985. *Small States in World Markets: Industrial Policy in Europe*. Ithaca, N.Y.: Cornell University Press.

Keating, P. J. 1993. "Speech to the Australian Institute of Directors." Melbourne, 21 April.

Keefe, Jeffrey H., and Rosemary Batt. 2002. "Telecommunications: Collective Bargaining in an Era of Industry Reconsolidation." In *Collective Bargaining in the Private Sector*, edited by P. Clark et al., 263–310 Champaign, Ill.: Industrial Relations Research Association.

———. 1997. "United States." In *Telecommunications: Restructuring Work and Employment Relations World-wide*, edited by Harry Katz, 31–88. Ithaca, N.Y.: Cornell University Press.

Kelly, D., and E. Underhill. 1997. "Australian Steel: A Corporatist Transformation?" In *Changing Employment Relations in Australia*, edited by Jim Kitay and Russell D. Lansbury, 158–84. Melbourne: Oxford University Press.

Kelly, Paul. 1992. *The End of Certainty*. Sydney: Allen & Unwin.

Kenworthy, Lane. 2001. "Corporatism and Unemployment in the 1980s and 1990s." Unpublished manuscript.

Kim, Sookon. 2000. "Korean Trade Union Movement, Manpower Policy and Labor Market." Paper presented at the 12th World Congress of International Industrial Relations Association, Tokyo, May 29–June 2.

Kim, Yong Cheol. 1994. "State and Labor in South Korea: Coalition Analysis," Ph.D. Dissertation. The Ohio State University.

Kim, Yeong-Soon. 1999. "Beyond Exceptionalism: The Working Class and the Development of the Welfare System in South Korea," Unpublished manuscript.

Kitay, James, and Russell D. Lansbury. 1997. *Changing Employment Relations in Australia*. Melbourne: Oxford University Press.

KLI. 1999. *Medium-Term Unemployment Measures: Future Prospects and Policy Agenda* (in Korean). Seoul: Korea Labor Institute.

Kochan, Thomas, Harry C. Katz, and Robert McKersie. 1994. *The Transformation of American Industrial Relations*, 2nd ed. Ithaca, N.Y.: ILR/Cornell University Press.

Kohaut, S., and C. Schnabel. 2001. "Tarifverträge—Nein Danke? Einflussfaktoren der Tarifbindung West- und Ostdeutscher Betriebe." Discussion Papers No. 8, Friedrich-Alexander-Universität, Erlangen-Nürnberg.

———. 1999. "Tarifbindung im Wandel." *IW–Trends* 2.

Koning, P. W. C. 2000. "Arbeid en Sociale Zekerheid: Participatie en Differentiatie." In *Trends, Dilemma's en Beleid*, edited by CPB, 163–81. The Hague: Centraal Planbureau.

Korpi, Walter. 1989. "Power, Politics, and State Autonomy in the Development of Social Citizenship: Social Rights during Sickness in Eighteen OECD Countries since 1930." *American Sociological Review* 54: 309–28.

———. 1980. "Social Policy and Distributional Conflict in the Capitalist Democracies." *West European Politics* 3: 296–316.

Kotani, Sachi. 2001. "Tokyo Kanrishoku Union Kumiaiin no Ishiki Henyō" (Changes in Union Consciousness of Members of Tokyo Middle Managers' Union). *Rōdō Shakaigakkai Nenpō* 12: 147–78.

———. 1999. "Josei no Atarashii Rōdō Undō" (The new labor movement of women). *Rōdō Shakaigaku Kenkyō* 1: 3–25.

Kujawa, Duane 1980. "Labor Relations of U.S. Multinational Abroad." In *Labor Relations in Advanced Industrial Societies*, edited by B. Martin and E. Kassalow, 15–17. New York: Carnegie Endowment for Peace.

Kume, Ikuo. 2000. "Rōdōseisaku Katei no Seijuku to Henyō" (The maturation and transformation of labor policy process). *Nihon Rōdō Kenkyō Kikō Zasshi* 475: 2–13.

———. 1998. *Disparaged Success: Labor Politics in Postwar Japan*. Ithaca, N.Y.: Cornell University Press.

Kyloh, R., ed. 1998. *Mastering the Challenge of Globalization: Towards a Trade Union Agenda*. Geneva: ILO.

Lang, K. 2001. "Bündnis für Arbeit—Jenseits von Ausstieg und Anpassung." *WSI-Mitteilungen* 54 (5): 294–98.

Lange, Peter, and Geoffrey Garrett. 1985. "The Politics of Growth: Strategic Interaction and Economic Performance in the Advanced Industrial Democracies, 1974–1980." *Journal of Politics* 47.

Lange, Peter, and Marino Regini, eds. 1989. *State, Market and Social Regulation. New Perspectives on Italy*. Cambridge: Cambridge University Press.

Lansbury, Russell D., and Greg J. Bamber. 1998. "The End of Institutionalised Industrial Relations in Australia?" *Perspectives on Work* 2 (1): 26–30.

Lawrence, Paul R., and Jay W. Lorsch. 1969. *Organization and Environment*. New York: Richard D. Irwin.

Lee, Joohee. 2001. "Structural Adjustment and Changes in Industrial Relations." Paper presented at the Korean Sociological Association Biannual Conference. Chunnam University, S. Korea. June 22 (in Korean).

———. 1998. "Micro-Corporatism in South Korea: A Comparative Analysis of Enterprise–Level Industrial Relations." *Economic and Industrial Democracy* 19 (3): 443–74.

Lee, Joseph J. 1989. *Ireland 1912–1985: Politics and Society*. Cambridge: Cambridge University Press.

Lee, Min Jin. 2000. *Chingin Kettei Seido no Kannichi Hikaku* (Korea-Japan Comparison of Wage Determination System). Chiba: Azusa Shuppansha.

Lee, Wonduck. 1997. *Labor Reform: A Choice for the Future* (in Korean). Seoul: Korea Labor Institute.

Lee, Wonduck, and Kang-Shik Choi. 1998. *Labor Market and Industrial Relations in Korea: Retrospect on the Past Decade and Policy Directions for the 21st Century*. Seoul: Korea Labor Institute.

Lee, Wonduck, and Byoung-Hoon Lee. 2001. "Korean Industrial Relations in the Era of Globalization," Unpublished manuscript.

Lee, Young-Myon and Seong Hee Lee. 2001. "Seoul Model: Public Sector Tripartism in Seoul Metropolitan City of Korea." Paper presented at the Korean Academy of Management Summer Conference, August 23.

Levy, Frank. 1998. *The New Dollars and Dreams*. New York: Russell Sage Foundation.

Lizzeri, Barbara. 2002. "Le Relazioni Industriali in Azienda: Grandi e Piccole Imprese tra Formalità e Informalità." In *Lavoro e Sindacato in Lombardia*, edited by Daniele Checchi et al., 175–90. Milan: Franco Angeli.

MacSharry, Ray, and Padraic A. White. 2000. *The Making of the Celtic Tiger: The Inside Story of Ireland's Boom Economy*. Cork: Mercier Press.

Manseragh, Martin. 1986. *The Spirit of the Nation: The Speeches and Statements of Charles J. Haughey*. Cork: Mercier Press.

Martin, John. P. 1998. "Labour Market and Social Policy." Occasional Papers. No. 35. Paris: Organization for Economic Cooperation and Development.

Matsuzaki, Tadashi. 1982. *Nihon Tekkō Sangyō Bunseki* (Analysis of the Japanese Iron and Steel Industry). Tokyo: Nihon Hyōronsha.

Mauer, A., and H. Seifert. 2001. "Betriebliche Beschäftigungs—und Wettbewerbsbündnisse—Strategie für Krisenbetriebe oder Neue Regelungspolitische Normalität." *WSI–Mitteilungen* 54 (8): 490–50.

McCallum, R. 2001. "Legislating Workers' Rights." *Worksite* (4) (Spring): 3–5.

———. 1997. "Crafting a New Collective Labour for Australia." *Journal of Industrial Relations* 39 (3): 405–22.

McIntyre, Stuart, and Richard Mitchell, eds. 1989. *Foundations of Arbitration*. Melbourne: Oxford University Press.

Mishel, Lawrence, et al. 2001. *State of Working America, 2000–2001*. Ithaca, N.Y.: ILR/Cornell University Press.

Miura, Mari. 2001. "The New Politics of Labor: Shifting Veto Points and Representing the Un-organized." F–93, Institute of Social Science, Domestic Politics Project No.3, Institute of Social Science, University of Tokyo.

Mjøset. Lars. 1992. "The Irish Economy in a Comparative Institutional Perspective." NESC Report no. 93: Dublin: NESC.

MOFE. 1999. "Recent Economic Indicators and Policy Direction" (in Korean). Policy Bureau, Ministry of Finance and Economy.
Molitor, K. 1998. "Kontrollierte Dezentralisierung." *Die Mitbestimmung* 6: 4042.
Morehead, A., M. Steel, M. Alexander, K. Stephen, and L. Duffin. 1997. *Changes at Work: the 1995 Australian Workplace Industrial Relations Survey*. Melbourne: Addison Wesley Longman.
Muller-Jentsch, W. 1995. "Germany: From Collective Voice to Co-Management." In *Works Councils: Consultation, Representation and Co-operation in Industrial Relations*, edited by Joel Rogers and Wolfgang Streeck, 53–69. Chicago: The University of Chicago Press.
NESC. 1996. "Strategy into the 21st Century." NESC Report no. 98: Dublin.
NESF. 1997. "A Framework for Partnership: Enriching Strategic Consensus through Participation." Dublin: National Economic and Social Forum.
Niphuis-Nell, M., and P. de Beer. 1997. "Verdeling van Arbeid en Zorg." In *Het Gezinsrapport*, edited by C. S. van Praag and M. Niphuis-Nell, 43–108. The Hague: SCP.
Obata, Yoshitake. 1996. "Community Union toha Nanika" (What Are Community Unions?). *Chingin to Shakai Hoshō* 1187: 18–22.
O'Donnell, R., and D. Thomas. 1998. "Partnership and Policy Making." In *Social Policy in Ireland*, edited by S. Healy and B. Reynolds, 117–46. Dublin: Oak Tree Press.
O'Donnell, R., and P. Teague. 2000. "Partnership at Work in Ireland: An Evaluation of Progress under Partnership 2000." Dublin: Department of An Taoiseach.
O'Dwyer, J. J., John O'Dowd, John O'Halloran, and Jean Cullinane. 2002. "A Formal Review of Partnership in the Civil Service." Dublin: Department of An Taoiseach.
OECD (Organisation for Economic Cooperation and Development). 2001. *Review of Labour Market Policies in Australia*. Paris: OECD.
———. 2000. *Economic Surveys: Australia*. Paris: OECD.
———. 1998. "OECD Economic Surveys: 1997–1998, Korea." Paris: OECD.
———. 1997. *Economic Outlook*. Paris: OECD.
———. 1994a. *The Jobs Study*. Paris: OECD.
———. 1994b. "OECD Economic Surveys: 1993–1994, Korea." Paris: OECD.
Office of the Employee Advocate. 2001. www.oea.gov.au.
Ogino, Noboru. 2002. "Nihongata WorkSharing no Genjō to Kanōsei" (The Present Condition and Problems of the Japanese-Style Work-Sharing Schemes). *Gekkan Rōdō Kumiai*: 24–31.
OISR (Ohara Institute for Social Research). Various years. *Nihon Rōdō Nenkan* (Japan Labor Yearbook). Tokyo: Junpō Sha.

Onomichi, Hiroshi. 1998. "Rōkihō Kaisei to Rengō no Taiō" (The Revision of the Labor Standards Law and Responses of Rengō). *Kokusai Rōdō Undō* 324: 8–13.
Osterman, Paul, Thomas A. Kochan, Richard M. Locke, and Michael J. Piore. 2001. *Working in America*. Cambridge, Mass.: MIT Press.
Paping, R., and K. Tijdens. 2000. "Meer Keuzevrijheid: Haalbaar en Wenselijk?" *Economisch-Statistische Berichten*: 613–15.
Parker, Eric, and Joel Rogers. 2001. "Building the High Road in Metro Area." In *Rekindling the Movement*, edited by Lowell Turner, Harry Katz, and Richard Hurd, 256–74. Ithaca, N.Y.: ILR/Cornell University Press.
Peetz, David. 1998. *Unions in a Contrary World*. Melbourne: Cambridge University Press.
Pempel, T. J., and Keiichi Tsunekawa. 1979. "Corporatism Without Labor? The Japanese Anomaly." In *Trends Toward Corporatist Intermediation*, edited by Philippe Schmitter and Gerhard Lehmbruch, 231–70. London: Sage Publications.
Plantenga, Janneke. 2000. "Deeltijd in de Polder: Collectieve Belangen en Individuele Preferenties." In *De houdbaarheid van het Nederlandse 'Model': Verder met Loonmatiging en Deeltijdarbeid?* edited by Wiemer Salverda, 43–56. The Hague: Elsevier.
Poole, M., R. D. Lansbury, and N. Wailes. 2001. "A Comparative Analysis of Developments in Industrial Democracy." *Industrial Relations* 40 (3): 490–525.
Purcell, John, and Bruce Ahlstrand. 1984. *Human Resource Management in the Multi-Divisional Company*. Oxford: Oxford University Press.
Regalia, Ida. 2003. "Decentralizing Employment Protection in Europe: Territorial Pacts and Beyond." In *Governing Work and Welfare in a New Economy: European and American Experiments*, edited by Jonathan Zeitlin and David M. Trubek, 158–87. Oxford: Oxford University Press.
———. 1995. "Italy: The Costs and Benefits of Informality." In *Works Councils, Consultation, Representation, and Cooperation in Industrial Relations*, edited by Joel Rogers and Wolfgang Streeck, 217–41. Chicago: The University of Chicago Press.
Regalia, Ida, and Marino Regini. 1998. "Italy: The Dual Character of Industrial Relations." In *Changing Industrial Relations in Europe*, edited by Anthony Ferner and Richard Hyman, 459–503. Oxford: Blackwell.
———. 1995. "Between Voluntarism and Institutionalization: Industrial Relations and Human Resources Practices in Italy." In *Employment Relations in a Changing World Economy*, edited by Richard Locke, Thomas Kochan, and Michael Piore, 131–63. Cambridge, Mass.: MIT Press.
Regalia, Ida, and Rossella Ronchi. 1988–92. "Le Relazioni Industriali nelle Imprese Lombarde." Milan: Ires Papers Nos. 14, 20, 24, 31, 34.

Regini, Marino. 2000. "Between Deregulation and Social Pacts: The Responses of European Economies to Globalization." *Politics and Society* 28 (1) March: 5–33.

———. 1997. "Still Engaging in Corporatism? Recent Italian Experience in Comparative Perspective." *European Journal of Industrial Relations* 3 (3): 259–78.

———. 1995. *Uncertain Boundaries. The Social and Political Construction of European Economies*. Cambridge: Cambridge University Press.

———. 1984. "The Conditions for Political Exchange. How Concertation Emerged and Collapsed in Italy and Great Britain." In *Order and Conflict in Contemporary Capitalism,* edited by J. Goldthorpe, 124–42. Oxford: Clarendon Press.

Regini, Marino, and Charles Sabel. 1989. *Strategie di Riaggiustamento Industriale*. Bologna: Il Mulino.

Rengō. 1997. *Dai 5 Kai Teiki Taikai Ippan Katudō Hōkoku* (The General Report of Activities Presented at the Fifth Ordinary Convention). Tokyo: Rengō.

Reyneri, Emilio. 1989. "The Italian Labor Market: Between State Control and Social Regulation." In *State, Market and Social Regulation. New Perspectives on Italy*, edited by Peter Lange and Marino Regini, 129–45. Cambridge: Cambridge University Press.

Rhodes, Martin. 2001. "The Political Economy of Social Pacts: Competitive Corporatism and European Welfare Reform." In *The New Politics of the Welfare State*, edited by Paul Pierson. Oxford: Oxford University Press.

Roche, W. 1997. "Pay Determination: The State and the Politics of Industrial Relations." In *Irish Industrial Relations in Practice: Revised and Expanded Edition*, edited by T. V. Murphy and W. K. Roche, 126–205. Dublin: Oak Tree Press.

Rōdōshō (Ministry of Labor). 1972. *Shōwa 46nen Rōdō Keizai no Bunseki* (Analysis of Labor Economics in 1971).

———. 1964. *Rōdō Kumiai Kihon Chōsa* (Basic survey of labor unions in Japan).

———. Various years. *Shiryō Rōdō Undō Shi* (Documentation on the History of the Labor Movement).

Rojer, Maurice F. P. 2000. "De Wondere Wereld van de CAO." *Tijdschrift voor HRM* 4: 87–114.

Rowley, Chris, and John Benson. 2000. *Globalization and Labour in the Asia Pacific Region*. Portland: Frank Cass.

Rusciano, Mario. 1990. "Lavoro Pubblico e Privato: Dalla "Separatezza" all"Unificazione' Normativa." In *Stato Sociale, Servizi, Pubblico Impiego*, edited by AA.VV., 7–32. Naples: Jovene.

Sako, Mari. 1997. "Shunto: The Role of Employer and Union Coordination at the Industry and Inter-sectoral Levels." In *Japanese Labour and Management in Transition: Diversity, Flexibility and Participation*, edited by Mari Sako and Hiroki Sato, 236–64. London: Routledge.

Salmon, I. 1996. "A Business Perspective." National Summit on the Future of Work in Australia. Sydney, May.

Schmitter, Phillipe. 1981. "Interest Intermediation and Regime Governability in Contemporary Western Europe and North America." In *Organizing Interests in Western Europe*, edited by S. Berger, 285–327. New York: Cambridge University Press.

———. 1979. "Still the Century of Corporatism?" In *Trends Toward Corporatist Intermediation*, edited by Phillipe Schmitter and Gerhart Lehmbruch, 7–49. London: Sage.

Schmitter, Philippe C., and Jürgen R. Grote. 1997. "The Corporatist Sisyphus: Past, Present and Future." EUI Working Paper SPS No. 97/4. European University Institute, Florence, Department of Political and Social Sciences.

Schnabel, C., and J. Wagner. 1996. "Ausmaß und Bestimmungsgründe der Mitgliedschaft in Arbeitgeberverbänden: Eine Empirische Untersuchung mit Firmendaten." *Industrielle Beziehungen* 3: 293–306.

Schroeder, W., and B. Ruppert. 1996. "Austritte aus Arbeitgeberverbänden: Motive-Ursachen-Ausmaß." *WSI-Mitteilungen* 49: 316–28.

Seifert, H. 2000. "Betriebliche Bündnisse für Arbeit—Beschäftigen Statt Entlassen." *WSI-Mitteilungen* 7 (53).

Seifert, Wolfgang. 1988. "Some Thoughts on the Problem of Internal Union Democracy in Japan." *Economic and Industrial Democracy* 9 (3): 373–95.

Sengenberger, W., and D. Campbell, eds. 1994. *The Role of Labour Standards in Industrial Restructuring*. Geneva: International Institute for Labour Studies.

Shafer, D. Michael. 1990. "Sectors, States and Social Forces: Korea and Zambia Confront Economic Restructuring." *Comparative Politics* 22: 2.

Shikata, Katsuichi. 1999. "Rengō no Shutō Kaikaku Rongi" (Rengō's debate over the reform of Shuntō). *Chingin to Shakai Hoshō* December: 15–26.

Shimada, Haruo. 1983. "Wage Determination and Information Sharing: An Alternative Approach to Incomes Policy?" *Journal of Industrial Relations* 25 (2): 177–200.

Shimamura, Seiki. 1995. "95 Shuntō ni dou Torikumuka" (How Can We Negotiate in the 1995 Shuntō). *Rōdō Keizai Junpō* 1528: 4–7.

Shinkawa, Toshimitsu. 1993. *Nihongata Fukushi no Seiji Keizai Gaku* (The Political Economy of the Japanese-Style Welfare). Tokyo: Sanichi Shobō.

Shinoda, Tōru. 1997. "Rengo and Policy Participation: Japanese-style Neo-Corporatism?" In *Japanese Labour and Management in Transition: Diver-*

sity, Flexibility and Participation, edited by Mari Sako and Hiroki Sato, 187–214. London: Routledge.

———. 1989. *Seikimatsu no Rōdō Undō* (The Labor Movement at the End of the Century). Tokyo: Iwanami Shoten.

Shinoda, Tōru, Go Ryōtarō, Ashida Jinnosuke, and Takanashi Akira 1989. "Keizai, Shakai no Henyō to Sangyō Seisaku no Tenkai" (The Transformation of Economy and Society and the Development of Industrial Policies). *Nihon Rōdō Kyōkai Zasshi* 356: 31–45.

Shirai, Taishirō. 1983. "A Theory of Enterprise Unionism." In *Contemporary Industrial Relations in Japan*, edited by Shirai Taoshirō, 117–43. Madison: University of Wisconsin Press.

Sisson, Keith, and Paul Marginson. 2002. "Coordinated Bargaining: A Process for our Times?" *British Journal of Industrial Relations* 40 (June): 197–220.

Slomp, Hans. 2000. "The Netherlands." In *Trade Union Education in Europe*, edited by Jeff Bridgford and John Stirling, 223–46. Brussels: ETUCO.

———. 2001. "The Netherlands in the 1990s: Towards 'Flexible Corporatism.' in the Polder Model." In *Policy Concertation and Social Partnership in Western Europe*, edited by Stefan Berger and Hugh Compston, 235–47. Oxford: Berghahn.

Snijkens, Marcel, and John Miltenburg. 2000. "De Ontwikkeling van een Decentrale CAO Bij Unilever." In *Innovatie of Imitatie? CAO–vernieuwing op Ondernemingsniveau*, edited by Marc van der Meer and Evert Smit, 87–100. The Hague: Elsevier.

Sōmuchō. 1995. *Rōdōryoku Chōsa Tokubetsu Chosa Hokoku* (Report on the Special Survey of Labour Force Survey).

Sōmushō. 2001. *Rōdōryoku Chōsa Tokubetsu Chosa Hokoku* (Report on the Special Survey of Labor Force Survey), http://stat.go.jp.

Soskice, David. 1999. "Divergent Production Regimes: Coordinated and Uncoordinated Market Economies in the 1980s and 1990s." In *Continuity and Change in Contemporary Capitalism*, edited by Herbert Kitschelt, Peter Lange, Gary Marks, and John Stephens, 101–34. Cambridge: Cambridge University Press.

———. 1990. "Wage Determination: The Changing Role of Institutions in Advanced Industrialized Countries." *Oxford Review of Economic Policy* 16 (4): 36–61.

SRN (Shōkan Rōdō News, Weekly Labor News). 2002. "Shuntō Saikōchiku ga Shidō" (The Start of the Shuntō Restructuring), September 23.

———. 2001a, "Rengō Bea Tōitsu Yōkyō Miokuri e" (Rengō Decided Not to Make a Unified Demand for Base-Up), October 22.

———. 2001b. "Aitugu bea Yōkyō Dannen" (Many Unions Decided Not to Make Base-Up Demands), November 5

---. 2001c. "Jidōsha, Zōsen wa Bea Yōkyō e" (Auto and Shipbuilding Workers' Unions Made Base-Up Demands), November 26.

---. 1999a. "Gutaisaku o Seifuni Yōsei, Rengō to Nikkeiren" (Rengō and Nikkeiren Asked the Government to Make a Concrete Plan), February 22.

---. 1999b. "Koyō Taisaku Hosei Yosan Heisei Motomeru" (Employment Measures, Requesting a Supplementary Budget), May 31.

---. 1998. "Rengō Nikkeiren, Kyodō de Koyō Sōshutsuno Gutaiteki Teigen" (Rengō and Nikkeiren Presented a Joint Proposal for a Concrete Plan for Job Creation), December 14.

---. 1995. "Nikkeiren Hōkoku, Teiki Shōkyō ha Minaoshi" (Nikkeiren Report, Regular Wage Raises Reconsidered), May 22.

Streeck, Wolfgang. 2001. "Kontinuität und Wandel im Deutschen System der Industriellen Beziehungen: Offene Fragen." *Die Arbeit* 10 (4): 299–313.

---. 1995. "From Market Making to State Building? Reflections on the Political Economy of European Social Policy." In *European Social Policy: Between Fragmentation and Integration*, edited by Stepan Leibfried and Paul Pierson, 389–431. Washington, D.C.: The Brookings Institution.

---. 1993. "The Rise and Decline of Neo-Corporatism." In *Economic and Political Changes in Europe*, edited by IIRA, 27–62. Bari: Cacucci.

---. 1984. *Industrial Relations in West Germany: A Case Study of the Car Industry*. London: Heinemann.

---. 1982. "Organizational Consequences of Corporatist Cooperation in West German Labor Unions." In *Patterns of Corporatist Policy-Making*, edited by Gerhard Lehmbruch and Phillipe Schmitter, 29–81. Beverly Hills, Calif.: Sage.

Streeck, W., and R. Heinze. 1999. "An Arbeit fehlt es Nicht." *Der Spiegel* 19 (S): 38–45.

Sweeney, Paul. 1999. *The Celtic Tiger: Ireland's Economic Miracle Explained*. Dublin: Oak Tree Press.

Takagi, Ikuī. 1999a. "Community Union no Genjō to Kadai Jō" (The Present Situation and Problems of Community Unions [1]). *Rōdō Keizai Junpō* 1632: 4–8.

---. 1999b. "Community Union no Genjō to Kadai Ge" (The Present Situation and Problems of Community Unions [2]). *Rōdō Keizai Junpō* 1633: 75–80.

Takai, Akira. 1997. "Community Union Zenkoku Network no Undō to Kadai" (The Movement of Community Union Nationwide Network and Its Agendas). *Rōdō Keizai Junpō* 1589: 8–12.

Teague, Paul. 1995. "Pay Determination in the Republic of Ireland: Towards Social Corporatism?" *British Journal of Industrial Relations* 33 (2): 253–73.

Thelen, Kathleen. 2000. "Why German Employers Cannot Bring Themselves to Dismantle the German Model." In *Unions, Employers and Central Banks*, edited by Torben Iversen, Jonas Pontuson, and David Soskice, 138–72. Cambridge: Cambridge University Press.

Thurm, Scott. 2001. "CISCO Helps Train a Union's Workers in New Ways." *Wall Street Journal* July 3: B1 and B6.

Tijdens, Kea. 2000. "Het Ontstaan van Ondernemingscao's Bij de Banken." In *Innovatie of Imitatie? CAO–Vernieuwing op Ondernemingsniveau*, edited by Marc van der Meer and Evert Smit, 63–73. The Hague: Elsevier.

Totsuka, Hideo. 1995. "The Transformation of Japanese Industrial Relations: A Case Study of the Automobile Industry." In *Lean Work: Empowerment and Exploitation in the Global Auto Industry*, edited by Steve Babson, 108–28. Detroit: Wayne State University Press.

Traxler, Franz. 1996. "Collective Bargaining and Industrial Change: A Case of Disorganization? A Comparative Analysis of Eighteen OECD Countries." *European Sociological Review* 12: 271–87.

———. 1995a. "Farewell to Labour Market Associations? Organized versus Disorganized Decentralization as a Map for Industrial Relations." In *Organized Industrial Relations in Europe: What Future?* edited by Colin Crouch and Franz Traxler, 3–19. Avebury, Ashgate.

———. 1995b. "From Demand-side to Supply-side Corporatism? Austria's Labour Relations and Public Policy." In *Organized Industrial Relations in Europe: What Future?* edited by Colin Crouch and Franz Traxler, 271–86. Avebury, Ashgate.

———. 1994. "Collective Bargaining: Levels and Coverage," In *OECD Employment Outlook*. Paris: OECD.

Trentini, Marco. 2001. "The Distribution of Income in the 1990s: What Has Changed since the Agreement of 23 July 1993." *European Industrial Relations Observatory On-Line* Ref: IT0109301f.

Tros, Frank. 2000. *Schuivende Marges: Trends in Arbeidsvoorwaardenvorming en Arbeidsverhoudingen*. Alphen: Samson.

Tsujinaka, Yutaka. 1987. "Rōdōkai no Saihen to 87 nen Taisei no Imi" (The Restructuring of Organized Labor and the Meaning of the 1987 System). *Leviathan* 1: 47–72.

Turner, Lowell. 1998. *Defending the High Road: Labor and Politics in Unified Germany*. Ithaca, N.Y.: Cornell University Press.

———. 1991. *Democracy at Work*. Ithaca, N.Y.: Cornell University Press.

van den Toren, Jan Peter. 1998. *De Collectieve Arbeidsovereenkomst: Sleutel Tussen Belang en Beleid*. Amsterdam: Welboom.

van der Meer, Marc. 2000. "De Philips-CAO: Innovatie Zonder Algemene Toestemming." In *Innovatie of Imitatie? CAO–Vernieuwing op Onderne-*

mingsniveau, edited by Marc van der Meer and Evert Smit, 39–50. The Hague: Elsevier.
van der Wiel, H. P. 1999. "Loondiffferentiatie Tussen Bedrijfstakken." *Economisch-Statistische Berichten* 492–94.
van Vleuten, Anna. 2001. *Dure Vrouwen, Dwarse Staten*. Nijmegen: Nijmegen University Press.
Visser, Jelle. 2002. "Why Fewer Workers Join Unions in Europe." *British Journal of Industrial Relations* 40 (September):403–30.
——. 1992. "The Strength of Union Movements in Advanced Capital Democracies: Social and Organizational Variations." In *The Future of Labour Movements*, edited by Marino Regini, 17–52. London: Sage.
Visser, Jelle, and Anton Hemerijck. 1997. *"A Dutch Miracle": Job Growth, Welfare Reform, and Corporatism in the Netherlands*. Amsterdam: Amsterdam University Press.
Wagner, G. 1998. "Einige Bemerkungen zur Diskussion einer 'Dienstleistungslücke' in West-Deutschland." *Beihefte zur Konjunkturpolitik, Zeitschrift für angewandte Wirtschaftsforschung* 48, Berlin.
Walton, Richard, and Robert McKersie. 1965. *A Behavioral Theory of Labor Negotiations: An Analysis of a Social Interact*. New York: McGraw-Hill.
Watson, B. 1996. "Commentary." National Summit on the Future of Work in Australia. Sydney, May.
Weathers, Charles. 1999. "The 1999 Shunto and the Restructuring of Japan's Wage System." *Asian Survey* 39 (6): 960–85.
Weekly Rengō. 1999. "Matamoya Kako Saiaku o Kōshin" (The Unemployment Rate in February Set a New Record Gain), April 2.
Wilkinson, Barry. 1994. "The Korean Labor Problem." *British Journal of Industrial Relations* 32: 3.
Wiseman, J. 1998. *Global Nation? Australia and the Politics of Globalisation*. Melbourne: Cambridge University Press.
Wooden, M. 2000. *The Transformation of Australian Industrial Relations*. Sydney: Federation Press.
Yamamoto, Kiyoshi. 1981. *Jidōsha Sangyō no Rōshi Kankei* (Capital-Labor Relations in the Auto Industry). Tokyo: Tokyo Daigaku Shuppan Kai.

Contributors

MARIAN BAIRD is senior lecturer in work and organizational studies at the University of Sydney. She received her Ph.D. in industrial relations from the University of Sydney and is currently researching changes to maternity leave and work and family arrangements in Australia.

GERHARD BOSCH is vice president of the Institute of Work and Technology in Gelsenkirchen, Germany, and professor of sociology at the University Duisburg-Essen. He received his Ph.D. from the University of Dortmund and his Habilitation from the University of Osnabrueck.

JAMES DONAGHEY is lecturer in management in the School of Management and Economics, Queen's University, Belfast. He is currently completing a Ph.D. on social partnership and labor relations in Ireland at Queen's University.

HARRY C. KATZ is the Jack Sheinkman Professor and director of the Institute of Collective Bargaining at the Industrial and Labor Relations School, Cornell University. He received his Ph.D. in economics from the University of California at Berkeley.

RUSSELL D. LANSBURY is professor of work and organizational studies and associate dean (research) in the Faculty of Economics and Business at the University of Sydney, Australia. He received his Ph.D. in industrial relations from the London School of Economics.

JOOHEE LEE is research fellow and coordinator of the Labor Forum at the Korea Labor Institute (KLI). She received her Ph.D. in sociology from the University of Wisconsin–Madison.

WONDUCK LEE is the president of the Korea Labor Institute (KLI). He is also on the Standing Committee of the Tripartite Commission and is the president-elect of the Korea Industrial Relations Association (KIRA). He received his Ph.D. in economics from Boston University.

IDA REGALIA is professor of industrial relations at the Institute for Labor Studies at the University of Milan and is president of the Institute for Economic and Social Research (IRES) in Lombardia.

MARINO REGINI is professor of industrial relations and dean of the Faculty of Political and Social Sciences at the University of Milan, Italy. He is the past president of the Society for the Advancement of Socio-Economics (SASE) and of the union-sponsored Institute for Economic and Social Research (IRES) in Lombardy.

HANS SLOMP is associate professor at the Nijmegen School of Management of the University of Nijmegen, the Netherlands. He received his Ph.D. in political science from that university.

AKIRA SUZUKI is associate professor at Ohara Institute for Social Research, Hosei University, Japan. He received his Ph.D. in sociology from the University of Wisconsin–Madison.

PAUL TEAGUE is the Martin Naughton Chair of Management at the School of Management and Economics, Queen's University, Belfast. He holds a Ph.D. from the London School of Economics.

Index

Activity integration, 202–3
Adversarial model, 13, 15, 62–63
Advisory committees, 132, 140, 193
Alliance for Work (Germany), 92–93, 113–16, 118, 228n.7
Annual improvement factor (AIF), 196–97, 200
Arbitration, 166–67, 180
Asian financial crisis, 145–46, 150, 157, 216, 231n.3
Australia, 191, 218
  arbitration, 166–67, 180
  centralization, 166–67
  compensation structure, 166–71, 183–84, 190
  consequences of change, 181–84
  decentralization, 185, 188
  economic performance, 173, 180, 183, 185
  employee participation, 178–79
  employers, 168–69, 172, 176–79
  enterprise bargaining, 6–7, 168–69, 185–86
  Enterprise Bargaining Agreements, 170–71
  Enterprise Flexibility Agreements, 169
  globalization and, 184–88, 191
  government role, 172–73, 175–76, 185, 188–89
  industrial conflict, 176–78, 182
  maritime workers, 176–78, 187
  microcorporatism, 174–75
  national pay agreements, 168–69, 171
  National Wage Cases, 168, 169, 171
  policy implications, 188–90
  tripartite agreements, 7, 171–75
  unions, 168–69, 172, 179–81, 187–88
  Workplace Relations Act, 1996, 170–71, 175–77, 182, 187
Australia Labor Party (ALP), 168, 172, 181
Australian Council of Trade Unions (ACTU), 168–69, 172, 180–81, 187
Australian Industrial Relations Commission (AIRC), 166, 167–70, 175, 177, 188–89, 214–15
Australian Workplace Agreements (AWAs), 170, 171, 189, 222
Authorizing clauses, 76, 84, 91, 108–9
Auto industry, 204
  Germany, 98–99, 103
  United States, 197–200, 233nn.5, 6

Benchmarking strategies, 89, 115, 152
Britain, 6, 124, 172
Business Council of Australia (BCA), 185

Canadian Autoworkers Union (CAW), 204
Capitalism, varieties of, 3, 219–21
Cascade model, 52
Centers of excellence, 206
Centralization, 79
  Australia, 166–68, 171
  Japan, 127–28, 137–39
  Korea, 152–58

Civil associations, 13, 17, 217
Civil society, 2, 4, 39, 217
Collective bargaining, 3. *See also*
    Company-level bargaining;
    Enterprise bargaining; Industry-level
    bargaining; National-level
    bargaining
  Ireland, 14, 17–23
  local, 5, 7, 9, 19, 64, 214
  pattern bargaining, 49–50, 54, 129, 196–98, 200, 214–15
  plant-level, 51, 85–88, 195–96, 210, 214
  shifts in power, 8–9
  Shuntō, 3, 6, 119–24, 129–31, 141, 229nn.10, 11
  two-tier system, 59–60, 64–66, 70, 79–80, 225n.2
Commonwealth Court of Conciliation and Arbitration, 166, 172
Communications Workers of America (CWA), 195, 200–203
Company agreements
  Italy, 66, 69
  Netherlands, 41, 50–52
Company-level bargaining, 196
  Germany, 84, 90–93
  Italy, 65–66, 72–73, 75–76, 214
Confederazione Generale Italiana del Lavoro (CGIL), 60–61, 63, 65, 71, 226n.3, 227n.10
Confederazione Italiana Sindicati Lavoratori (CISL), 61, 71, 226n.3
Confindustria, 61, 68, 71
Coordinated decentralization, 11–13, 220
Coordinated flexibility, 168–69
Coordinated market economies, 3, 81, 181, 219–20
Corporatism, 2, 34, 37, 160, 173, 215
  Japan, 125–26
Cross-national unionism, 112–13, 187–88, 203–5

Decentralization, 2, 6–8, 119, 220. *See also* Collective bargaining 1990s, 81–82
  Australia, 181–82, 185, 188
  coordinated, 11–13
  Germany, 89, 93–108
  hypotheses, 139, 230n.18
  individualization and, 213–15
  Italy, 69–70, 79, 81–82
  of management, 199–200

  Netherlands, 49–54
  organized *vs.* disorganized, 3, 81
  United States, 195–97, 199–200
Decision-making, 12–13, 56–57, 179
Deregulation, 141
  Japan, 133–35, 141
  Netherlands, 47–49
DGB (Germany Trade Union Federation), 89, 109–11
Diagnostic review, 30–31
Discretionary work arrangements, 133–35, 230n.12
Doorn Declaration, 112–13
Dunlop Commission, 194

East Germany, 90–91, 94–96, 117
Employee participation, 178–79, 190, 196
Employers
  Australia, 176–79
  decentralization and, 8, 199–200
  Ireland, 13–14, 16, 26, 30, 33–34
  Italy, 69–70
  Japan, 120–21, 138–39, 228n.3
  Korea, 154, 156
  Netherlands, 42, 45–46, 48
Employers' associations, 14, 228n.3
  Germany, 84, 87, 89, 96, 108–9, 111–12
  Italy, 61, 68–71, 75
  Korea, 161–62, 232n.15
  Netherlands, 39–40, 48–50, 54
Employment security, 220
  Japan, 126–30, 139
  Korea, 147–48, 161, 164
Enterprise agreements, 49–51, 169–71
Enterprise bargaining, 119
  Australia, 6–7, 168–69, 185–86
  Ireland, 14–15, 29–34
  Netherlands, 41, 49–51
Enterprise partnerships, Ireland, 11, 29–34
Enterprise unions
  crisis of representation, 141–42
  Japan, 120–22, 130, 135–36, 138, 228nn.1, 2, 234n.6
  Korea, 145, 150–53, 156, 164
  membership, 151–52
Europe, falling wage share, 21–22
European Commission, 45, 102
European Monetary Union (EMU), 82, 215–17
  Ireland and, 16, 23, 35
  Netherlands and, 43, 45, 58

Index

European Union (EU), 4, 15, 35, 80–82
Experimental public policy, 30
Export-led industrialization (ELI), 143–45

Federation of Korean Industries (FKI), 157, 161–62, 232n.15
Federation of Korean Trade Unions (FKTU), 152, 155–58, 160–61, 164
Federations, Japan, 122, 127–31, 136, 228n.3
FNV-Bondgenoten (Netherlands), 41–42, 49
Focused-factory managers, 206
Foreign workers, 97, 100–102, 136–37
Fragmented flexibility, 167, 170, 214
Framework agreements, 11
France, 113, 228n.6

Germany, 6, 8, 116–18
  academics, 115–16
  authorizing clauses, 76, 84, 91, 108–9
  collective bargaining structure, 86–89
  compensation structure, 95–96, 100–102
  construction industry, 95, 101–2, 113
  economic performance, 86, 92, 94
  employers' associations, 84, 87, 89, 96, 108–9
  foreign workers, 97, 101–2
  globalization and, 85, 93–94, 97–100
  government role, 86, 88–89, 102, 108, 113–15
  hardship clauses, 94–97
  industrial restructuring, 94, 100–104
  legal framework, 86–87
  metal industry, 112–14
  national alliance for work, 92–93, 113–16, 118, 228n.7
  plant-or company-level bargaining, 85–88
  political issues, 114–15
  reasons for decentralization, 93–108
  responses to decentralization, 108–13
  stagnation in reform process, 106–8
  statistics on collective bargaining, 90–93
  unemployment, 93, 94–97
  unification, 93–94, 106–8, 116
  unions, 85–87, 89, 104, 109–12
  wage drift, 84–85
  wage moderation, 42, 114
  working time, 93–95, 98–99, 105–6, 116, 227n.3
  Working Time Directive of 1993, 113
  work organization, 92–93, 105–6, 116
  Works Constitution Act, 88, 117
  works councils, 32, 87–88, 214
Globalization, 146
  Australia, 184–88, 191
  cross-national unionism and, 203–5
  Germany, 85, 93–94, 97–100
  Italy, 82–83
  standardization, 206–7
  United States, 203–9, 211
  U.S.-based multinationals and, 205–9
Government role
  Australia, 172–73, 175–76, 185, 188–89
  Germany, 86, 88–89, 102, 108, 113–15
  Italy, 62–63, 65–68
  Japan, 124–27, 131–36
  Korea, 143–44, 148–49, 151, 156–63

Hancock Report, 168
Hardship clauses, 94–97
Hidden microconcertation, 63–64
Human resources management (HRM), 32–34
Hyundai Motor Company (HMC), 151, 232n.8

IG Metall, 86, 103, 104, 109, 115
IMF-JC (Japan), 124, 229n.6
Income inequality, 219
  Ireland, 22, 28, 35, 219
  Korea, 162–63
  United States, 209–10, 219
Incomes policies, 2–3, 7, 213
  Germany, 86, 113
  Italy, 62, 64–66
Individualization, 2, 6, 152, 213–15, 222
  Australia, 170–71
  Netherlands, 54–66
  United States, 201–2, 211
Industrial conflicts, 68
  Australia, 172, 176–78, 182, 189
  Germany, 41, 87, 109
  Ireland, 26–29
  Japan, 122–23
  Korea, 144, 150–53, 160–61, 164, 231n.2
  Netherlands, 39–42
Industrial Relations Act, 1986 (Australia), 169

Industrial Relations Reform Act, 1993 (Australia), 169
Industrial tribunals, 166, 167–70
   changing roles, 171–72
Industry agreements
   Italy, 66, 71–72
   Netherlands, 41, 50–52, 54
Industry-level bargaining, 14
   Europe, 81–82
   Germany, 84–85, 89–91, 93, 105–6, 108
   Italy, 63–66, 70–75, 79–80
   Korea, 154–56
   Netherlands, 41, 49–51, 54
Information technology industry, 53–56, 104
Interest representation system, 60–61
International Monetary Fund (IMF), 157, 165, 231n.3
Ireland, 216, 217. *See also* Social partnership
   civil associations, 13, 17
   coordinated decentralization, 11–13
   economic performance, 15, 19, 21–25, 34–35, 38, 219
   employers, 13–14, 16, 26, 30, 33–34
   employment disputes, 26–29
   enterprise bargaining, 14–15
   enterprise partnerships, 11, 29–34
   Federated Union of Employers, 16–17
   income inequality, 22, 28, 35, 219
   living standards, 19, 22, 35
   management-employment interactions, 13–16, 26
   minimum wage, 15, 18, 25
   National Centre for Partnership and Performance, 29, 30
   national pay agreements, 16–22
   Partnership 2000, 16–17, 19, 29, 216
   Program for Economic and Social Progress (PESP), 16, 19
   Program for Prosperity and Fairness (PPF), 16, 29, 225n.2
   Sustaining Progress, 35–36
   tripartite agreements, 4, 6, 16–17, 216
   unions, 14, 16, 25–26, 30
   wage bargaining, 17–23
   wage increases, 19–20
   wage moderation, 19–23, 216–17
Irish Business and Employers Confederation (IBEC), 26, 30
Irish Congress of Trade Unions (ICTU), 14, 16, 30

Italy, 214, 216–17
   changes in public-sector collective bargaining, 77–79
   Clean Hands investigation, 65, 226n.7
   collective bargaining reform, 64–65
   Communist party, 63, 226n.3
   company-level bargaining, 72–73, 75–76, 214
   economic performance, 62–66, 66, 73–74, 82, 226n.5, 227n.12
   employers' associations, 61, 68–70
   employment pact, 1996, 64, 69, 76
   European Union and, 81–82
   government role, 62–63, 65–68
   hidden microconcertation, 63–64
   incomes policies, 62, 64–66
   industry-level bargaining, 63–66, 70–75, 79–80
   instability of collective bargaining, 80–81
   interest representation system, 60–61
   legal framework, 77–79
   macroeconomic indicators, 73, 74
   Milan Employment Pact of 2000, 76–77
   pension reform, 66–69, 216–17
   scala mobile, 61–62, 64–65, 72, 226n.5
   second-level negotiations, 75–77
   social pacts from mid-1990s, 69–71
   structure of bargaining before and after tripartite agreement of 1993, 71–79
   traditional features of collective bargaining system, 60–62
   tripartism and regulation of collective bargaining, 62–71
   tripartite agreement of 1983, 62
   tripartite agreement of 1984, 64
   tripartite agreement of 1992, 64, 65, 68
   tripartite agreement of 1993, 60, 64, 68, 70, 73–77, 81, 226n.8
   tripartite agreement of 1998, 70
   tripartite agreements, 4, 6, 59–60
   two-tier bargaining system, 59–60, 64–66, 70, 79–80, 225n.2
   union democracy, 221–22
   Unione Italiana del Lavoro, 61, 71, 226n.3
   unions, 60–62, 67–68, 72, 77, 226n.4
   wage increases, 66, 73–74, 75–76
   weak regulation, 59, 61
   welfare issues, 61, 63, 66–69, 227n.9

workplace representation system (RSUs), 79–80, 216–18, 226n.8

Japan
Central Employment Stability Committee, 132–34
centralization tendency, 127–28, 137–39
Central Labor Standards Committee, 132–35
characteristics of industrial relations, 120–24
collective bargaining structure, 119–20
deregulation, 133–35, 141
development of industrial relations from mid-1970s to late 1980s, 127–28
development of tripartite dialogue, 131–36
discretionary work arrangements, 133–35, 230n.12
dispatched workers, 120, 133–35, 142, 229n.9
economic performance, 6, 128–32, 139, 141, 221
employers, 120–21, 138–39, 228n.3
employment security, 126–30, 139
enterprise unions, 119–22, 130, 135–36, 138, 228nn.1, 2, 234n.6
federations, 122, 127–31, 136, 228n.3
government role, 124–27, 131–36
Heisei recession, 131–32, 139, 141, 221
industrial relations from mid-1970s to late 1980s, 124–28
industrial relations in 1990s, 128–37
interunion coordination, 139–40
labor market deregulation, 133–35
Labor Standards Law, 133–35
macrocorporatism, 125–26, 139
national-level bargaining, 119–20, 125–26, 131–36, 138–39
nonstandard workers, 128, 136, 141
part-time workers, 136, 142, 230n.19
Pension Reform Act, 133, 135
pensions, 133–34
regional unions, 136–37, 230n.14
Sanrōkon, 125, 140
Seisui Kaigi, 127
Shuntō wage bargaining, 3, 6, 119–24, 129–31, 141, 229nn.10, 11
Tripartite Council on Employment Policy, 131

tripartite dialogue at national level, 124–27
unemployment, 128, 131
unions, 127–28
wage increases, 129, 229n.5
Worker Dispatching Law, 133–35
work-sharing schemes, 131–32
Japanese Electrical, Electronic, and Information Union (JEIU), 121, 130
Japan Federation of Steel Workers' Unions (JFSWU), 122, 129–30, 229n.6
Job creation, 69, 131, 148–49, 220

Kok, Wim, 40
Korea, 120–21, 231n.7, 234n.6
Asian financial crisis and, 145–46, 150, 157, 216, 231n.3
banking sector, 149, 153–54, 232n.11
chaebols, 144, 148, 158
compensation structure, 150, 152, 158, 232n.14
decentralized bargaining structure, 144–45
decline of enterprise unionism, 150–52
democratic transition, 145–46, 231n.5
economic performance, 146–49, 157–58, 162
employers, 154, 156
employers' associations, 161–62
employment security, 147–48, 161, 164
enterprise unions, 145, 150–53, 156, 164
experiments with tripartism, 156–63
export-led industrialization, 143–45
government role, 143–44, 148–49, 151, 156–63
income inequality, 162–63
industrial conflicts, 144, 147–48, 150–53, 160–61, 164, 231n.2
job creation, 148–49
Labor Dispute Adjustment Law, 145
labor law reform, 1996, 147–48, 157
labor market after crisis, 148–50
Labor Standards Act, 158
legal framework, 144–45
National Wage Council, 157
oyong labor leaders, 145, 156
precrisis labor reform, 146–48
Presidential Commission on Industrial Relations Reform, 157, 231n.4
pressure toward centralization, 152–58

Korea *(continued)*
  security concerns, 143–44
  tripartite agreements, 159, 161
  Tripartite Commissions, 145, 148, 158, 160–61, 165, 218, 232n.17
  unemployment, 158, 163–64
  union density, 146, 150–51, 161
  unions, 143–44, 146, 150–53, 156–64
  wage increases, 144, 150
  welfare issues, 162–63, 232n.16
Korea Employers Federation (KEF), 156–58, 161–62
Korean Confederation of Trade Unions (KCTU), 147–48, 152, 155–56, 158, 160–61, 163–64, 218

Liberal market economies, 81, 181, 219–20
Local bargaining, 5, 7, 9, 19, 64, 214

Maritime Union of Australia (MUA), 176–77, 187
Microcorporatism, 157, 174–75
Multiemployer bargaining, 195
Multi-industry unions, 49, 179–80
Multinational corporations, 15, 22, 152, 206–7
  Germany and, 97–98
  U.S.-based, 39, 205–9
Multiple trade unions, 127–28, 161

National emergencies, 82–83, 215–16
National-level bargaining
  Germany, 85–86
  Japan, 119–20, 125–26, 131–36, 138–39
  Korea, 156–63
National-level tripartism, 1–2, 213
  Japan, 124–27
  revival of, 215–17
National pay agreements, 86
  Australia, 168–69, 171
  Ireland, 16–22
Negative externalities, 33–34
Netherlands, 215
  Agenda 2002, 42
  banking sector, 51, 56
  care sector, 53, 54
  Central Planning Bureau, 39, 40
  cross-country links, 112–13
  decentralization, 49–54
  deregulation, 47–49
  economic forecasts, 40–41
  economic performance, 37–38, 57, 219

  employers, 42, 45–46, 48
  employers' associations, 39–40, 48–50, 54
  individualization, 54–66
  industry agreements, 41, 50–52, 54
  minimum wage, 42–43
  "More is Needed," 42, 56
  "New Course," 42
  overleg, 38–39, 42–47, 51–52, 214
  part-time employment, 38, 43–47, 51, 54–55, 57–58
  Polder model, 38–40, 44–45, 217
  public sector, 42, 47, 53–54
  social security, 43, 47, 48–49
  STAR (Foundation of Labor), 39, 41–42, 46–47, 55–56
  structure of bargaining, 40–41
  tripartite agreements, 4, 6, 38, 42–43, 47
  unemployment, 37–38, 43, 46
  unions, 40–41, 49
  wage moderation, 38, 42–43, 47–49
  Wassenaar Agreement, 38, 42–43, 47
  women's employment, 38, 43–47, 57–58
  Working Hours Act, 48
  working time, 38, 46, 48, 52, 54–55
  Working Time Adaptation Act, 48
  works councils, 41, 52–53
Nikkeiren, 123, 129, 131, 230n.17
Nixon, Richard, 143–44
Nonstandard employment, 222, 227n.13.
See also Part-time employment
  dispatched workers, 120, 133–35, 142, 229n.9
  foreign workers, 97, 100–102, 136–37
  Japan, 120, 128, 136–37, 141–42
  Korea, 149, 161, 163, 231n.6
  seconded workers, 100–102, 113
  temporary agencies, 50, 69, 75, 152
North American Free Trade Agreement (NAFTA), 204

OECD countries, 162, 182, 184, 233–34n.4
Oil crisis, 1970s, 62, 123, 138
Opening clauses, 76, 84, 91, 108–9
Open method of coordination, 12–13, 29, 34–35
Organizing model, 180
Outsourcing, 50, 100–102, 198, 227–28n.4
Overleg (Netherlands), 38–39, 42–47, 51–52, 214

Part-time employment, 2
  Italy, 69
  Japan, 136, 142, 230n.19
  Korea, 147, 149
  Netherlands, 38, 43–47, 51, 54–55, 57–58
Pattern bargaining, 49–50, 54, 129, 196–98, 200, 214–15
Pay-for-knowledge, 199
Performance-based pay, 55–56
Plant-level bargaining, 51, 85–88, 195–96, 210, 214
Polder model, 38–40, 44–45, 217
Policy learning, 57–58
Power, 8–9
Private sector, 44, 47, 170, 176
Privatization, 73–75, 77–79, 102–3, 185
Production systems, Germany, 105–6, 116
Public sector, 14, 18, 53–54, 77–79, 108

Regional Bell Operating Companies (RBOCs), 200–202
Regionalization, 192, 194, 209, 211
Regional unions, 62, 69, 136–37, 230n.14
Rengō, 127–36, 230n.15

Sanrōkon, 125, 140
Scala mobile (wage-indexation system), 61–62, 64–65, 72, 226n.5
Seconded workers, 100–102, 113
Second pay bargaining rounds, 84
Security concerns, 143–44
September 11th terrorist attacks, 47, 211
Service industries, 22, 45, 50, 100–102
Shared services, 207–8
Shinkawa, Toshimitsu, 126
Shop stewards, 14, 88
Shuntō wage bargaining, 3, 6, 119–24, 141, 221, 229nn.10, 11
  reform of, 129–31
Skills-related pay, 174–75
Social dialogue, 1–2, 70–71
Social movement unionism, 136–37
Social partnerships, 10–11, 16–17, 34–36, 62. *See also* Tripartite agreements
  employment relations under, 25–29
  enterprise level, 29–34
  labor market performance and, 23–25
  negative externality, 33–34
  as neoliberal, 22, 28
  open coordination, 12–13, 29, 34–35
  stability of, 26–28
  wage bargaining and, 17–23
Social security. *See* Welfare issues
Sōhyō (General Council of Trade Unions), 122, 123, 127, 229n.6
Special Act on National Security (Korea), 145
STAR (Foundation of Labor) (Netherlands), 39, 41–42, 46–47, 55–56
Streeck, Wolfgang, 115, 117
Strikes, 68
  Australia, 172, 182, 189
  Germany, 41, 87, 109
  Japan, 122–23
  Korea, 144, 151, 153, 231n.2
  Netherlands, 41–42
Structural efficiency principle, 168

Taylorism, 105–6
Teamwork, 9, 99, 198–99, 233n.6
Technology, 174, 206–7
Temporary employment, 50, 69, 75, 152
Territorial bargaining, 66, 69–70, 75–77, 79
Territorial principle, 97
Thelen, Kathleen, 80–82, 117
Third Way social democracy, 22–23, 35
Training, 89, 117, 194, 211
Tripartism, 1–2, 233n.3
  Australia, 189–90
  connections with previous research, 2–3
  decentralized collective bargaining and, 6–7
  economic performance and social policy reform, 217–19
  Korea and, 156–63
  nature of dialogue and labor policy making, 4–5
  suggestions, 70–71, 165, 189–90
Tripartite agreements. *See also individual agreements*
  Australia, 7, 171–75
  Germany, 89
  Ireland, 4, 6, 16–17, 216
  Italy, 4, 6, 59–60, 62–65, 68, 70, 73–77, 81, 226n.8
  Korea, 159, 161
  limitations, 70–71
  Netherlands, 4, 6, 38, 42–43, 47

Unilever, 51–52
Union democracy, 5, 121, 145, 221–22

Union density, 39, 221
  Australia, 179–80, 189, 221
  Ireland, 25, 35
  Korea, 146, 150–51, 161
Unione Italiana del Lavoro (UIL), 61, 71, 226n.3
Unions. *See also* Enterprise unions
  activity integration, 202–3
  Australia, 168–69, 172, 179–81, 187–88
  bargaining structure and, 40–41
  centralization and, 152–58
  competition between, 52–53, 60–61, 69, 71, 109–10
  cross-national activities, 112–13, 187–88, 203–5
  decentralization, United States, 195–97
  Germany, 85–87, 89, 104, 109–12
  Ireland, 14, 16, 25–26
  Italy, 60–62, 67–68, 72, 77
  Japan, 120–27, 130, 135–36, 228nn.1, 2, 234n.6
  joint business-trade, 39, 41
  Korea, 143–44, 146, 150–53, 156–64
  mergers, 109–11
  Netherlands, 40–41, 49
  recognition, 26, 175–76
  regional, 136–37, 230n.14
  Shuntō wage bargaining and, 123–24
  United States, 194–97, 199–203
  vertical structure, 61, 226n.4
Unitary Federation (Italy), 61
United Autoworkers (UAW), 197, 200
United States, 210–12
  auto industry, 196–200, 233n.5
  decentralization, 192, 195–97
  economic performance, 197, 209–10
  financial scandals, 210–11
  globalization and, 203–9, 211
  historical lack of national-level tripartism, 193–95, 211–12
  income inequality, 209–10, 219
  individualization, 201–2, 211
  multinational corporations, 39, 205–9
  National Labor Relations Act, 194
  pattern bargaining, 214–15
  plant-level bargaining, 195–96, 210, 214
  regional tripartism, 192, 194, 211
  telecommunications industry, 200–203

union decline, 201–2
union revitalization, 202–3
unions, 194–97, 199–203
work rules, 196–98

Value adding working time, 98–99
Varieties of capitalism literature, 3, 219–21
Vereinigte Dienstleistungsgewerkschaft, 110–11
Verification and assurance focal points, 30
VNO-NCW (Netherlands), 39–40
Vocational training, 89, 117
Volkswagen, 103, 118
Volkswagen model, 97, 98–99
Voluntarism, 13–14, 60, 63, 80–81, 193

Wage indexation, 61–62, 64–65, 72, 168, 226n.5
Wage moderation, 4
  Germany, 42, 114
  Ireland, 19–23, 216, 217
  Netherlands, 38, 42–43, 47–49
Wassenaar Agreement, 38, 42–43, 47
Welfare issues
  Ireland, 23–25, 35
  Italy, 61, 63, 66–69, 227n.9
  Korea, 162–63, 232n.16
  Netherlands, 43, 47–49
Whipsawing, 7, 8, 196, 198
Wisconsin Regional Training Partnership, 194
Women, 88, 136–37, 183, 231n.6
  Netherlands, 38, 43–47, 57–58
Working time, 2, 147, 215
  Germany, 93–95, 98–99, 105–6, 116, 227n.3
  Italy, 69, 72
  Netherlands, 38, 45–48, 52, 54–55
  value adding, 98–99
Work organization
  Australia, 168, 174–75
  Germany, 92–93, 105–6, 116
Workplace representation system (RSUs), 79–80, 216–18, 226n.8
Works councils, 33, 61, 190
  Germany, 32, 84, 87–88, 91–92, 94, 109, 214
  Netherlands, 41, 52–53
Work-sharing, 131–32